GAME DESIGN

Learning Centre ot issue
re charged a day

EDITION

THOMSON
━━━━━━━✦━━━━━━━
COURSE TECHNOLOGY

Professional ■ Trade ■ Reference

GAME DESIGN

SECOND EDITION

Premier
Press

BOB BATES

ISBN: 1-59200-493-8

Library of Congress Catalog Card Number: 2004108015

Printed in the United States of America

05 06 07 08 BH 10 9 8 7 6 5 4 3 2

THOMSON

COURSE TECHNOLOGY

Professional ■ Trade ■ Reference

Thomson Course Technology PTR,
a division of Thomson Course Technology

25 Thomson Place

Boston, MA 02210

http://www.courseptr.com

SVP, Thomson Course Technology PTR:
Andy Shafran

Publisher:
Stacy L. Hiquet

Senior Marketing Manager:
Sarah O'Donnell

Marketing Manager:
Heather Hurley

Manager of Editorial Services:
Heather Talbot

Acquisitions Editor:
Mitzi Koontz

Senior Editor:
Mark Garvey

Associate Marketing Managers:
Kristin Eisenzopf and
Sarah Dubois

Project Editor:
Jenny Davidson

Thomson Course Technology PTR Market Coordinator:
Amanda Weaver

Copy Editor:
Sean Medlock

Interior Layout Tech:
Marian Hartsough

Cover Designer:
Mike Tanamachi

Indexer:
Sharon Shock

Proofreader:
Sara Gullion

For Peggy,
with love and admiration

Credits

ACKNOWLEDGMENTS

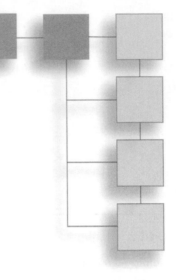

It's hard to acknowledge all the people who have helped you without starting to sound like an actor at the Oscars, but the fact is, no one writes a book without a lot of help.

In more or less chronological order, I would like to thank my parents and family for the support and encouragement they have given me, and for all the games we played along the way. Steve Lauder, Joe Joyce, and Sue Thimmesch also must share the credit (or blame) for shoving me down the writerly path.

Next are all the people at Infocom and Legend Entertainment, especially Mark Poesch and Duane Beck, who taught me more about game development than I ever taught them about game design. A special thanks to Mike Verdu, who was the best business partner a guy could ever hope for, and who was also kind enough to make valuable suggestions about the first edition of this book while it was in progress.

At Course Technology, Stacy Hiquet, Mitzi Koontz, Jenny Davidson, and Sean Medlock all have my appreciation for shepherding the material from manuscript to book.

Most of all, I would like to thank my wife, Peggy Oriani, and our children, Alex and Malia, from whose lives were extracted the countless hours it took me to write the book. I love you all.

ABOUT THE AUTHOR

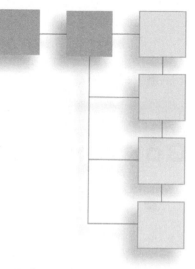

Bob Bates began his game writing career at the legendary Infocom in 1986. His design and development credentials include more than 25 games that have won over 40 industry awards, including the 1993 Adventure Game of the Year, *Eric The Unready*.

In 1989 Bob co-founded Legend Entertainment and served as its President until the company's 1998 sale. He continued as Legend's Studio Head and as an active designer/producer until the studio closed in January of 2004.

On the publishing side, he has at various times been responsible for marketing, PR, sales, and business development. His industry activities also include a term on the Board of Directors of the IGDA (2004-2006), and frequent speeches on design and production at conferences and events around the world.

Bob is a co-founder and organizer of the Game Designer's Workshop, an annual invitation-only conference attended by many of the top storytelling game designers in the business. He is also the editor of the *Game Developer's Market Guide* from Premier Press.

Bob is still an active game designer, producer, and industry consultant. His website is www.bobbates.com.

CONTENTS AT A GLANCE

Contents

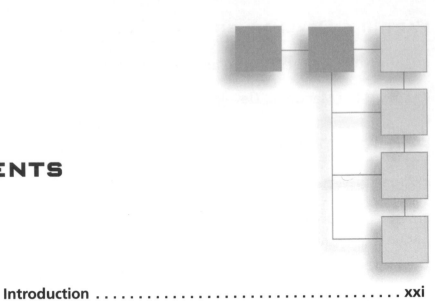

PART V   CONCLUSION 265

PART VI   APPENDIXES 269

INTRODUCTION

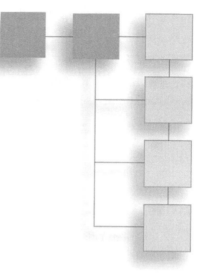

Game design is a highly collaborative art. Each of us who works in the industry is a game designer, whether he knows it or not. From testers and producers to programmers, artists, marketers, and executives, we all shape the games that pass through our hands. The product that appears on the shelves is the sum of all our efforts.

This book explains how a game gets designed and developed from the day the idea is born to the day the box hits the shelves.

Above all else, it is a *practical* guide that covers everything from the fundamentals of game design to the trade-offs in the development process to the deals a publisher makes to get a game on the shelves.

No matter what your role is in the industry, understanding this entire process will help you do your job better. And if you're looking to break in, you'll find knowledge here that is usually attained only after years in the trenches.

Introduction to the Second Edition

The first edition of this book was adopted as a textbook by various colleges and universities, and it soon became clear that some sections needed updated and strengthening.

Although all the chapters in this edition have been revised, the primary changes from the first edition are:

- Genre-specific advice from some of the industry's leading game designers
- A general re-working that acknowledges the advent of "Agile Development" techniques and the emergence of rapid-iterative-prototyping as the best development model for most new games

- The addition of Appendix A, which contains very useful templates for most of the documents that will be needed during product development
- A greatly expanded set of resources in Appendix B

My goal remains to deliver *practical* information on every page, and my hope is that the book will be of use to game developers everywhere.

Bob Bates
Centreville, Virginia
July 2004

How This Book Is Organized

Chapter 1 describes how to develop a mere idea into a project that a publisher will agree to fund.

Chapter 2 lays out the fundamental rules of good game design.

Chapter 3 analyzes different genres and deals with category-specific design issues. It also contains sidebar interviews with top designers from twelve different game genres.

Chapter 4 is about storytelling and how to apply its rules to interactive media.

Chapters 5 and 6 cover level design and how to create good puzzles.

Chapter 7 explains how to work with franchises, both those licensed from the outside and those created internally.

Chapter 8 discusses the duties of the members of the development team, how each of them participates in and affects game design, and how the team works together to create the finished product.

Chapter 9 gives guidance on working with external resources like voice actors, musicians, language localizers, and so on.

Chapter 10 describes the game development lifecycle, from the initial design documents through proof of concept and technical development all the way to alpha, beta, code freeze, and release.

Chapter 11 covers the fundamentals of good software development.

Chapter 12 brings in the marketing, PR, and sales groups and explains what they do with a game after it leaves the developer's hands. It explains how games are sold into the retail channel and promoted to consumers, and it discusses the kinds of materials these departments need to help make the game a hit.

Chapter 13 contains advice on breaking into the business.

Chapter 14 is a brief reflection on whether it's all worth it.

Appendix A is a very useful collection of project document templates and outlines.

Appendix B is a treasury of useful resources including books, magazines, schools, web sites, conferences, and organizations.

At the end is a Glossary of game development terms.

A Note on Gender

Throughout the book I refer to players, designers, programmers, and everyone else using the pronoun "he." I do this strictly for readability of the text. I have considered the alternatives (s/he, he or she, alternating gender pronouns between paragraphs, and so on), but unfortunately, our language has not yet settled on gender-neutral terminology that is not jarring. Therefore, with apologies to the many women game-industry professionals and the many more women game-players, I have opted for the less intrusive "he."

PART I

DESIGN

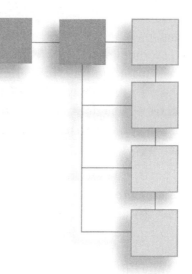

CHAPTER 1

GETTING TO "YES"

Before you can begin design work on a game, you must have a general idea of what the game is about, which genre it fits into, and what your publisher's goals are. When you know this, you can create a pitch document with the goal of getting a green light to develop the project, the magical "yes."

Concept Development

Most games begin with a single idea.

The idea can revolve around a character ("It would be cool to play James Bond!"), gameplay ("How about a squad-based action game?"), philosophy ("Explore the horrors of biology gone mad!"), or new technology ("Let's create a dancing game that captures the player's movements in the real world and superimposes them on a model in the game world.").

The idea might come from a friend, coworker, or publisher, or from deep in your own subconscious. It might come while you're walking down the beach or driving to work. Perhaps it will come only after many days of anxious worrying that if you *don't* come up with an idea, you'll be fired and your team will be out of work.

Sometimes the idea is completely original, but more often it builds on the work of game designers who have gone before. Beginning designers often fret about this, but it's not something to worry about. Why? Because usually when game publishers say that they're looking for a "new" idea, what they really want is a new wrinkle on something that's established already.

From a business point of view, this makes good sense. Consumers, too, are always look-ing for something new and different, yet paradoxically they don't want to take a chance on something they don't already know about. That's why you can always walk into a gro-cery store and buy "new" Tide. Proctor & Gamble has been selling Tide for almost 60 years (it first appeared in 1946 as the "New Washday Miracle"). People like Tide. They know what it does. However, they also want to be up-to-date. Therefore, Proctor & Gam-ble makes sure to tell consumers that this is the same reliable product, but it also has the latest scientifically engineered, state-of-the-art clothes-cleaning capabilities.

This is the exact reason why game publishers pay big money for movie licenses, fund countless sequels of a popular title, and work so hard to establish and build brand aware-ness. Consumers want the latest scientifically engineered, state-of-the-art technology in their games, but they also want to know *in advance* that they're going to have fun for the $20 to $60 they're about to spend. How can they be assured of this? By knowing that the game, although new, is similar to one they've already enjoyed. "New" Tide.

This is not to say that you should give up before you start, and just design another "me, too" clone or boring sequel. You do need innovative and interesting ideas. Just don't despair if your game follows the conventions of an existing genre or has gameplay ele-ments similar to those of existing products.

Of course, if you *do* have something truly original, it might be worth fighting for. It took Will Wright four years to find a game company willing to distribute *SimCity*, before Broderbund finally took it on in 1989. Why did so many publishers turn down a blockbuster like *SimCity*? (See Figure 1.1.) Because they didn't know what to make of it. It wasn't "new" Tide.

So the goal of the first phase of develop-ment is to come up with your idea, which will eventually evolve into the *high concept* of the game.

The high concept is the one-or two-sen-tence response to the question, "What is your game about?" Many publishers believe that if your game cannot be boiled down to this quick summary, it has no chance of success.

They have a point.

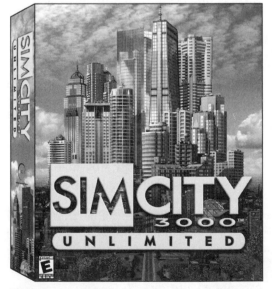

Figure 1.1 SimCity has become one of the most recognized franchises in gaming. © 2000 Electronic Arts Inc. All rights reserved.

You might think that your game is so huge, complex, and chock-full of gamerly goodness that it couldn't *possibly* be summed up in two measly sentences. Yet, someone in the marketing department will eventually have to do precisely that, because a couple of sentences are all you'll get on the game box to tell a prospective customer why he should put it in his shopping cart rather than back on the shelf.

Think of how many people shop for PC games. They stand in the aisles and look at the boxes (most of which, depressingly, are only spine out). They pick up a game and look at the front cover for, say, 10 seconds. Then they flip it over, look at the two or three screen shots, read the two-sentence description of the game, and check out the features. Finally, it goes either into the shopping cart or back on the shelf. The situation is even worse for console games, whose packaging is limited to the size of a 5 × 5-inch jewel case.

Now, think of a game executive as one of those shoppers. He's a busy guy. Hundreds of game proposals cross his desk each month. What does he read first? The high concept. If that doesn't grab him, the rest of the proposal goes unread and you don't get to "yes."

Here are some sample high concepts:

- A busty female archaeologist pursues ancient treasure. (*Tomb Raider*)
- Ping-Pong on the computer. (*Pong*)
- An ordinary technician battles trans-dimensional monsters after an accident at a secret research facility. (*Half-Life*—see Figure 1.2.)
- A street-racing game where you drive a getaway car for the mob. (*Driver*)

As you work on the high concept, try to make it something that's interesting to *you*. You're going to spend a year or more on this project, so you need something to keep you fresh and inspired throughout the long development cycle. You need something to keep you going when it's two o'clock in the morning, you're tired, everything is going wrong, and everyone is asking, "Why are we doing this?" With a good high concept, your answer will be, "Because it's interesting and we like it, and if we can only do *this*, it will be so cool."

Figure 1.2 *Half-Life's* clear high concept helped it become Game of the Year. Used with permission of Sierra On-Line Inc.

Genres

Your high concept might fall neatly into an existing genre, but more and more games are *hybrids*, combining elements from different categories. If you're creating a game that crosses genres, make sure that you're familiar with the conventions of each genre so that you end up with the best of both, instead of the worst.

The following sections describe various genres. Your game should probably belong to a genre that you enjoy playing yourself, so that you've already internalized the genre's conventions. For more on genres, read Chapter 3, "Genre-Specific Game Design Issues."

Adventure Games

Adventures are story-based games that usually rely on puzzle-solving to move the action along. They can be text-based (such as the early adventures from Infocom like *Zork* and *Planetfall*) or graphical (Sierra's *King's Quest*—see Figure 1.3—and *Gabriel Knight* series). They can be told from a first-person perspective (*Seventh Guest*), second-person (most text games in which the hero is "you"), or third-person (*Monkey Island*).

Generally, adventure games aren't in real-time, unless they're an action-adventure hybrid. The player usually takes as much time as he wants between turns, and nothing happens in the game world until he enters a command.

Figure 1.3 The latest in a long line of *King's Quest* games from Sierra. Used with permission of Sierra On-Line Inc.

The original adventures were *parser-based*, accepting simple sentence commands from the keyboard. More modern adventures are *point-and-click*, in which the player indicates what he wants to do by moving the mouse around the screen. An active community of hobbyist developers still make parser-based text adventures, but they're rarely published commercially.

Players generally expect an adventure game to have a large, complex world to explore, along with interesting characters and a good story.

Action Games

Action games are real-time games in which the player must react quickly to what's happening on the screen. The category is dominated by first-person shooters (FPS) such as *Quake*, *Unreal*, and *Halo* (see Figure 1.4).

The action-adventure hybrid, however, is often a third-person game, such as *Tomb Raider*, in which you can see the hero or heroine as he or she moves through the environment. Typically, the gamer has much more to do than just shoot and kill enemies.

In general, action games are far less cerebral than adventure, strategy, or puzzle games. Players are looking for the adrenaline rush of fast-paced action that calls for snap judgments and quick reflexes. Opponents can be computer-generated artificial intelligences (AIs), or other human players connected to the game over a local network or the Internet.

Figure 1.4 The action category is dominated by first-person shooters like *Unreal Tournament*. Used with permission of Epic Games Inc.

Role-Playing Games (RPG)

In role-playing games, the gamer generally directs a group of heroes on a series of quests. Gameplay revolves around gradually increasing the abilities and strengths of these heroes. Classic RPGs include *Ultima*, *Might and Magic*, and *Final Fantasy* (see Figure 1.5).

Like an adventure game, an RPG features a huge world with a gradually unfolding story. Players expect to be able to micro-manage their characters, all the way down to the weapons they carry and the specific armor for each part of their bodies. Combat is an important element, by which the heroes gain strength, experience, and money to buy new equipment.

Figure 1.5 The *Final Fantasy* games are popular console role-playing games. © 2001 Square Co., Ltd. All rights reserved.

Fantasy RPGs also feature complex magical systems, as well as diverse races of characters that make up the player's party.

Strategy Games

Strategy games require players to manage a limited set of resources to achieve a predetermined goal. This resource management frequently involves deciding which kinds of units to create and when to put them into action.

In the classic *Command & Conquer*, for example, the player has to continually balance which kind of unit to build, how much tiberium to harvest, how many resources to allocate to offense and to defense, and so on (see Figure 1.6).

Older strategy games were typically *turn-based*. The player could take his time as he made each decision, and the computer acted only when the player indicated he was ready. Now, real-time strategy (RTS) games set the computer AI in motion against the gamer whether he's ready or not.

Multiplayer versions of RTS games substitute human opponents for the computer's AIs. These games are enormously popular on the Internet.

Figure 1.6 Strategy games like *Command & Conquer* are all about resource management. ©1999 Electronic Arts Inc. All rights reserved.

Simulations

Simulations, or sims, are games that seek to emulate the real-world operating conditions of complicated machinery, such as jet fighters, helicopters, tanks, and so on.

The more serious the sim, the higher the premium that's placed on absolute accuracy, especially with equipment controls. Players expect to spend hours learning the intricacies of the machine, and they expect a thick manual to help them with the finer points.

Less serious sims, however, just let the player "get in and go." These are sometimes referred to as *arcade* sims. Controls are simplified, the player has less to learn, and he's punished less often for making mistakes.

Sports Games

Sports games let players vicariously participate in their favorite sport, either as a player or a coach (see Figure 1.7). Prowess in a real-world sport isn't required for success in its computer-game counterpart, but then, that's sort of the point. One of the things we want from a computer game is wish fulfillment, the opportunity to do things we can't in real life.

Figure 1.7 Sports of all kinds make for popular games. Used with permission of Eidos Interactive Ltd.

These games must accurately reproduce the rules and strategies of the sport. One gameplay session can cover an individual match, a short series, or an entire season.

Some titles focus on emulating an athlete's actions, on actually *playing* the game. Others approach the sport from the management side, allowing the user to be a coach or general manager, sending in plays or making trades.

Fighting Games

Fighting games are two-person games in which each player controls a figure on the screen, using a combination of moves to attack his opponent and defend against his opponent's attacks. These games are generally viewed from a side perspective, and each session lasts only a few minutes.

Players expect to find a basic set of attacks and counters they can learn right away, as well as more complicated combinations they can master over time.

Casual Games

Casual games include adaptations of traditional games such as chess, bridge, hearts, and solitaire. They also include easy-to-play, short-session games on the Web, such as *Slingo, Poker*, and *Concentration*.

Television game shows are also represented in this category, with the very popular *Jeopardy, Wheel of Fortune*, and *Who Wants to Be a Millionaire?*

Players generally want to drop into and out of these games quickly. They're already familiar with the rules of the real-world game and expect to find those rules emulated here. These games generally have an extremely simple user interface, with little or no learning curve.

God Games

God games (sometimes called *software toys*) are games that have no real goal, other than to encourage the player to fool around with them just to see what happens. Examples include *The Sims* (see Figure 1.8) and *RollerCoaster Tycoon*.

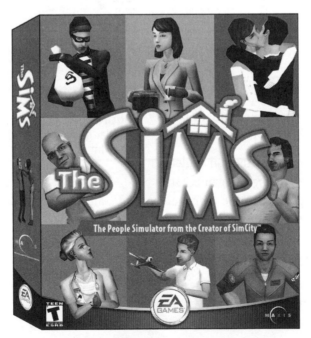

Figure 1.8 Software toys like *The Sims* encourage open-ended experimentation.
© 2000 Electronic Arts Inc. All rights reserved.

Designers in this genre try to create games in which the player can do no wrong. The games are very open-ended, with no correct way to play and no preset winning conditions.

Educational Games

Educational games are those that teach while they entertain. Sometimes called *edutainment*, examples of these games include *Oregon Trail* and *Reader Rabbit*.

Generally, these games are aimed at a much younger audience than most commercial products. Their designers work closely with experts on the subject matter to ensure that the content is appropriate for the target group.

Puzzle Games

Puzzle games exist purely for the intellectual challenge of problem solving, such as *The Castle of Dr. Brain* and *The Incredible Machine* (see Figure 1.9).

The puzzles are an end in themselves and aren't integrated into a story, as is common in adventure games.

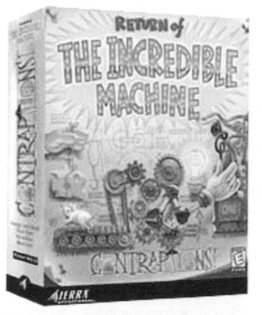

Figure 1.9 *The Incredible Machine* provides hours of Rube Goldbergesque puzzle-solving. Used with permission of Sierra On-Line Inc.

Online Games

Online games can include any of the pre-ceding genres, but their distinguishing feature is that they're played over the Internet. Entire communities grow around the most successful of these games, and the designers of games like *Everquest* and *Ultima Online* are constantly creating features that encourage those communities to flourish (see Figure 1.10).

Online gaming is still in its infancy, and publishers are still groping for a solid profit model. This has important game-play implications, which are discussed in Chapter 3.

Client Goals

Before designing a game, you need to know what the publisher hopes to achieve by funding it.

Figure 1.10 Games like *Ultima Online* are sometimes called MMPORGs (massively multiplayer online role-playing games).
© 2000 Electronic Arts Inc. All rights reserved.

Some companies try to develop many inexpensive games each year, in the hope that one or two will break through and sell enough copies to pay for the duds. Others put their money into fewer games, hoping that the increased budget and longer schedule for each one will create games of such high quality that they can't help but be hits. These companies are all engaged in risk management. Is it riskier to spread out your eggs across a bunch of inexpensive baskets, or to place them all in a few costly ones?

To some extent, moviemakers are faced with the same dilemma. Do they fund one $100-million action extravaganza, and rely on expensive special effects to give it an extra boost at the box office? Or, with that same money, do they make two or three "little" pictures, any one of which could take off by word of mouth and become a sleeper hit?

During concept development, you need to know what your client wants. If he's looking for a blockbuster that will dominate the category, you have to design a game that excels in all areas, requiring a large budget and a long schedule. If he wants a sequel to a franchise title in time for Christmas, perhaps you should concentrate on one or two new features and leave other portions unchanged, because you know the schedule is inflexible.

Sometimes you'll be working on a *conversion*—an existing game that's being ported to a new hardware platform. In this case, the publisher probably wants a few new wrinkles that take advantage of the different hardware, but basically he wants to see the same game again. This is usually a low-cost effort, in which the publisher is trying to leverage the investment from the initial game across as many platforms as possible.

Sometimes the publisher's overriding goal is to ship a game by a certain date. Many agendas can be at work here. It might be that the company's stock price is riding on how much revenue it books in a given quarter. Perhaps the genre's giant-killer is coming out the following month, and going head to head with it would be suicide. Occasionally, a publisher has a contract with a licensor that requires a certain number of games to be published by a certain time in order for the license to be renewed. Then you find yourself in the unfortunate position of designing a game that must be on store shelves by a certain date, no matter what.

In all these situations, knowing what your client wants is essential during the concept development phase. The key elements you can manipulate at this time are *gameplay*, *scope*, and *technical risk*.

Good gameplay is the cheapest weapon in your arsenal, and you can wield it effectively on any project, no matter the schedule or budget. Just as cool explosions won't save a movie with a lousy script, special effects won't save a game with lousy gameplay. Conversely, a game with mediocre graphics but great gameplay can still become a big hit.

Good designers take up this challenge with every game they build, and they recognize that sometimes it's the limitations that drive the greatest creativity. Like an artist who can afford only a few colors on his palette, a good game designer turns the limitations of the project to his own advantage and creates something new and interesting.

Your second big variable is scope. Gameplay doesn't determine how expensive a project is or how long it takes to finish. Scope does. How big is the game? How many levels? How many creatures? How many weapons? How many tracks and cars do you put in a racing game? How many moves do you put in a fighting game?

Making the game big enough while keeping it affordable is a constant battle. Perhaps the only thing reviewers, publishers, designers, and game players all agree on is that they would rather play a small, well-polished game than a large clunky one.

What you must realize is that every single thing you add to a game design will take someone else time to draw, program, test, and debug. There's no such thing as a free feature.

The best time to attack the problem of scope is up front. If you decide halfway through the project that the design is too ambitious, you'll throw out man-years of work on material that will never see the light of day. If you narrow your scope during the design phase, your artists, programmers, and level designers will have the time to concentrate on quality, not quantity.

The third important variable is technical risk. If the success of your game will depend on the development of new technology, it will be more expensive, take longer to produce, and have a harder schedule to predict than a game that's built using existing technology.

It's vital that you and your client agree on how to deal with these three variables before you kick off the project.

The Game Proposal Document

The result of the concept development phase is the game proposal. If you're an internal developer, the proposal's goal is to get you the go-ahead to proceed to preproduction. If you're an independent, your goal is to get funding for the *proof of concept* phase. This phase is when you demonstrate that your team can deliver on the concept, and that you're the type of partner with whom the publisher will want to continue working.

Think of the proposal as the executive summary of what you want to accomplish. You must quickly convey how the game is played, what will make it great, how long it will take to develop, and how much it will cost. At this stage, the information is imprecise. Later, if the project is approved, you'll refine this information into a project plan (see Chapter 10, "Project Lifecycle and Documents"). For now, you need to deal in broad strokes.

The format of this document changes from company to company, but all formats seem to include the following elements.

High Concept

You already looked at the high concept earlier in this chapter. It's "the vision thing." State what your game is about, in one or two sentences.

Genre

A single sentence that places the game within a genre, or a hybrid of genres.

Gameplay

This section summarizes what the player will do when he's playing the game. Typically, this section leads off by placing the game within a genre, and then explains how it departs from genre conventions in creative and entertaining ways.

Features

List the major selling points of your game. Identify the technical advancements and what they mean to the game (that is, why they'll help sell more units). These selling points are likely to end up as a bulleted list on the back of the game box. It's a shorthand way of telling people what's inside the box.

Setting

Summarize in a few paragraphs what makes your gameworld and its occupants interesting and unique.

Story

If your game has a story, this is the place for a quick synopsis of what happens.

Target Market

For whom are you developing the game? Is it a niche market of specialized genre fans? The mass market? Kids? Sports fans?

This section should also include some historical information about how games of this type have traditionally sold to the target demographic.

Target Hardware Platforms

Identify the target platforms on which your game will be played. As development costs rise, more and more games are *cross-platform* projects released on several gaming systems to leverage the costs and create a greater chance of financial success.

If it's a PC game, list the target hardware requirements, including memory and processor speed.

Estimated Schedule and Budget

This is one of the hardest parts of the game proposal to put together. Estimating the schedule and budget of a software project is part science, part art. Entire books have been devoted to the topic, and we *still* get it wrong.

This document comes too early in the game development cycle to enable any precision, so the best thing to do is to consult with the leads of your technical and art teams to come up with some rough estimates.

Competitive Analysis

What games have come out in this genre? How did they sell? Why will yours do better or worse? What competition will your game have to face when it comes out? How will your game stack up against the competition and survive the fierce battle for shelf space?

The Team

What publishers invest in is not so much game ideas as people. Ideas are cheap and plentiful—it takes good people to turn them into reality.

List the major credentials of your team. If your team has been together for a while, this is easy—you just list the games you've produced together. If you're assembling a new team, list the credits for the major team players (designer, tech lead, art lead, and so on).

Document Summary

Reiterate why this will be a great game, and why your team is the one to pull it off. Show that you understand the publisher's goals for the product, and give him the confidence he needs to say yes.

CHAPTER 2

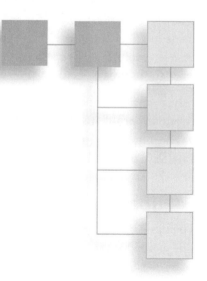

PRINCIPLES OF GAME DESIGN

Anybody can recognize problems in a game after it has been created (reviewers are especially good at this), but how do you avoid errors ahead of time? Even though our business is young, the principles of good game design have already been established, and paying attention to them will make yours a superior game.

This chapter deals with design principles that are broadly applicable to all game genres. For design tips about specific genres, see Chapter 3, "Genre-Specific Game Design Issues."

Player Empathy

A good designer always has an idea of what's going on in the player's head.

This empathy for the player is crucial. You must develop the ability to put yourself in the player's shoes and anticipate his reaction to each element of the game. You must be able to close your eyes and see the game unfolding like a movie in your head, all before a single line of code has been written.

At any given point in the game, you must be able to say, "Here's the situation the player faces, and here are the range of choices he can make . . . Now, what will he likely want to do?" Then, your job is to let him try, and to make the game respond intelligently to his attempt, even if it's only to steer him toward a different course of action.

Naturally, no designer has completely accurate foresight. That's one reason you have testers. Testers not only hunt for bugs, but also provide feedback on things they want to try in the game but can't.

One of the hardest things for a designer to do is to keep his mouth shut while watching someone play his game. The urge to tell the tester to go *this* way instead of *that* way can be overwhelming. If you steer the tester in one direction, though, you'll never discover what thousands of actual gamers will encounter when they go the other way instead.

Player empathy not only helps you create good gameplay, but also lets you identify and eliminate problems during the design phase rather than during production, after code has been written and graphics have been created. With good player empathy, you'll write a better game, and you'll build it faster and more cheaply as well.

Feedback

The basic interaction between a player and a game is simple: The player does something. The game does something in response. This feedback is what distinguishes a game from every other form of entertainment. It's the *interactivity* that makes our games unique. Without it, the player would just be watching a movie on the screen.

Every input the player makes in the game should give him a discernible response. No input should go unanswered. This "answer" can take many forms. It can be visual feedback, aural feedback, or even tactile feedback (if the controller is so equipped). It can be positive feedback or negative feedback, but there must be *some* feedback.

Generally, this is easy when the player "gets" the game and is progressing nicely through it. It becomes more difficult when he's doing something "wrong." Nothing is more frustrating for a player than pressing a key, clicking the mouse, or pushing on the controller and having *nothing* happen. For every conceivable input, be sure to give the player some feedback about it.

If you can detect what the player is doing and know how to steer him in the right direction, do so. Give him a message about what he has done. If you simply don't understand the input, at least send a *BOOP* noise back to him. He'll quickly learn that this noise means, "I know you tried to do something, and I heard you, but I don't know what to do about that."

Grounding the Player

The player should always know where he is in the game and why he's doing what he's doing. At any given point, he should have a long-term goal, a medium-range goal, and an immediate goal. (This is true even of *software toys*, games that ostensibly have no goals, but in reality have a series of goals the player creates for himself.)

Computer games are huge, and it's easy for a player to feel lost. Also, usually games aren't played start-to-finish in one sitting. If a player has an overall map in his head, it encourages him to come back to the game again and again until he's done. Physical maps also help (see Figure 2.1).

In a strategy game, the long-term goal can be to conquer the world. In an action/adventure or RPG, it can be to defeat the ultimate bad guy. In a golf game, it can be to win an individual match.

Medium-range goals are good-sized steps toward the long-term goal. For the strategy game, perhaps it's establishing a home base. For the RPG, perhaps it's the completion of a simple quest. For the golf game, it can be the battle to win the first hole. Frequently, these medium-range goals turn out to be embodied in levels.

An immediate goal is the problem that's right in front of the player. In the strategy game, it can be figuring out which units to build to fend off an impending attack. In the RPG, it can be ordering a party before marching into the next battle. In the golf game, it can be figuring out which club will carry the ball over the water hazard without rolling it into the bunker on the far side of the green.

Throughout the game, as the player wrestles with the problem in front of him, he should always have some idea of how this single step fits into the longer path that will eventually lead to success.

Figure 2.1 This map of Raymond Feist's *Krondor* helps keep the player oriented toward his goals. Used with permission of Sierra On-Line Inc.

The Moment-to-Moment Experience

At any instant while he's playing the game, the player has the option to turn it off and do something else. You can't let that happen. You have to hold his attention constantly and entertain him from moment to moment.

This is far more important than most designers realize. At every point in the game, the player should have something interesting to do. One of the worst things you can do to a player is to bore him.

Verbs

The positive side of creating a good moment-to-moment experience is giving the player a constant stream of interesting choices that have significant outcomes.

It's useful to think of the things the player can do as "verbs." In early shooters, the player had two main verbs: *move* and *shoot*. He also had some adverbs: move *slowly* (walk), move *quickly* (run), shoot *quickly* (machine gun), shoot *accurately* (sniper). As the genre expanded, it was primarily through the addition of more verbs, which allowed players to do new and interesting things: *climb, rappel, zip-wire, set explosives, unlock, move stealthily,* etc. In essence, every time you give the player an inventory item, you're giving him another new verb.

Each genre uses verbs. In an RTS, the player *builds, researches, surveys the terrain, gives orders,* etc. In an RPG, he *moves, talks, fights, buys, sells,* etc.

No matter what the genre, the more verbs you can give a player, the more you allow him to do. It's the doing that's at the heart of good gameplay and a positive moment-to-moment experience.

Hazards

The hazards that will destroy a good moment-to-moment experience are easy to design around, once you're aware of them. Here are several experience-killing pitfalls and how to avoid them.

Don't make the player perform a complex action twice. In an adventure game, after he has completed the steps to a puzzle, don't make him do it again. For example, after he has figured out the combination to a safe and opened it, don't make him reenter the combination. Just give him an Open Safe command to use.

In an action game, don't make him travel back and forth across the world for frivolous reasons. Today's games have big, beautiful environments, but no matter how pretty the pictures are, they wear thin after a while. If you have large environments, build in shortcuts to get from one end of the world to the other, and don't design the gameflow so that the player has to constantly backtrack or crisscross your world.

If you have rendered transitions, let the player bypass them by pressing the Esc key or a button on the controller.

The same principle applies to audio and dialogue trees. Don't make the player listen to every line of dialogue over and over to get a bit of information he forgot. Instead, let him abort each piece of dialogue as it begins, so he can get quickly to the line he wants to hear and then leave the dialogue altogether.

The same applies to cutscenes. No one wants to sit through the same cutscene over and over. God gave us the Esc key for a reason. Use it.

Restarting the game can also be tedious for the player. You might have created the most beautiful introductory movie known to man, but hey—he's seen it already. Let him bypass it.

Avoid text or dialogue dumps. Instead, dole out information in bits and pieces. Don't make the player sit through long, boring screeds.

In general, have the computer do set-up tasks the player might find boring. In an RPG, for example, allow the gamer to have the computer generate his character and party automatically. In a racing game, give him a default car that will perform acceptably without having to be tweaked. In a basketball game, don't make him select each player on each team before he can begin a game.

Make the game entertaining, moment to moment, by keeping it interesting. Give the player a lot to do—but also make sure that what he does is fun.

Immersion

Immersion is what happens when you make the moment-to-moment experience so compelling that the player is drawn completely into the game and the real world disappears. It isn't until he hears birds chirping that he realizes he's spent the whole night playing the game (again!). This can be as true of chess games as it is of action games.

John Gardner, in *The Art of Fiction*, writes that a good book creates "a continuous dream" that's bolstered by providing a constant stream of concrete detail. Immersion works the same way. You bathe the player in a constant stream of images that pull him into your world, and you avoid gaffes that jar him out of his reverie. If you break the dream, you lose the immersion.

These gaffes can be anything from typos to bad voice acting. Modern slang in a medieval world will destroy the player's suspension of disbelief in a heartbeat, as will graphical styles that change from scene to scene, or stupid AIs.

A successful game entices the player into the gameworld, and then never lets him go.

Writing

Good writing is invisible. Bad writing draws attention to itself and instantly destroys the player's sense of immersion.

Every game uses words somewhere. The player might see them as text on the screen or hear them as spoken dialogue. The writing can be confined to cutscenes between levels, or it can be an integral part of gameplay. Regardless, you can be sure that at some point, someone will be sitting down with pen in hand (keyboard on lap?) to put words into your game.

It turns out, though, that writing well is hard. People spend a lifetime learning how to do it. If you've never given writing much thought before—*don't write*.

This doesn't mean that you can't be a good game designer. It just means that if you've never studied writing, if you've never struggled to learn the difference between good writing and bad, you should bring in someone else to do it.

Design Within Limits

Designers often forget that building a game is actually a software development project. It has a cost and a schedule, and its ultimate success or failure hinges not just on good gameplay, but on whether you can deliver that gameplay on time, on budget, with technical features that work, and without crashing the player's machine.

The person who makes this happen is the tech lead, and you must work with him to make his job easier. Even if you're not a programmer, you should read books about the software development process and adapt your design to the tech specs and the budget.

As a designer, you must limit yourself to features that can be implemented on the target machine, so you don't find out at the end of the project that the game runs like a dog.

Removing Impediments

Another way to enhance the moment-to-moment experience is to remove technical impediments to the player's enjoyment, such as excessive disc swapping, long load times, game interruptions, limited saves, bugs, a poor interface, and so on.

You might think of these as technical problems, not design issues, but they're areas where programming and design meet. The practitioners of both areas have to work together to create an enjoyable game for the player.

Disc Swapping

If you design a multiple-disc game with a huge world and give the player complete access to the entire world at any time, it will result in annoying disc swaps. If he shuttles back and forth between two locations that have graphics and sound on different discs, he'll be faced with the onerous task of swapping discs every time he crosses the boundary.

One solution to that problem is to dump everything onto the player's hard drive, but this creates a huge footprint that will drive your sales and marketing people crazy. The system requirements will go up, thereby driving sales down.

The better solution is to design *choke points* in the game. These are points beyond which the player can't go back, other than by restoring a saved game. This allows the programmers to organize the game's data on successive discs, put fewer core assets on the hard drive, and eliminate the need for the player to swap discs continually.

By doing this, you give up a theoretical design advantage (total freedom for the player to go anywhere at any time) in favor of a practical gameplay advantage (gameplay uninterrupted by annoying disc swaps).

Load Times

Another potential impediment is long load times. This, too, is something you can address in your design. If you suspect that load times will be an issue (your tech lead should be able to give you a good feel for this), perhaps you should alter your design to allow smaller levels. Or you can designate points along the way where you pause the game for just a second or two for a quick load. This is a technique that *Half-Life* has used with much success.

Game Interruptions

In every game there are breaks in the action. Perhaps the player has come to the end of a level. Perhaps his character has died or otherwise hit a failure condition. Regardless of what causes the break, try to keep him involved. If he fails, don't kick him all the way back to the opening screen. Instead, as quickly as you can, cycle him back to a point just before the failure and let him try again. Always give him the sense that just one more try will bring success. Make it hard for him to give up. If he masters a level, tease him right away with the challenge of the next one. Always have another goal waiting just around the corner.

Saving the Game

It's astonishing that games are still being designed that allow no saves (or only one save at a time), or that let you save only at infrequent junctures, such as between levels.

This is horrible. It condemns people to replaying sections of the game they've already completed, which is a huge disincentive for them to pick up the game again when they've been interrupted.

In a PC game, you simply *must* allow the player to save his game whenever he wants, wherever he wants, and as many times as he wants. You should also let him name the save files whatever he wants. In a console game, where the size of the memory card is restricted, you should still try to give him as many save slots as you can, allow him to name them, and let him save as often as he wants.

Autosave, undo, and autorestore-on-death are all nice features, but they don't make up for preventing the player from saving the game when he wants to. This is a design requirement you must communicate to your tech lead at the very start of the project, so he can design the game's architecture around it. Mentioning it to him halfway through development might be too late.

Housekeeping

There are a few activities that the player should be able to perform at virtually any point in the game. If you handle these activities gracefully, no one will notice, but players will subconsciously appreciate it. If you handle them poorly, everyone will notice and they'll complain.

The player should be able to *pause* at any point. The phone rings, he has to go to the bathroom, the boss walks by. . . . There are any number of reasons why he might need to suspend your game world temporarily in favor of the real world.

It should be easy for the player to *quit*. (Mechanically easy, that is—psychologically, you want to make it as hard as possible for him to leave the game.) It's very frustrating to finish a session of gaming and not be able to clear the game off the screen.

The player should be able to *save/load* whenever he wants (see the preceding section).

The player should have easy access to the *options screen* so that he can customize the game controls and settings.

Help should be available to the player at all times. The initial help screen should be easy for the player to bring up, and the subsequent screens should answer as many of the player's questions as possible. You should tell the player how to save and load the game, how to customize the game by going to the Options menu, where to find additional information, and so on.

Bugs

Nothing knocks a player out of a game like a bug. Many designers think that bugs are the exclusive domain of programmers. Not so. There are many ways you can help keep the game bug-free.

Be clear in your design documents. If you're unclear and the programmers do things the wrong way, they'll have to go back and do it again. This reduces the amount of time they have to address other problems, and vestiges of the incorrect way are certain to remain and will be hard to stamp out. The more you can get it right the first time, the more they can too.

Be flexible in creating your design. Consult with your tech lead and listen to his advice. If he says of a particular feature, "It will be hard to code and buggy as hell," *believe* him. Perhaps there's some other way to accomplish what you want. Stay involved throughout the whole development cycle. You can't create a design document and walk away.

A bug doesn't have to be a crash. It can be anything that deviates from what you intended: a weapon that's too powerful, a line of dialogue that's spoken in jest but that you meant to be taken seriously, or an inappropriate lighting scheme that creates the wrong mood for a room. The earlier you catch these problems in the development cycle, the easier they are to fix. The later you discover them, the more likely they are to remain in the game.

Keep a level head. As the game comes down to its final days in development, everyone's life revolves around managing the bug list. Deciding what gets fixed and what doesn't is the joint responsibility of the test lead, the tech lead, the producer, and the designer.

When everyone is working 20-hour days in a superheated atmosphere, it's easy for problems to be blown out of proportion, arguments to erupt, and friendships to shatter. At this stage, you must distinguish between problems that are a matter of taste and problems that will actually hurt the game. Yield on the former. Stand firm on the latter. Remember that yours is not the only voice in the room, and try very hard to check your emotions at the door.

Interface Design

Creating a good-looking yet functional interface is one of the most underrated tasks of game design—but it's vital to get it right. You must decide what the game looks like on the screen, how information is passed along to the player, and how the player uses the controller or keyboard/mouse to input commands.

Influential game designer Brian Moriarty tells us a game interface should be "desperately simple." (And anyone who has met Brian will recognize the passion he puts behind the word "desperately.") Designer Noah Falstein refines this idea by quoting Albert Einstein: "Make things as simple as possible, but no simpler." Noah's point is to keep paring away elements of the interface until it's as simple as possible, but don't go so far in the name of simplicity that you remove something the player needs to play the game easily.

Vital information must always be easy to find (see Figure 2.2). The player should be able to understand what's going on at a glance. For some games, this means creating a *HUD (heads-up display)* that overlays information on the action screen. For others, it might be best to display status information and control buttons in a wrapper around a smaller active area. For still others, the information doesn't have to be visible at all, as long as the player can bring it up quickly.

The controls must be clear. The actions that the player takes most often should be physically easy for him to perform using the controller or keyboard/mouse. You must hone these inputs to a minimum number of nonawkward clicks, keypresses, or button pushes.

In his excellent book, *The Design of Everyday Things*, Donald A. Norman insists that the physical appearance of an object must tell us how it works. In a sentence that's directly applicable to game interfaces, he writes, "Design must convey the essence of a device's operation; the way it works, the possible actions that can be taken, and, through feedback, just what it is doing at any particular moment." He also goes on to emphasize the importance of constraints: "The surest way to make something easy to use . . . is make it impossible to do otherwise—to constrain the choices."

Figure 2.2 The interface of *The Sims* is clear and easy to use.

You cannot rely on your instincts to get this right. You have to try out the interface, first with team members and later with testers. What's intuitive to you can be awkward to someone else.

Pay attention to the conventions of your genre, and use them to your advantage. Don't try to reinvent the wheel. If there's an established way to play the kind of game you're designing, and you like it, and it works, *don't change it!*

Elegance and ease of use are more important than increased functionality. Achieving this compromise is never easy, however. Frequently, the team will argue about it for months. If including a nonvital feature comes at the cost of messing up the interface, you're better off without it.

Prototype the interface early, and keep noodling with it. Usually, there are several interfaces within a game. Look at all of them. Get people to test them early, and listen to their feedback. Most importantly, *play your own game*. If the start-up menu annoys you, it will annoy others. If the options menu is clunky, you'll be the first to know about it. If saving and loading is awkward and drives you nuts, you should fix it before a customer ever sees it.

You need to come back to this over and over again throughout the development process. The game must be easy to play. The player should not have to fight the interface. The whole point is to let the player do things quickly and simply. If the interface looks good and its theme is well integrated into the game, you get plus points. If making a "cool" interface confuses the player or makes it harder for him to play the game, it's not worth it.

One day, voice recognition and speech synthesis may revolutionize the way we interact with our games. But until then, the whole point of the interface is to let the player do what he wants without having to think about it. After a while, his fingers should move unconsciously on the controller or keyboard/mouse so that he's thinking only about *doing* it, rather than *how* to do it.

The Start-Up Screen

When the game boots, you have no way of knowing anything about the person sitting at the controls. Is he a complete novice for whom this is the first videogame ever? Is he an expert in the genre who can't wait to get to the tough stuff? Is he the gamer's roommate, who's only on the first level while his roommate is halfway through? Is he the proud but battered gamer who's firing it up for the zillionth time, hoping to finally defeat that last level?

You must design a start-up sequence that will accommodate all these users.

Your start-up screen should give the player the option of

- Going right into the game for the first time ("new game")
- Loading a saved game
- Going to the tutorial or practice area
- Opening the options menu to tweak features
- Replaying the opening movie (just in case he bypassed it unintentionally in a frenzy of button-pushing while trying to make the game load faster)

If you have an opening movie, let the player bypass it with a keystroke or button-click.

Customizable Controls

Give the player as much control over the interface as possible. Make everything as adjustable as you can. This includes game controls, monitor settings, volume . . . everything. Give him the best default settings you can arrive at, but then let him change whatever he wants.

Different things are important to different players. One player might want to optimize for speed instead of graphics, because he's an action addict. Another might prefer a higher resolution, even though it slows down the game, because he likes to look at the pictures. A third might want to remap the commands to different buttons or keys, because that's what he's used to. Whenever possible, let the player customize the game to his liking.

On the options screen, explain what each option does (see Figure 2.3). Don't assume that the player knows what gamma intensity or mouse inversion is. Explain each feature or setting, and tell him how changing it will affect the game.

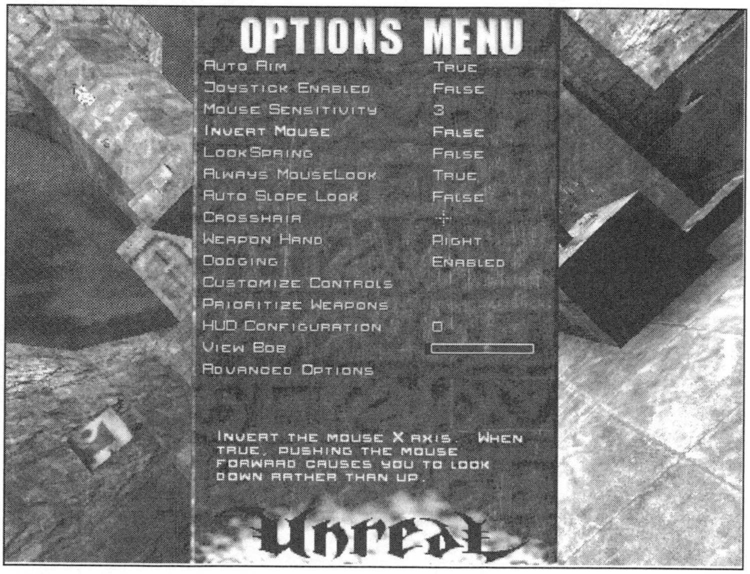

Figure 2.3 The highlighted option on this screen from *Unreal* is explained at the bottom of the screen so the player knows what it does. Used with permission of Epic Games Inc.

Cheat Codes

Include as many cheat codes as you can, while acknowledging that they break the play-balancing rules.

Entire third-grade classes are playing *Age of Empires*. Do they play by the rules? No, but those nine-year-olds are enjoying the game anyway. Not only that, but every one of them made his parents buy him a copy, and many of them will continue buying games in the future. This is a good thing for game designers everywhere.

In other words, let the player decide what's fun for himself. If he wants to get the biggest monster weapon there is and go around flattening everyone else with no challenge at all, *let him*. In an action game, include god mode and the cheats to get all the weapons or walk through walls. In an adventure game, give him the cheats to get around puzzles.

These cheats need to be tested, however. The more hierarchical the game (especially something like an adventure game), the more the game designer depends on the player having followed a certain path to get to where he is. If you let him jump there directly via a cheat, make sure that the cheat simultaneously sets all the game parameters as if he arrived there legitimately, especially in terms of objects in his inventory and flags set in the environment.

If you can't preserve the design integrity of the game while allowing the player to cheat, let him do it anyway, but make sure that he knows he's breaking the rules. You need to let customer support know about this, however. They're sure to get calls from confused gamers who've used the cheat codes and can't figure out why the game isn't behaving the way it should. (Even though you warned them!)

Tutorial or Practice Mode

Some players like to jump right into a game. Others need a chance to get their feet wet in a nonthreatening atmosphere.

A tutorial gives the player hands-on experience without endangering him. A good example of this is Lara Croft's house in the original *Tomb Raider*, where the player is slowly introduced to the running, jumping, and climbing skills he'll need later in the game. If he fails at any one stage, he can simply try again. Even if he succeeds, he can go back and do it again to become more comfortable or to learn the limits of the move.

The *Tomb Raider* tutorial is especially good because, in addition to teaching those skills, it also introduces the player to the character and the world. Thus, he's hooked from the start.

You cannot assume that the player will actually play the tutorial, however. (You also can't assume that he's read the manual. Many people just slam the game disc in and start it right up.) This presents difficulties if he must learn a certain skill in order to advance, but he hasn't gone to the right place to learn it. Probably the best way around this is to have some other character show him this skill, or tell him that there's something he clearly hasn't learned and that he should go back to basic training (or whatever it's called in the game) in order to pick it up.

Structure and Progression

"A game should be easy to learn, but difficult to master."

It's the cliché you hear most often about game design.

It's true.

It's true for arcade games, where the entire design philosophy is built on getting players hooked quickly and then escalating the challenges just enough to continue sucking quarters out of their pockets. It's true for board games. It's true for console games, where you have young kids who pick up the controller and drop it in a second if they can't figure out how to play the game. It's true for PC games, where busy people want to get into the game experience as quickly as possible without a steep learning curve.

Easy to learn, difficult to master. Anyone can sit down at *Quake* and start shooting things. As he gains more experience, he realizes that if he stands in one place, he'll get killed, so he learns to start moving while shooting. Then he learns to circle-strafe. Then to shoot while running backwards. Then to figure out which weapons are better up close or far away. Then he learns to rocket jump. As he progresses, he learns the characteristics of each weapon. He learns to "lead" his opponent. Anyone can pick up *Quake* and start having a good time within minutes, yet the longer he spends mastering the game, the more enjoyable it becomes.

In an adventure game, you should make the first puzzles easy. In an action game, make the first opponents fall over when the player even looks at them. In a fighting game, give the player some easy attacks that are effective right away. In a racing game, make the controls easy enough that the player can get out onto the track and start moving around. Save the esoteric adjustments for later, or at least don't *require* the novice to customize his car before he's ready to do so.

"Let the game begin" should be your motto. The first few minutes of a game are like the first moments of a movie. They're supposed to grab the audience. If you don't get a player involved in your game within the first 15 minutes, you've probably lost him forever.

Later, after the player has figured out the basic gameplay mechanics, it's time to raise the ante. If the intermediate levels are too easy, people will lose interest in the game almost as quickly as they do if the first levels are too hard.

As the player advances through the game, slowly introduce the intricacies you've built into it. If he must acquire a special skill to defeat the boss monster late in the game, give him some lesser creatures to practice on in the intermediate levels. If a puzzle calls for an intuitive leap, scatter examples of that kind of leap elsewhere before the player encounters that puzzle.

The final levels should be the hardest of all. You must find that delicate balance between the challenging and the impossible. A game that's too hard is no fun. A game that's too easy is no fun either (except to the very young). People don't want to play a game they have no chance of winning, nor do they want to play a game that's so easy there's no challenge to it. The trick is to design something in-between. Something that frustrates the player just enough that he enjoys it.

This sense of gradually acquiring mastery over a game is a pleasure that cannot be had in traditional media. (One doesn't get better at watching TV, for example.) The feeling is more like learning a sport—increased skill brings increased pleasure. What you must do is design a game where the better the player plays, the more he wants to play it.

Throughout the process, you must listen to your testers. Remember that you're one of the most skilled people who will play your game. You know its ins and outs, its strengths and weaknesses, its guts. A level or puzzle you think is ridiculously easy can prove impossible to others. By cycling fresh testers onto the game, you get feedback that's impossible to obtain from more jaded testers who've played the game as much as or more than you. You need both kinds of testing to make the game successful.

Taking Care of the Player

You're not the player's adversary. Your job is to help him enjoy the game you've created. It's easy to lose sight of this, especially when so many of your tasks involve challenging the player and finding that delicate balance between frustration and pleasure. Remember, though, that you're not in competition with him. Although *his* goal may be to beat the game, *your* goal is not to beat *him*.

One of the biggest mistakes young designers make is trying to prove that they're smarter than the player. There's no point to this, and it would be an unfair fight anyway, because you hold all the cards. Anyone can design a puzzle based on obscure knowledge or create a path that's almost impossible to traverse. The skill comes in creating problems that are just challenging enough, and in confining the player's frustration to the problem at hand, rather than making the playing of the game itself a challenge.

A good designer tries to help players get through the game, take care of them along the way, and protect them from time-wasting traps and pitfalls that take the fun right out of the whole thing.

Dead Man Walking

Don't put your player in a position where he can't win and doesn't know it. This is a familiar problem in adventure game design, but the phenomenon is now creeping into action games.

Let's suppose that in the fourth level of a game, the player needs some special goggles to spot the laser beams crisscrossing a narrow hallway. The designer put the goggles behind a crate on level 2, but the player didn't see them because it was dark back there. He went merrily on his way through level 3 and halfway through level 4, unaware that he missed something. Now he runs into this laser beam problem. He does everything he can to get around it. He becomes frustrated. He finally buys the strategy guide and learns for the first time that a) There's equipment he's missed, b) He's going to have to go back and get it, and, worst of all, c) He's been a "dead man walking" since the middle of level 2, and the last several hours of gameplay have been wasted.

What's the mindset of the player? He might decide that it's not worth it to go back and play through the game again. Even if he does continue, from there on out, he's going to play with one eye on the strategy guide, never trusting the designer to do the right thing again.

Instead, you want the player to trust you, to believe at any given moment that if he does the right thing, he can somehow win.

Protect Newbies

When the game begins, take it easy on the player. Ease him in until he acquires some confidence. Nothing is worse than to be a newbie in an online game and have some experienced player come along and kill you. Nothing is worse in a first-person shooter than to have the first set of opponents kill you over and over, while you struggle just to move around and can't figure out why you're always staring at the ceiling. Nothing is worse in an adventure game than a first puzzle that's so hard that you're made to feel like an idiot.

All these problems have design solutions. Devise a punishment for experienced players who kill newbies, or cordon off an area of the game where new players can fumble around safely. Make the first opponents easy. Make the first puzzle even easier.

Play It Again, Sam

Have you ever played a game where you come to a long, tricky sequence of moves that you have to get just right? And every time you get one move wrong, you die and have to go back and do the whole thing again? Often, entire levels have to be played this way. No matter how close the player is to completion, one false step sends him back to start over.

A special section of Hell should be reserved for game designers who do this. These same designers probably think that Sisyphus clapped his hands with glee every time his rock rolled back down to the bottom of the hill.

It needs to be stated once and for all, unequivocally, with no room for doubt:

This is not fun.

As the player repeats the sequence, pushing one step deeper into it each time, he comes to resent it, as well he should. He's demonstrated his ability to complete the early steps— why should he be condemned to repeat them? Why should he spend his time doing the same thing over and over again? What's new and exciting about that? Where's the entertainment?

Nothing makes a player want to fling down the controller and put his fist through the screen like dying for the hundredth time near the end of one of these sequences and having to go back and do the whole damn thing *again*! Nobody gains anything by this torture.

This problem has many solutions. The simplest is to allow the player to save the game at any point. That way he never has to return to the very start, but can pick up from just before he was killed.

Another solution is to code in checkpoints along the way. If the player dies, quickly cycle him back to the last checkpoint so that he can have another go at it.

The best solution is to avoid designing one of these sequences in the first place.

Give the Player the Information He Needs

All the knowledge a player needs in order to play a game should be included within that game. You cannot expect him to rely on strategy guides, Web sites, or word of mouth to pick up critical information. Whenever possible, the information should be on the disc itself, rather than in the manual. However, some games (especially simulations) are so complex that a beefy manual cannot be avoided.

Many games have *undocumented features*, special moves or tricks that aren't mentioned anywhere in the manual. These frills can be fun, but you must make sure they aren't essential to the completion of the game, because not everyone will discover them.

It's also a tricky problem for a designer to figure out what "everyone knows." It used to be that gamers were computer hobbyists with a scientific or mechanical bent, and you could rely on them to have a certain body of common knowledge. You could make jokes based on pop-culture references and devise puzzles using the order of colors in the spectrum. Now the person playing your game could be a teenager in Italy or a grandmother in Sweden. You can't be sure what these people know. So if your gameplay relies on specialized knowledge, you must make that knowledge available to the player.

Reduce Player Paranoia

Players spend much of a game worrying that they're doing the wrong thing. You need to reassure them when they're doing okay. Give them small, incremental rewards as they make progress toward their goals. Gently steer them in the right direction, and let them know when they're straying from the path.

Offer Levels of Difficulty

Another way of taking care of the player is to include different levels of difficulty in your game. These usually come in three flavors—novice, intermediate, and expert. In an action game, for example, the novice level has fewer opponents, who die more easily and might not have the smartest AI. At the intermediate level, you can provide less ammunition for the weapons you give the player, or make the player's health packs less powerful. At the expert level, there are many opponents with good AI, sparse ammunition, and perhaps no armor or health kits.

Similar gradations can be made in other genres. Driving games can vary the performance of the other cars, adventure games can scatter more clues to the puzzles, and sports games can demand greater or lesser adherence to the rules. In every case, you're allowing the player to choose the degree of challenge that will provide the most enjoyment for him.

How to Design

With all these principles in mind, how do you actually go about designing your game?

Create an Integrated Whole

Game design doesn't have to be as hard as people make it out to be. Once you have an original inspiration (the high concept), a lot of the design process is mere logic. If you've settled on the central nugget around which the game revolves, a lot of design comes down to iteratively answering this question: "For this interesting thing to be true, what *else* has to be true?"

As you answer this question over and over, your world slowly grows into an integrated whole. "If we're doing a farming simulation, we're going to need tools. How does the player use these tools? What do they look like on the screen? How does the player select them? How does he manipulate them? What does he see after he's used them?" And so on.

Economy of Design

Good design in any field is distinguished by simplicity (see Figure 2.4). A good designer includes only those things that are necessary to create the effect he desires. Anything else is superfluous and detracts from the overall goal.

In game development, economy of design also helps your schedule and budget. If you know exactly what you want to build, you won't waste time and money creating material that ends up on the cutting room floor.

The high concept is also useful in this regard. While a project is in development, features will pop up that the team wants to implement. You can't do *everything*, so how do you decide what to put in and what to leave out? One very good benchmark is to assess the proposed feature against the high concept. If it doesn't help you achieve the game's basic goal, leave it out.

The best games aren't big and sprawling; they're tight and focused. They don't distract the player with irrelevancies.

Figure 2.4 The Barcelona Chair, designed by Mies van der Rohe (originator of the phrase "Less is more").

Where Do You Get Your Ideas?

This is the question most frequently asked of writers and game designers. The answer is that if you're designing something of interest to *you*, the ideas will come naturally. This was mentioned in the preceding chapter, but it bears repeating. The game should be about something you're interested in, and it should be in a genre you're familiar with.

However, even though one person might set the game design in motion, there must still be a balance between his ideas and those of the rest of the team. Every game needs a "vision guy"—the person who holds the central idea in his head and evaluates all proposals and suggestions against that idea. In some cases, it's not even the game designer who fills this role, but the project leader or the producer.

One of the major tenets of this book is that no one person can come up with all the creativity necessary to make a game successful. Game design is a collaborative art, and you need contributions from all the disciplines, including story, art, programming, gameplay, sound, music—even sales and marketing. Everyone involved in the production of the game has a claim on the design, and the design process must be flexible enough to include each person's contributions.

Some endorse the *cabal* approach. This method sets up highly focused teams, each of which addresses one specific area. Each group usually includes one member from each of the areas of production (programmer, artist, level designer, tester, and so on). They have a series of meetings and are empowered to make decisions on behalf of the entire team.

A less formal approach to group design is brainstorming. In *The Art of Innovation*, Tom Kelley writes about the success of IDEO, a Silicon Valley product development firm. "The best way to get a good idea," Kelley writes, "is to get *lots* of ideas." A brainstorming session gathers team members in an open discussion that generally follows established rules. No ideas are labeled good or bad; they're merely recorded. No decisions are made during the meeting; the group tries to get a flow going, and they record the session without interfering with it. For example, they might photograph the whiteboard as they go along.

Keep the size of your brainstorming group small, preferably fewer than seven people. Larger groups tend to ramble and are less productive. Small groups stay more focused, kicking around many variations of one idea before moving on to the next.

When a brainstorming session is over, the designer is free to mull over the ideas, accepting some and rejecting others. This system takes advantage of the creativity of the entire team, but relies on the vision guy to keep the focus.

Finally, don't talk about your ideas too soon. A small flame can easily be extinguished by a puff of wind. If it grows into a fire, the stronger the wind, the more fiercely it burns. When an idea is born, it can easily be extinguished by a single puff of derision. After it's established, though, conversational buffeting only makes it stronger, requiring it to adapt, change, and grow. When you get an idea, nurture it along before exposing it to the winds of discussion. When the spark becomes a fire, bring it out for others to see, and then you'll discover whether it's strong enough to survive.

CHAPTER 3

GENRE-SPECIFIC GAME DESIGN ISSUES

eople play games for different reasons. Some look for a casual, quick escape from the real world, and others want a challenge or a simulation of a real-world activity. Various genres have sprung up to satisfy these desires, and each genre has its own design peculiarities.

Action Games

Your goal in an action game is to keep the player moving and involved at all times. You want to create an adrenaline rush that makes his heart pound and his palms sweat. The primary skills the player needs are hand/eye coordination and quick reflexes. Deep thinking is generally not required, although the better games in this category do call for quick tactical thinking on the fly.

Point of View

Your first design choice is to select the point of view. First-person games put the camera in the character's head. the player sees what his character sees. In third person, the camera is outside the main character, usually floating just above and behind but sometimes moving to different positions to provide a better view of the action (see Figures 3.1 and 3.2).

This choice has important implications for your game. First-person games tend to be faster-paced and more immersive. There's a greater sense of being "in the world," because the player sees and hears along with his character. Third-person games allow the player to see his character in action. They're less immersive but help the player build a stronger sense of identification with the character he's playing.

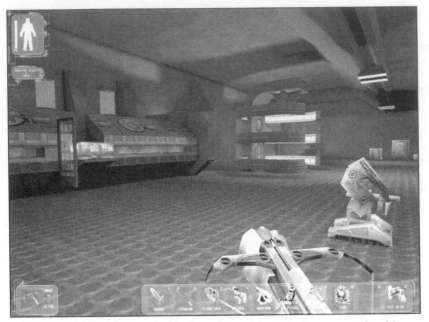

Figure 3.1 *Deus Ex* is a first-person game, where the player sees what his character sees. Used with permission of Eidos Interactive Ltd.

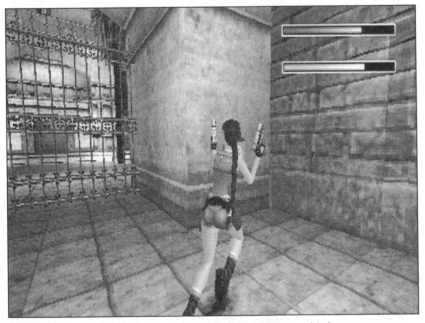

Figure 3.2 The *Tomb Raider* series, also from Eidos, are third-person games where the camera is outside the main character. Used with permission of Eidos Interactive Ltd.

First-person games tend to have more beautiful game environments and higher-detail nonplayer characters (NPCs). This is because the game engine doesn't have to devote any of its resources to drawing the main character. Third-person games chew up a lot of resources drawing the main character and the animations that go along with it, leaving correspondingly fewer resources to render the game world and the creatures in it.

If your main character is a generic "everyman" whose look and identity are not of great importance, consider using first person. First person is also useful if your main character's identity is so well established that players don't need to see him to identify with him (for example, James Bond). However, if your emphasis is on the main character instead of the world around him, consider using third person. (If a publisher is trying to establish and build a character-based franchise, such as Lara Croft, Mario, or Sonic, he will most likely request you to create a third-person game.)

Level Design

Good level design is crucial to the success of an action game. See Chapter 5, "Level Design," for an extensive treatment of this topic.

Weapons

Weapons are extremely important in an action game. They must be appropriate to the game fiction you have created, whether fantasy, science fiction, or real world. They must have interesting characteristics that encourage players to master their quirks. They must be well balanced, which means that there cannot be one *uber-weapon* that will automatically guarantee victory.

Give your player more powerful weapons as the game progresses and opponents become more formidable. These weapons should not only look interesting on the screen but also be accompanied by flashy graphics and sound effects when the player uses them. Although this sounds simple, it requires close coordination between you and the weapons AI programmer, the special effects programmer, the texture artist who creates the weapon, the artist who creates the special effects, and the sound engineer.

Generally, designers start off players with a basic weapon they can fall back on throughout the game. This weapon is only moderately effective, but plenty of ammunition is available for it. As weapons become more powerful, their ammunition becomes scarcer, which encourages players to become proficient in their use.

Engine

In all probability, you will be working with a licensed 3D engine from a developer such as Epic (*Unreal*), id (*Quake*), or Monolith (*Lithtech*). For console games, you'll be working with middleware supplied by a company such as Criterion (*Renderware*) or Alias (*Check Six*). Each game engine has its advantages and disadvantages, and you should consider several criteria when making your choice:

- **Ease of use.** Each game engine has its own editor, and each editor has its quirks. Check out the user community for a vigorous discussion of plusses and minuses.

- **Cross-platform capability.** If your game is to appear on more than one piece of hardware (for example, PC and PlayStation 2), your engine must support those platforms. Because every engine is built on compromises, make sure that the engine is best suited to your lead platform but can also handle the other platforms gracefully. For example, some engines are texture-heavy, whereas others emphasize polygons. The former tend to require a lot of memory, which make them better suited to PCs than consoles.

- **Look-and-feel.** Games developed in a particular engine tend to resemble one another. During the evaluation process, play games that use the various technologies, and see which appeal to you the most.

- **Support.** One engine can have an active user community and receive ongoing support from its creators, whereas another can have poor documentation and be incomprehensible to anyone but the people who wrote it. Again, the user community is helpful here.

- **Availability.** Do you select an engine that is still in development, or one that has already come to market? Using a new engine is risky, because your schedule is tied to the notoriously unpredictable progress of an engine team. If you require bleeding-edge technology, however, the risk might be worth it. Selecting a stable engine instead eliminates that danger but introduces a different one—your game might look dated by the time it appears.

- **Extendibility.** How easy is it for your programming team to modify and add features to the engine?

- **Cost.** Engines are expensive, but they're almost always cheaper than building the technology yourself. Pricing structures vary. Some companies charge a single (usually hefty) upfront fee. Others lower this fee but ask for a back-end royalty. Work with your business department to create a P&L (profit and loss) model with varying sales projections to see which cost structure is right for you.

Graeme Devine

Graeme Devine has been making games since the late '70s, having worked at Atari, Lucasfilm, Activision, Virgin, id, and now Ensemble. Perhaps his best known game was The 7th Guest, *but he has worked in virtually every genre including titles ranging from the PC port of* Double Dragon, *to* Quake III: Arena. *Here are some of his thoughts on the action genre.*

Action games fall into so many categories. The first few (*Space Invaders, Asteroids*) dealt with a one-on-one situation and slowly added more chaos to the fire until the player couldn't handle the situation anymore and died. Later games like *DOOM, Quake, Tomb Raider,* etc., still had that "one vs. the world" approach to gameplay but changed the point of view for the player to the third dimension. Other action games such as *Warcraft* and *C&C* took the approach of adding chaos for you to control, as well as chaos coming in to fight you, which multiplied the factors involved in gameplay.

On advances in technology

Technical design generally limits game design. Technology improvements do change the immersion factor of games, but it comes so often at the expense of good design and gameplay. We've seen a flattening of this curve over the last couple of years (good games with good technical design) and I'm hoping this trend will continue and flourish. We're at a point now where we can just about represent anything well in a computer/console game, and that frees the designer up to do some wonderful things. Unfortunately, as an industry we make far too many games with poor designs, and the good ones sometimes get lost in the pack (for example, *Beyond Good and Evil*).

How market conditions affect game design

I think the marketplace affects production more than design. Art and level design is so much more complex than it was just a few years ago, and takes so much longer, that it's become hard to schedule full-time people around the process of making a game. Also, publishers are so driven to the three threes (RPG, RTS, and FPS), that they are unwilling to try new game designs out. Long term, this will hurt our industry as people get bored with variations on the same designs.

> ### On story
>
> An increased focus on story can only be a good step, and I don't think we've even scratched the surface here, because we're not using real storytellers yet to spin the yarns within our games. Just as programmers created all the art for games back in the early '80s, the stories in our games are not yet well-produced (In most cases, that is—there are exceptions).
>
> ### Books that game designers should read
>
> Well, besides lots of comic books, I would recommend *The Writer's Journey: Mythic Structures for Writers* by Christopher Vogler.

RPGs

Role-playing games (RPGs) revolve around characters, story, and combat. They take place in large, expansive worlds and are frequently played out over hundreds of hours.

Character Growth

RPGs have a slow, delicious build that starts the player's character as a weakling in a strange and dangerous world. Through carefully managed encounters and alliances, the hero and his party slowly grow in competence and power until they are able to take on the baddest of the bad guys.

You must give players a range of choices in the attributes of the characters in their party. Some attributes should be shared by many classes of characters, but a few should be unique to a particular class. This allows players to balance the team yet bias it towards their own style of gameplay.

Although you should allow the player to select his party individually and to allocate attributes among them (within preset limits), you should also be prepared to generate reasonable parties automatically for the player who wants to skip this step.

By the end of the game, the characters will be a peculiar blend created by both you and the player. In no other genre do the players form a more personal attachment to the characters who play out the story on the screen.

Character Attributes and Skills

Traditionally, the outcome of a character's attempt to perform a particular action has been determined by a behind-the-scenes dice-roll that has a binary result. He either succeeds or fails, depending on some combination of his attributes (skill, luck, health, etc.).

Recent games have introduced a variation that brings these attributes out from behind the curtain and integrates them more elegantly into gameplay. Instead of getting binary succeed/fail results, the player performs various activities with more or less efficiency, depending on the current state of his attributes and skills.

For example, in *Unreal2: XMP* (an action game with RPG elements), designer Scott Dalton presents the activity of "hacking" a door not as a binary succeed/fail activity, but as one that progresses more quickly or slowly, depending on factors like the character's class, his health, his team's energy, etc. All the characters can hack a door, but some are better (faster) at it than others.

This method eliminates the hidden dice-roll and makes the player much more aware of how his skills and attributes are affecting him from moment to moment. The result is a much more satisfying and immersive experience.

Statistics

If you are designing a game in this genre, you should have a love of figuring out details, such as how many damage points a halberd will inflict instead of a pike and how those points will be affected by the target's armor class, spells of protection, or the luck of the wielder.

Some players share this love of statistics and want to micromanage their characters and how they are equipped (see Figure 3.3). Others want to get right to the action. You should allow for both. Give the player the ability to micromanage the characters, but also enable an auto-equip option that will automatically upgrade each character to better armor and weapons as he acquires them.

Statistics lie at the heart of the game, but you must be prepared to hide them if the player doesn't want to play by the numbers.

Story

Generally, storytelling in RPGs is accomplished through a series of quests. As the player carries out the missions, he explores the world and learns more about its inhabitants and his place among them.

To deal with the never-ending conflict between linearity and nonlinearity, don't give the player the quests one at a time. Instead, group the missions in a series of small clusters so that, although he has a choice of what he is working on at the current moment, he isn't overwhelmed with too many possibilities. At any given time, the player should have several immediate goals, one or two midterm goals, and one final goal.

More story basics are covered in Chapter 4, "Storytelling."

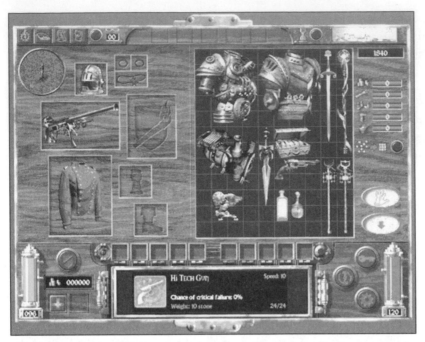

Figure 3.3 In the RPG *Arcanum,* players can choose how they want to equip their character. Used with permission of Sierra On-Line Inc.

Combat

Early RPGs were called *hack-and-slash* games, and combat still plays an important role in this genre. If you don't handle combat well, you won't have a good RPG. Here are some quick pointers:

- Design an interface that gracefully handles the encounters and makes the player feel that he's always in control.

- Whether your game is in real time or is turn-based, give the player a chance to make meaningful choices as the combat progresses.

- Don't overwhelm the player right away. Give him a training area where he can acquire competence. Carefully sequence his first several combats so that he can win and acquire a sense of mastery.

- If the game is a sequel, educate the player in the series' conventions and peculiarities (which you probably take for granted by now). The first hour he plays the game will be crucial. If it is hard to learn and he is killed again and again, he will return the game to the store and move on to something else.

Warren Spector

Warren Spector joined Origin in 1989. There he co-produced Ultima VI *and* Wing Commander, *and produced* Ultima Underworld 1 and 2, Ultima VII: Serpent Isle, System Shock, *and others. In 1997, after a year as producer of* Thief *and GM of the Looking-Glass Austin office, Warren started Ion Storm-Austin. Warren was project director on Ion's award-winning action/RPG* Deus Ex. *As Studio Director of Ion Storm-Austin, he also supervised development of* Deus Ex 2: Invisible War *and* Thief: Deadly Shadows.

I fundamentally disagree with your assertion that RPGs require large worlds and hundreds of hours of play. Nowadays, I think the trend is toward shorter games, even in the RPG space, and some of us believe that huge, contiguous worlds just mean lots of aimless (and dull) running around. I'd say an RPG is about, well, playing a role.

To me, RPGs should be about character development through player choice in the collaborative telling of a story. Character classes, stats, and combat are a throwback to our paper game roots. Even if, historically, we've defined electronic RPGs in terms of their paper game forebears, we must—and we have begun to—create our own conventions that don't derive from those earlier works.

I live for the day I can make an RPG that doesn't include any combat. . . . And I'm convinced someone will do that someday, even if it isn't me.

On the differences between U.S. and Japanese RPGs

The ways that U.S. and Japanese RPGs offer players control over the flow and pacing of game and story differ radically. U.S. RPGs tend to be more open-ended, freeform, and player-choice-driven, while Japanese RPGs tend to be more linear in their storytelling style, allowing players to interact only during party-building, power-customization, and combat. An obvious oversimplification, but something that's always intrigued me.

Advice to RPG designers

Always think in terms of player intention. Offer players the information and capability to make a plan based on their current situation and execute that plan. Make sure the world responds to that plan-execution in ways that are obvious to the player, ways that either change the player character or drive the story in a new direction. Opportunities to influence story or character growth are critical, I think.

Games that designers should play

I'm highly prejudiced here. . . . At least one of the "middle" *Ultimas* (4-6, maybe 7 . . .), *Ultima Underworld*, *Baldur's Gate*, *Diablo* or *Diablo 2*, a *Final Fantasy* game (7 or more recent), *Suikoden* (a personal favorite), *Knights of the Old Republic*, *Morrowind*. I like to think *Deus Ex* belongs on that list, if only to prove just how hard it is to define game genres!

Recommended reading

Zimmerman and Salen's *Rules of Play*. I'm quite enamored right now of a book called *First Person* (Wardrip-Fruin & Harrigan). There's always Brenda Laurel's *Computers as Theatre* and Janet Murray's *Hamlet on the Holodeck*. And you kind of have to read Chris Crawford's books, even if only so you can disagree violently! (Seriously, he gets *so* much right . . .) Outside the game/computer space, I'm a huge fan of Christopher Alexander's *The Timeless Way of Building* and Christopher Vogler's *The Writer's Journey*. Beyond that, I'd say read some psychology books and maybe some economics books. They'll stand you in good stead.

On moving forward

We need better actors. We can count on players to do interesting things. Wouldn't it be nice if NPCs behaved (and looked) more interesting, too? Wouldn't it be nice to get a sense of what an NPC is feeling through facial expression, posture, subtle changes in the way they move based on circumstances? Let me see a tear or a smile or a frown, caused by my choices. . . . And how about characters who speak believably, rather than in the stilted branching tree dialogue we're stuck with today? Give me all that and we'll really be onto something special.

Adventure Games

You are standing in an open field west of a white house.

The famous opening line of *Zork* is a call to adventure. The original adventure games combined exploration with puzzle-solving. They were stories in which the player was the hero.

Adventure games have evolved from their static, text-based origins to include more and more real-time elements. Whether you're designing a "pure" adventure game or an action/adventure hybrid, the defining characteristics of the genre are still story and puzzle.

Story

If you don't have a good story, you don't have a good adventure game.

It's up to you, the game designer, to decide what the story is. You cannot "harness the power of the computer to let the player create his own characters and write his own story."

Chapter 4 gives an in-depth treatment of storytelling, but the quick summary is that you must decide what your story is about and build the player's activities around that central theme. You must create interesting people, in interesting places, doing interesting things.

If you do not approach your story with this kind of purpose, you will simply write another Tab A in Slot B adventure game, and we have plenty of those already.

Puzzles

After you have the story, it's time to create a threat to the hero's world and put obstacles between him and his goal. These obstacles are the puzzles, and they must flow naturally from the setting and story.

Some designers think that this requirement is unique to our genre. It's not. Putting obstacles in the way of the hero has always been a fundamental part of storytelling. Ulysses didn't get back from the Trojan wars in a weekend.

A good puzzle provides a pleasant, temporary frustration that leads directly to the rush of the "AHA!" moment. A bad puzzle leaves the player angry, frustrated, and distrustful of the designer.

Puzzle design gets its own treatment in this book (Chapter 6, "Designing the Puzzle"), but here are some quick tips:

- Each puzzle must be appropriate to its setting, it must be reasonable for the obstacle to be there, and when the player solves it, he should know why what he did worked.

- To get puzzle ideas, think about the villain. He is the one who does not want your hero to succeed—how is he likely to try to interfere with the hero's progress?

- The puzzles must make sense. Give the player enough clues that he can solve them, don't make them too hard, and make sure that every puzzle advances the story.

- Don't think of puzzles as roadblocks to slow down the player so that he "gets more hours of gameplay." Instead, help him along.
- Every puzzle is a storytelling opportunity.

Interface

Simplify your interface.

The interface you design determines the kinds of activities, puzzles, and interactions the player will have—not the other way around.

Your interface must allow the player to do as much as possible with the minimum amount of effort. Effort, in this case, is defined by the number of clicks it takes to perform actions such as talking with people, examining the environment, doing object-on-object interactions, using inventory, and so on.

If allowing a particular interaction means increasing the number of clicks the player must make for all other activities, abandon that interaction. The player will be happier to have a streamlined interface with basic functionality than to struggle with a clunky interface loaded down by bells and whistles.

If there are well-established protocols for the style of game you are building, use them. The interface is not the place to experiment. The highest compliment a player can pay to the interface is not to notice that it is there.

Linearity versus Nonlinearity

The biggest complaint you hear about adventure games is that they are too linear. "I felt like I was being led by the nose." "I might as well have been reading a book." Players don't like it if they can't make choices. But if you give the player *too* many choices at once, he gets lost.

The solution is to design a linear series of open environments. In each open area, the player has many activities he can pursue in any order he likes. When he has accomplished them all, the designer closes off the area, does a little storytelling, and then moves on to the next.

Exploration

People are curious. They want to see what's around the next bend. Your adventure game should scratch this itch and take the player on a journey through a landscape of visually interesting places.

Be careful how you dole these out. If you open the entire environment to the player within the first ten minutes of the game, he has no surprises left.

Instead, use access to new places as a reward for the player and to show him that he is making progress. Tease him with hints and glimpses of areas he can't get to. Try to make the first view of each new area memorable—start with a bang, not a whimper.

Implementing this strategy also means that you must work closely with your PR people to determine which screenshots to publish ahead of time and which to hold back. The PR and Marketing departments will want to shout to the world about the great game you are creating, and there is an insatiable demand for screenshots from magazines and fan sites. It is not uncommon to see several hundred shots appear before a game comes out, causing some gamers to feel a letdown when they actually play because they've seen everything already.

Ron Gilbert

Ron Gilbert worked at LucasArts from 1985 to 1991, where he created such classic adventures as Maniac Mansion *and the first two* Monkey Island *games. In 1992 he founded Humongous Entertainment and was the Creative Director as well as the lead designer of the Junior Adventure Series, including the* Putt Putt *and* Freddi Fish *games, and the* Backyard Sports *series of games. He also created Cavedog Entertainment, which produced* Total Annihilation. *After leaving Humongous, he founded Hulabee Entertainment, and is now working on a RPG.*

I always put puzzles into one of two categories, plot puzzles and normal puzzles. Plot puzzles advance the story in some major way—they reveal something about the game or the main character. When designing, I always design the plot puzzles first, then fill in the others. That's not to say the other puzzles don't involve the plot. I see plot puzzles much the same way a screenwriter looks at plot points.

On linearity versus nonlinearity

I disagree (in theory) that there needs to be any openness. I think the story and design should be so damn good the player never wants to do anything other than what you want him to. I see my games not as "interactive," but "participatory." You are not "interacting" with my story (which implies some degree of choice). Rather, you are participating in it. Roller coasters never leave the track, but they are still damn fun. A guy I worked with in the early days of LucasArts had this saying: "Learn to love the track".

Games you should play

Zork. Kings Quest I. Myst (as an example of really bad adventure game design that sold billions, and no, I'm not bitter). And honestly, I'm having a hard time thinking of any others. If you're serious about adventure game design, you should play all the Infocom, Sierra, and LucasArts stuff. Not because it's that good (some is, most isn't), but just because you need to understand them.

On advances in technology

I don't think technology has had any effect on what we do. Yeah, there is 3D and all, but that doesn't change anything about how a good adventure game should be designed. It's all just glitter. Fifty years from now, we might have really good AI that can make NPCs a little more than script readers, but that's a long way away.

On the state of the genre

During recent meetings with publishers, even bringing up "adventure games" was a deal-killing move. Right now I am designing a role playing game, taking the elements of adventure gaming that work (story, character and plot puzzles) and putting them in the game, and of course, not mentioning any of this to the publisher. I think that soon, adventure game designers are going to need a secret handshake.

Strategy Games

The key to strategy game design is balance.

Balance is everything, and it can be achieved only through thousands of hours of playing. Play a little, tweak a little; play some more, tweak some more. More than any other genre, it is vital to have a strategy game up and running early so that months can be spent on polish and on play balancing. A strategy game cannot come together at the last moment. If you get this just right, your game may well become a classic (see Figure 3.4).

Figure 3.4 The *Command & Conquer* games are the epitome of balance. ©1999 Electronic Arts Inc. All rights reserved.

This balance extends to everything in the game. There can't be only one right way to do things. No one strategy can always succeed; otherwise, the game quickly ceases to be fun. In a well-balanced game, one's success is almost completely determined by one's skill.

Resources

Balance the amount of raw material available. Too much, and the player will never need to make decisions about it. Too little, and the player will spend his time worrying about that, to the exclusion of all else.

You must also balance the rate of production. It's no fun if the Red Team can build 100 tanks in five minutes, but the Blue Team can build only three anti-tank bazookas in the same time span.

Teams

Most strategy games have two teams opposing each other, but some have more. Regardless, each side in the game must have an equal chance to win. It was said of Robert E. Lee that he could take his soldiers and beat yours, or take your soldiers and beat his. The good strategy player must feel the same about the teams available at the start of the game. The sides must be balanced.

Units and Weapons

If all your testers wind up using the same weapon or unit, it is too strong, and you need to make it less effective. If there is another weapon that no one uses, it's too weak—beef it up.

Give each unit or weapon a single distinguishing characteristic, both visually (so that the player can quickly pick it out on the screen) and functionally (so that he can categorize its use in his head). In addition to its main function, however, include a few other minor capabilities as well.

You don't have to give the same units to both sides, but you do have to create a defensive weapon or strategy for every offensive weapon you create.

An effective design tool to keep in mind is the idea of rock, paper, scissors. This three-way dynamic leads to far more interesting choices for the player than two-dimensional design. *A* versus *B* is simple. *A* versus *B* versus *C* is much more complex and interesting, especially if the units are well balanced and have a circular flow of power among them. (See *Return Fire* for a classic example. The armored support vehicle, tank, and helicopter are perfectly balanced units.)

Realism versus Fun

Do you make it real, or do you make it fun? The answer is almost always to make it fun.

Even though you can base your weapons on actual ordinance, it's better to make them fun than to have them correspond exactly to their real-world counterparts. The physics of a certain weapon may confine it to a restricted range in the real world, but if it would balance the game better to give it a longer range, do so.

How much ammunition does a particular gun hold? How long does it take to reload? You can start with the real world in answering these questions, but what survives in your game must always be what's the most fun for the player.

Real combat is made up of hours and days of boredom, followed by 15-minute bursts of real terror. You must capture and extend those 15 minutes.

Artificial Intelligence (AI)

Programming interesting and convincing AI is one of the toughest tasks in the business. If the computer opponent always does the same thing, or is too difficult or too easy, the game will suffer. AI is a job for an expert in the field, not a game designer. Nevertheless, you can help the AI programmer by giving him a clear idea of how you would like the computer opponents to behave in various situations. Talk with him throughout development, and rework designs that he says will be too hard to implement.

Testing

Throughout the development cycle, you must constantly search for flaws that will lead to unbeatable strategies. If one team is inherently superior or always has an insuperable advantage, your game is out of balance. Similarly, if nothing can defend against a particular unit or weapon, everyone will use it to the exclusion of all others. This quickly ceases to be a fair game, and the player will lose interest and move on to something else.

You must rely on your testing corps to ferret out those imbalances. For testing that is even more thorough, consider holding an open beta, but do so only if you have the infrastructure to administrate it and make use of the feedback.

Missions

Organize a level or mission around one major premise, whether it is a particular style of gameplay or an unusual goal.

Because variety is the spice of life, change the themes and underlying structures of missions as the player goes through the game. Vary the strategies for success from mission to mission. One could be, "Build up your units and make a rush," the next could be, "Send in a small but powerful unit on a sneak attack," and a third could be, "Defend the base against an enemy rush." Mix it up so that the player doesn't become bored.

Quality here is more important than quantity. If you have to choose between giving the players lots of the same kinds of levels, or fewer levels with a greater variety, choose the latter.

Make sure that the player knows what his objectives are for each mission. This can be done either in a cutscene prior to the mission or within gameplay as the mission gets underway. It's also good to give the player access to a screen with his current status and a simple restatement of his mission.

Create visually distinctive landmarks to keep the player from getting lost as he navigates through your world. It's especially helpful if some of these landmarks appear as a result of the player's actions, so he can orient himself if he has to do any backtracking. This applies to both 3D worlds and tiled worlds.

Within a level, as within a game, start easy and build up the difficulty as the player goes along. Don't make the hardest part of the level the first thing he has to do. Ease him into it. Also, avoid the "restore" puzzles that plague adventure and action games. In theory, it should be possible for a player to win a level on his first try, rather than failing repeatedly in order to gain the knowledge he needs to win.

Mike Verdu

Mike Verdu co-founded Legend Entertainment in 1989 and was its Chairman and Studio Head until 2002, when he left to join Electronic Arts as Senior Producer of Command and Conquer: Generals. *His design credits at Legend included* Frederik Pohl's Gateway, Gateway II: Homeworld, *and* Mission Critical. *He is now the Senior Producer of EA's strategy game,* Lord of the Rings, The Battle for Middle-Earth.

The number and variety of strategy games can be intimidating—but I believe there is a simple and easy way to reduce some of the complexity in understanding strategy game design.

Draw a line on a piece of paper. Label one end of the line "resource management and building". Label the other end "combat". Most PC strategy games fall somewhere on this line—which is a spectrum that defines how much time is taken up by each of these fundamental strategy game play activities.

Some of the most popular strategy games in the history of our medium are nonaggressive resource management games that draw on the urge to be creative. Think of *Sim City*, *The Sims*, or *Roller Coaster Tycoon*. When you play one of these games you are generally figuring out how to use limited resources to make something cool (which might be building a city, shaping the lives of a family in a simulated household, or designing the world's best theme park). The act of creation is important—as is the challenge of managing the game resources.

In the middle of the spectrum are classic real-time strategy games such as *Command & Conquer*, *Age of Empires*, *Warcraft*, and *Starcraft*. The fundamentals of these games are pretty similar: they generally have maps or levels to explore and fight over, resources that can be harvested to build structures and units, armies that move and fight, and a technology or "research" tree that unlocks more powerful units and capabilities over time.

The balance between "resource management and building" and "combat" is critical in a real time strategy game. It's a bit of an exaggeration to say that *Age of Empires* players like micro-managing resource collection and *Command & Conquer* players like massive tank battles—but there is truth there. "*Age*" players do tend to prefer resource management and building while *Command & Conquer* fans like fast action and fighting. The market has actually segmented based on these preferences.

On the far right side of the line—almost pure "combat"—are strategy games like *Myth* and *Close Combat*. The player spends most all of his time moving and fighting. There is little or no resource management and building to be done.

Games every designer should play

Civilization, *Dune 2*, the original *Command & Conquer*, and *Warcraft II* are canonical strategy games that combine resource management, building, and combat. These games came out in the early to mid-nineties, the "golden age" of PC strategy games. More than ten years later, you'll find that best-selling modern strategy games like *Command & Conquer Generals* from EA, *Warcraft III* from Blizzard, and *Rise of Nations* and the *"Age of . . ."* series from Microsoft are direct descendents of these original classics. You'll find the basic hybrid formula of "explore—gather resources—build a base—build an army—fight to the death" present in all. The "technology tree" is also a key element.

The various incarnations of *Sim City*, *The Sims*, and *Roller Coaster Tycoon* are canonical games for non-combat oriented strategy games.

On advances in technology

What's interesting to me is how little the evolution of technology has really changed the fundamentals of strategy game design up to this point. Even the advent of true 3D didn't do much to change the isometric top down view on the game world—basically because it's the ideal way to look at the level you're playing and control your units. The games are certainly much prettier, but the dynamics in a real-time strategy game are very similar to what existed in the first incarnations of these titles.

The future holds the promise of breakthroughs on multiple fronts. Units in real-time strategy games are moving away from being little robots and are becoming real characters that act on their own emotions—fear, excitement, triumph, greed, anger, or empathy. The game worlds are coming to life as well; units are starting to interact with their surroundings in very cool ways. Improvements in game physics promise to finally fulfill the promise of truly interactive environments. Improvements in processing power will allow strategy games to take place in giant dynamic simulations with many possible outcomes rather than forcing the player through a series of pre-scripted levels. Finally, the widespread acceptance of broadband will allow us to develop a rich on-line experience with persistent campaigns that span worlds.

> **On designing for a larger audience**
> The holy grail for strategy game designers—at least this one—is to move the core strategy game experience to the next generation consoles. Up to now the best strategy games have been exclusively on the PC—but we're pushing to solve the design and control issues that come with the consoles, use the processing power and on-line capabilities to create cool new experiences, and eventually widen our audience far beyond what it is now.

Simulations

Casual games are often described as "a mile wide but only a foot deep." A simulation (*sim*), by contrast, is only about a yard wide but miles deep. It focuses on only one piece of equipment or activity and mines that experience for all it's worth.

Wish Fulfillment

Of all the genres, simulations are the purest examples of wish fulfillment. Your goal is to fulfill the player's fantasy of doing things he can't do in real life.

The catch is that players have different fantasies, and you must decide which ones your game will fulfill. One player might consider himself a student of mechanical physics and approach the sim as an exercise in the precise re-creation of reality. Another might be looking only for the adrenaline-filled rush of operating high-performance machinery in demanding situations.

The differences between the serious sim and the casual sim usually cannot be bridged in a single product, so you must decide at the outset which you're going to design and then must signal that decision clearly to the marketing and PR departments.

Hard-Core versus Casual

After you decide on your target gamer, tune the reality of your game accordingly.

For the hard-core, no detail is too small to get right. The physics model must be accurate. Measurements and tolerances must be precise. The controls must respond as they would in real life. The people whom magazines hire to review the game are likely to be subject matter experts, and they'll be merciless when you stray the slightest bit from reality.

If you yourself are not absolutely fascinated with this sort of minute detail, you probably shouldn't design a serious sim.

The casual gamer, however, wants to "get in and go." He doesn't want to be bothered with learning a million controls before he can *do* something. For casual sims, you must simplify the controls and simulate the fantasy the gamer has in his head, instead of the reality.

It's important that the casual gamer be able to have immediate success. In a driving game, for example, it should be very easy for him to at least maneuver the car around the track. Then, when he has a feel for the controls, it shouldn't be too hard for him to finish in the middle of the pack. To progress, however, it becomes legitimate to require him to know the fine points: which car to select based on the style of track, how much air to put in the tires, camber, pit-stop strategy, fuel management, and so on (see Figure 3.5).

Remember: The serious gamer wants real life; the casual gamer wants it to be like the movies.

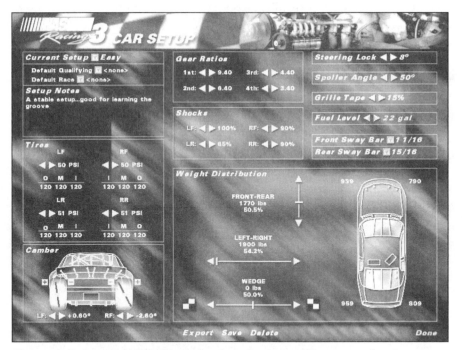

Figure 3.5 In *NASCAR Racing 3,* the player has an amazing range of options to fine-tune his car. Used with permission of Sierra On-Line Inc.

Interface

The more functionality you put in the hands of the gamer, the more complex the interface becomes. Even if you're designing a hard-core sim, keep the interface as simple as possible. Hide any game controls that don't have to be on the screen by nesting them inside menus, rather than clutter the basic view with too many options.

Keep It Fun

Whether serious or casual, your sim can't afford to be boring.

The player doesn't just want to operate the machinery; he wants to use it in pursuit of some goal. As in strategy games, the missions should be varied and can be linked in a campaign.

Beyond the emulation of the machinery, you have a wide degree of freedom in creating an entertaining ambience through convincing sound effects and scenery graphics. Take advantage of force-feedback controllers, and try to engage all the player's senses to help him feel immersed in the experience.

David Kaemmer

David Kaemmer co-founded Papyrus Design Group in 1987 and programmed the legendary Indianapolis 500: The Simulation. *He followed that up with a string of award-winning racing simulations:* IndyCar Racing, *the* NASCAR Racing *series, and* Grand Prix Legends. *Sometimes called the "John Carmack of Simulations," David recently co-founded FIRST-Racing.net, an online racing simulation venture. His interest in racing simulations has led him onto real racetracks as well. He has raced formula cars successfully for the past eight years.*

I always think of simulations as a very broad category, although within the industry *"sim"* usually refers to a vehicle simulator (originally just flight simulators). But there are golf sims, historical military sims, even suburban life sims (*The Sims*). To some degree, the more "casual" a sim becomes, the less of a simulation it is.

The notion that there are serious sims and casual sims is perhaps an oversimplification. In designing a simulation, you must always keep in mind what it is you are simulating. In the racing genre, for example, is the most important thing to simulate how it feels to drive the car, or simulate what it's like to manage a racing team? There will always be some aspects of reality that have to be glossed over while you concentrate on others. For example, in *Diamond Mind Baseball*, there are virtually no graphics, but it is considered to be one of the finest baseball simulations going. It doesn't simulate what it's like to face down a pitcher and hit a fastball, but it does give a good idea of what it's like to manage a team.

I think at the core of simulations is the idea that you are teaching the user something. There is an educational component to a simulation and the designer needs to know what that is. What new skill (or set of skills) will the user come away knowing? That helps to provide focus.

Tips for designers

Take the time to figure out an elegant interface. It can often take quite a bit of work to figure out what *not* to put in. Don't let technology drive your decisions about gameplay. Just because you can do 3D graphics doesn't make it the best choice for every sim. Development can get expensive very fast, often unnecessarily. Remember what it is you're teaching people.

Story & simulations

To my mind, the sim category is about focus on an activity that is difficult to participate in or practice in the real world, due to expense, or practical considerations. Story is usually used in games to provide a structure within which an activity takes on a purpose. People using a sim already have a purpose, so I've always felt that there's no need for story structure. Adding a story structure adds a lot of development cost, which could otherwise be used in increasing the fidelity of the sim. There are many who don't agree with me, who would like to add "career mode", or something like that. To me, that cheapens a simulation, and turns it too much into a game. The focus turns to success in the story, rather than success at the simulated activity.

Canonical simulation games

Microsoft's Flight Simulator, Diamond Mind Baseball, NASCAR Racing 2003 Season. Some older classics: *Red Baron, Battlehawks 1942* (for simplicity of interface and focus on the subject matter), *4D Boxing* (perhaps the first, and best, fighting game).

> **Books to read**
>
> Read books that focus on how to do the activity that you're simulating. For a flight sim, I would recommend a book like *Stick and Rudder* by Wolfgang Langewiesche. It's written by a pilot, for pilots. Similarly, *The Technique of Motor Racing* by Piero Taruffi or *Going Faster* by Carl Lopez are books written by race drivers for race drivers. If you're working on a baseball sim, focus on books about how to coach and play baseball. Of course, most sims involve physics, so you'll need to enjoy reading science and math textbooks.

Sports Games

Some people can't get enough of their favorite sport. They play it, they watch it on TV, they form fantasy leagues, and they buy videogames as well. These people are *fans* in the original sense of the word—*fanatics.*

Know the Rules

First and foremost in a sports game, you must get the rules right. Keep the official rulebook by your side as you design the game, and know the obscure ones just as well as the obvious ones.

Knowing the rules doesn't mean that you can't let the player change them! It's always a good idea to let him customize the game to suit himself. For example, he could decide that his soccer referee won't call offsides, that his National League team can use designated hitters, or that his NBA center won't be called for goaltending.

The Meta-Game

A sport isn't played only on the field. It's also played from the bench and in the front office.

Is your gamer going to be an athlete competing in a single event (on the court, making the plays)? Is he the coach of a single game (on the sidelines, sending in the plays and deciding whether to punt or kick the field goal)? Is he a manager trying to win a season of games (rotating starting pitchers and resting tired veterans)? Is he an owner trying to build a franchise (fantasy league play, trading players and worrying about the salary cap)?

Each of these activities results in a different game, and the user needs to know by looking at the box which of these games you have designed.

Licenses

The whole genre is fraught with license issues, so work closely with your legal staff to determine what you can or cannot use. Everything imaginable can be licensed these days, so you can't casually include anything. You must get written permission to depict everything from venues (major league baseball parks, football stadiums, racing tracks), logos (team names, mascots, uniform designs, even certain color schemes on equipment), player names, likenesses, and even signature moves.

The safe rule is that if you're showing *anything* that can be construed as being taken from real life, you must get it cleared. Remember, too, that these clearances cost money and must be calculated into your budget.

The Look

Sports games lead all other genres in the realistic depiction of human bodies in motion (see Figure 3.6). Here is where you find the best animation in the business. Practically speaking, this means that your game design, schedule, and budget must take into account the complexities of motion capture. With this technology, it's now possible to capture the signature moves of players so precisely that even a glance at the screen can reveal who each player is. Make sure your art director and tech lead are comfortable with this technology before moving forward.

Figure 3.6 Motion capture gives a sense of heightened realism to games like *Madden NFL 2000*. © 1999 Electronic Arts Inc. All rights reserved.

Managing the camera is also complicated. In some games all the action is in one spot. In hockey, the action is where the puck is. In other games, the action is spread out over a much wider area, especially when team formation is important, such as in football. Study the existing games in your genre and see how they approach these problems. Then consider the hardware you have at hand, and think about whether you can come up with a new and better approach or should stick with the tried and true.

Also, take the time to consider special imagery that's peculiar to your sport. It might be the ethereal beauty of early morning fog on a pristine golf course, or droplets of sweat flying off boxing gloves caught in the spotlight. Reproducing these strong visual images reinforces the fantasy.

Features and Interface

Don't load up the game like a Christmas tree. Select the most important features, and then tune and polish those, rather than including everything under the sun without having time to make sure that they all work.

Pay special attention to the user interface. Sit down with the controller for the game system, and think carefully about how its button layout matches the kinds of actions the user will have to emulate on the field.

If the hardware permits, allow the player to download the latest statistics, or to create his own images and import them into the game.

Finally, check out the peculiar activities associated with the real-world sport, and include that ambience in the game. When a football team scores, some fans do as many push-ups as their team has points, some stadiums fire off cannons, some have mascots that cavort across the field. Soccer fans sway back and forth throughout a match, and their wailing chant has become the soundtrack to the real-world game. On the golf course, announcers whisper and fans applaud politely, as if they were wearing white gloves at a tea party. If you capture these rituals, you will also captivate the player.

Dale Jackson

Dale Jackson joined Tiburon Entertainment in 1995, working as an artist on EA's first football products for the PlayStation. He moved through the roles of art manager, director of development, and senior producer before arriving at his current position as executive producer on the Madden series. Dale is extremely team-oriented, and he credits his success to "being at a great company and working with some of the best talent in the industry."

If you want new ideas, you must look in new places for inspiration. That's true for all genres, but it is probably most overlooked by sports game designers.

All designers have to consider what we want the user experience to be, how we want to pace the gameplay, usability, depth, replay value, etc. We have to analyze how and why gamers play the games they do. Sports game designers in particular must then apply those findings to our genre to give the users new ways to play and look at our games.

Fun versus realism

We often have to determine where to draw the line between what is real and what is fun. This is most often dictated by limitations of the hardware. For instance, we have the power to do some very realistic ball physics in a football game. However, unless all of the physical objects that the ball can react to (player, field, stadium, benches, goalposts, pylons, etc.) can be as precise and accurately modeled as the ball itself, there will be a big disconnect in how the game plays. Another common tradeoff is control vs. the visual look, especially animation. It is pretty easy to force a character in a game to perform a perfect-looking animation at the right time. But to do so, we might have to momentarily take control away from the player. Finding a happy medium where we can leave the player in control and still hit a quality level with the animation is where the balance has to occur. In the end, fun game play is more important than realism, so if a balance can't be found and a tradeoff is necessary, fun wins.

On technology

The biggest effect of technological advancements is how much they allow you to let the user experience the game itself, rather than the hardware. We are now able to create better graphics, AI, and animation, which allows us to focus on making a game where people lose themselves in the action and don't even feel as if they are playing a game. This requires focusing on the experience and how it naturally fits with the controls. The more that control can become a subconscious aspect of gameplay, the more the user is immersed in the sports experience itself.

Adding context

We are always looking for ways to bring emotion into the sports games we are creating. Traditional gameplay can only take the user a portion of the way to experiencing all of the emotion involved in a sport. Through adding story and a broader picture of the sport than just the single game experience we can begin to tap into some of the other areas that make sports great.

Games you should play

The range of games, both in style and gameplay, is so great that you need to play as many as possible. There are design takeaways from every game, even if it is only what *not* to do. Looking outside the sports genre itself is often the best way to really spark creative ideas in sports gaming.

Books you should read

I read everything. The more the better. Ideas come from the most unlikely of places. The last way I would expect to find a groundbreaking idea on developing sports games is by restricting my research to that specific area.

On the design team

Sports games are more often designed by a full team than by a single designer. While you often hear of great designers like Will Wright or Sid Meier in other game genres, you seldom hear someone designated as the key designer on a sports product. Our games are put together by teams with a lot of great designers who all make large contributions. I have been fortunate to work with some of the best sports game designers in the industry, and have had a lot of success based on the great teamwork involved.

Fighting Games

Fighting games are simple and direct, yet they can be very engaging. This is one of the few genres to assume that the players are physically sitting side by side and can talk to (and taunt) each other. Your goal is to create quick bursts of swift and intense action, followed by more of the same.

Because the focus is so tight, great graphics are a must. The only things players see are a confined fighting area, a relatively static backdrop, and the two fighters. These characters are the most visually developed of all the genres, because the processor can focus so much attention on them.

Each of the characters must have a unique look that conveys personality, and a set of distinctive moves that are interesting to watch. The animations must be perfect.

The characters and moves must be well balanced. If one character has unstoppable moves, everyone will want to play him. If another is too weak, no players will choose him as their avatar. Either case would be evidence of poor design.

Pay attention to weapons, special graphics effects and sound effects, because they add a large portion of the flash and dazzle of the games.

Manage the damage points so that the rounds are neither too short nor too long.

Start the player with a set of easy-to-learn moves. The button-presses should do approximately the same things for all the characters (for example, High Attack, Low Attack, Defend, and so on), but you should also build in special moves for each character that the players can learn as they slowly master the game.

Ed Boon

Ed Boon has been in the game industry for 17 years. After graduating from the University of Illinois at Champaign-Urbana, he began working for Williams Electronics, programming pinball machines. In 1990 he moved to the videogame department where he designed and programmed High Impact Football *and its sequel* Super High Impact. *Midway split from Williams Electronics, and in 1991 Boon began work on the first* Mortal Kombat *arcade game. The game spawned several sequels, two Hollywood motion pictures, two television series and has generated over a billion dollars in revenue. His most recent title* Mortal Kombat Deception *was released in October of 2004 for the PlayStation 2 and Xbox videogame systems.*

I disagree that the goal of a fighting game is "quick bursts of swift and intense action, followed by more of the same." The goal really is like a boxing game where each hit reduces the opponent's health by a certain percentage. The first player to get enough hits on his opponent to reduce his health meter to 0 wins the round. The first opponent to win 2 out of 3 rounds wins the match.

Also, it's not true that "the button presses should do approximately the same thing across all the characters." In fact, exactly the opposite is true. Some fighting games have been criticized for doing exactly that. If all of the basic attacks for the characters were approximately the same, then there really wouldn't be much distinction between different characters, other than their special moves. This results in the perception that all the characters are basically the same and the game quickly gets dull.

The goal with fighting games is to make the characters as diverse as possible in *all* areas: Basic attacks, defensive moves, special moves, speed, strength. The more variables you can introduce into the basic fighting mechanic, the more variables you can adjust to make as varied a cast of characters as possible. This is *very* challenging as the rosters of characters in fighting games has gone up from about 8 in the early 90's to 20+ in today's games.

Tips for designers

Animations in fighting games are perhaps the most critical element that can make the game "feel" great or horrible. More than any other game genre, fighting games are very reflex-sensitive and *absolutely require* that the controls be as responsive as possible for the player. Animations play a critical role in this formula. When a player presses an attack button, his character needs to begin his attack animation immediately. Players *need* to see their character begin their animation the instant they press the button. A delay of just a few frames will make the difference between a responsive and sluggish-feeling fighting game.

The same is true with maneuvering your fighter on the screen. There are periods in the game where control of the fighter is temporarily taken away from the player—in the middle of a punch attack, for example. The time window where you cannot interrupt with another command from your controller needs to be minimal. The instant your attack animation finishes, control of your character needs to resume. Both the animation speeds and the small time windows where the player controls are disabled contribute to the responsive feel of a fighting game.

Also, since so much of fighting games graphics are devoted to displaying these large character models, the design of the characters, their costumes, their size, and their styles all are very sensitive areas that require much more thought than just putting a guy in a white karate suit. Character design is much more critical in fighting games, and the bulk of the content is in the lineup of characters.

Games that designers should play

You can literally count on one hand the fighting games that have a major influence in this category (at least in the United States). These include *Mortal Kombat*,

Tekken, *Virtual Fighter*, as well as *Street Fighter* and *Soul Calibur*. Interestingly, all of these titles have been around for many years (some 10+) and have had many sequels. This genre is so competitive that it is very hard, if not impossible to introduce a successful new fighting game without putting a license on it.

On advances in technology

Sophistication in graphics presentation is probably the most noticeable feature that has changed fighting game designs. As the hardware systems become more powerful they allow games to present much more realistic graphics. Designers have over 10,000 polygons to represent their characters. Also, with motion capture technology these characters' movements can be exactly like a real human because the motions are taken from data created by human motion. I see this trend continuing. Each new generation of fighting game will make big leaps in the visuals and the advances will mostly be in the area of graphic presentation.

On story

Fighting games (for the most part) were originally made for the arcade, where games were designed to provide entertainment in short 2-3 minute spurts. When you only have the player's attention for such a short period of time, you need to entertain them enough that they want to put another quarter into the game and experience it again. This means you can't spend time telling an elaborate story. You need to bring them right into the action and give them the most exciting experience you can deliver in 3 minutes. This legacy of "short burst of entertainment" for the most part has remained intact with fighting games. But as they are being designed for the home, additional game modes have been added to provide the longer stretches of fun.

The team

The buzzword phrase that describes the development of a videogame today is "movie-like production," and the phrase is so often used because it's accurate.

It is very important for designers to acknowledge the massive amount of effort that goes into the creation of a video game. In just 10 years, the *Mortal Kombat* fighting games have gone from a 4-man team to about 60-70. Instead of just a couple of programmers, artists and a sound designer, we now also have writers, producers, directors, and designers. All these people have to understand the vision of the game and understand what their contribution will be.

Casual Games

The explosion you see at the top of the sales charts each December is the influx of "casual" gamers getting ready for Christmas. Often they are parents entering this bewildering marketplace for the first time to buy games for their children. The result is that brand names such as *Barbie* and *Monopoly* suddenly dominate.

As PCs and consoles penetrate more and more homes, though, casual games have expanded beyond their traditional Christmas niche and have become year-round sellers. Witness the phenomenal and sustained success of *Who Wants to Be a Millionaire?*

Your casual game should be "a mile wide and a foot deep." It should be easy to learn, but *not* difficult to master. Although the gamers' game generally offers increasingly difficult levels that require more profound strategic decisions or enhanced levels of skill, your casual game should simply provide "more of the same" to achieve additional hours of gameplay. This means that you must design a simple, uncluttered interface that presents the player's choices in an easy-to-understand format.

If the game is an adaptation of a real-world game such as Hearts, Solitaire, or Poker, you must also remain faithful to the rules (see Figure 3.7). However, give the player the option to customize those rules to his own liking.

Remember that a casual game is often played in short bursts, during lunch hour or a 15-minute break. The player wants to get in, have some quick fun, and get out. You cannot require him to retain information from session to session. He wants to start each time with a clean slate, although it's also good to provide features such as High Score and Best Time.

Figure 3.7 Some casual games are computerized adaptations of familiar real-world games. Used with permission of Sierra On-Line Inc.

Steve Meretzky

Steve Meretzky has been designing games in a variety of genres since 1982 for Infocom, Activision, Legend Entertainment, and his own development company, Boffo Games. His titles include Planetfall, The Hitchhiker's Guide to the Galaxy *(in collaboration with Douglas Adams),* Leather Goddesses of Phobos, Zork Zero, *and* The Space Bar. *He is currently Creative Content Director at worldwinner.com, where players can play games of skill in cash tournaments. He has served on the board of directors of the IGDA, and is a founder of the Boston IGDA chapter, known as Post Mortem.*

The best definition I've ever heard of this genre comes from Dave Rohrl (Senior Producer at EA.com): "A casual game is a game for someone for whom gaming is not a central focus of his or her life." These are people who buy retail games like *Tetris*, *Shanghai*, *Microsoft Arcade Pack*, and *Hoyle's Board Games*. They're also the people who play games at sites like pogo.com, zone.com, and games.yahoo.com. They're people who download (and sometimes pay for) games like *Bejeweled* and *Collapse*. They may play *Tetris* on their PDA and *Snake* on their cell phone. But most of all, you'll find them playing games that came free with Windows, such as *Solitaire*, *Free Cell*, *Hearts*, etc.

Here are rules for casual games we identified at the Casual Games Summit at the 2004 GDC:

- **Low barrier to entry:** Either the game should already be familiar to the player—so learning the game is nothing more than mastering what is hopefully a very intuitive UI—or the rules should be able to fit on one side of a 3 × 5 index card.

- **Forgiving:** The game should be informative if you do the wrong thing, not just play an annoying error sound. For example, "You can only swap adjacent pieces" or "Your king is in check! You must make a move that gets you out of check!"

- **Short playing time:** Casual games should be playable in a couple of minutes, up to perhaps 15 minutes. Unlike hardcore gamers, casual gamers are not interested in sitting down for a 6-hour marathon gaming session. Someone may play a casual game for hours, but that should be as a result of playing game after game after game. Again, to quote Dave Rohrl, "wasting your whole day, five minutes at a time."

■ **Highly replayable:** Because of the short playing time, games must be playable over and over without getting boring and without burning through all the content (puzzle levels, trivia questions, etc.). High score lists are a great way to achieve replayability by giving a goal that transcends a single game session.

■ **Convenient/quick-starting:** Casual gamers won't abide long boot times, complex install procedures, or annoying and unnecessary company logo "movies." They want to double-click an icon and be immediately playing.

■ **Inexpensive:** Whereas hardcore gamers will happily pay $40 or $50 for a game, casual gamers will rarely pay more than half that amount.

Games you should play

Card games—*Windows Solitaire, Windows Freecell*

Word games—*Text Twist* (Gamehouse, 2001), *Bookworm* (Popcap, 2002)

Sports games (e.g. Bowling, Golf, Miniature Golf, Pool)—*Pool* (games.yahoo.com, year unknown)

Casino games—Nothing definitive; all tend to be rather generic

Puzzle/strategy—*Shanghai* (Activision, 1985), *Tetris* (Spectrum Holobyte, 1987), *Collapse* (Gamehouse, 2000), *Bejeweled* AKA *Diamond Mine* (Popcap, 2000), *Cubis* (Fresh Games, 2002)

Trivia—*You Don't Know Jack* (Jellyvision/Berkeley Systems, 1995)

Classic arcade—*Breakout* (Atari, 1976), *Space Invaders* (Taito, 1978), *Pac-Man* (Namco, 1980)

Classic board games (e.g. Chess, Checkers, Backgammon)—*Chessmaster 7000* (Mindscape, 1999)

Modern board games—*Monopoly* (Westwood Studios/Hasbro Interactive, 1995)

Game shows—*Strike a Match* (Boxerjam.com, year unknown)

On advances in technology

The growth of Internet access has had a huge impact on casual games, which are ideally suited to the Internet mass market, thanks to their small downloads and their appeal to a broad audience. We no longer have lush 3D graphics and copious whimsical animations, but those elements are, basically, fluff; the core gameplay elements of casual games transfer easily from the CD-based retail channel to the virtual marketplace of the Web.

Technologies like Java, Flash, and Shockwave have helped make casual game development more platform-independent, and have also provided the tools that make game development possible by individuals or "garage companies" with only rudimentary programming abilities.

Another place where the casual games market is being buffeted by technical change is in mobile games. Because of cellphones' limitations as gaming devices, almost all mobile games being offered currently are casual games. The technical constraints of developing for the mobile market are intense; the different models of phones (even when running supposedly platform-independent environments, such as Brew or J2ME) represent many different incompatible platforms. In addition, the memory footprints are miniscule, and the displays are small and often monochromatic. Finally, because of the way mobile games are distributed, players often make buying decisions based on nothing more than a list of game names; therefore, licenses are critical to success.

How changing market conditions affect design

The most lucrative market for casual games right now is the downloadable market. Players are able to play a given game for free on a Website (such as the developer's own Website, or on a gaming site such as pogo.com). Players are also able to download a trial version for free. This trial version may be a fully-featured version, but playable for only a limited number of sessions or minutes; or it may be playable indefinitely, but missing certain features or content; or it may be both time-limited and feature-limited. Players must provide credit card information, paying an amount generally ranging from $15 to $25, to receive a software key that unlocks the full version.

When designing a game that will be distributed in a *session-limited* trial version, it is important to make sure the game is very fun and addicting in a very short span of time; if a player is still learning the ins and outs of the game when the trial runs out, he or she won't be very likely to purchase the unlocked version at that point. If the game will be distributed in a *feature-reduced* trial version, then it is important to design the game such that the feature-reduced version has enough there that it is fun and addicting, but not so much that there is no impetus to pay to unlock the full version. Some examples of missing features are lack of "undo" functionality or a high score list. Often the missing features are content, such as a trial version which contains only 10 of 100 levels, or 500 out of 10,000 trivia questions.

Books to read

Clean, simple, intuitive interface design is important in any game, but is particular crucial in casual games where the players want to be up and playing very quickly, where players will flee at the tiniest frustration, and where players are even more loath than hardcore gamers to read rules. Therefore, a good book on

UI design would be an excellent addition to your bookshelf; I don't have a recommendation, and in fact I'd love to get a recommendation from your readers to add one to *my* bookshelf!

Also, with little in the way of long-term goals, and with no time for any sort of story-related element, casual games are all about the moment-by-moment addictiveness of the gameplay. Therefore, books on how the human mind works may have lessons for the designer of casual games. Two that are in my reading queue, and come highly recommended, are *Flow: The Psychology of Optimal Experience*, by Mihaly Csikszentmihalyi, and *How the Mind Works*, by Steven Pinker.

Finally, the development of casual games harkens back to the early days of our industry in many ways: small teams, short development times, low budgets, the need to justify every byte, people wearing multiple hats, lots of exciting innovation instead of sequelitis and bloated "me-too" games, and a freedom from the bureaucracy of large publishers. So books that recount the early days of game development might be worth reading, such as *Hackers: Heroes of the Computer Revolution* by Steven Levy (especially the third part, on the early days at Sierra Online), and *Game Over* by David Sheff (especially the part about the birth of *Tetris*).

On breaking in

Casual games represent the best space today for a startup company to break into the game development biz. It's the only place where a "garage company" can hope to compete. The barriers to entry are still rather low. The person-hours that go into a typical casual game are still low enough that a few people can form a virtual company and create a game in their weekend and evening hours. And with the Web as a viable distribution method, there are no steep production costs to act as an additional barrier to entry.

God Games

God games have no preset "win" condition. Thus, they are sometimes called *software toys* or *sandbox games*. You must still design a compelling activity that is fun for the player, but instead of pushing him in a given direction and telling him when he has finished, you let him choose his own path.

Here are some design keys:

- Give the player a huge variety of interesting building blocks to play with—especially if it's a world-building game.
- Because you're giving the player so much to manipulate, make it easy for him to keep track of it all. Design a simple interface, and let him zoom in to concentrate on small details and zoom out to get the bigger picture.

- The interface should also allow him to jump quickly from one part of the world to another.

- The graphics should allow the player to distinguish between units at a glance, and should also convey status information.

- The heart of the game will lie in the AI—a very complex web of interrelated rules and subsystems that govern how the computer responds to the player's actions.

- Give the player instant feedback to let him know that his commands have been understood and that the game is working on carrying out his orders. It is important that he feel in control and that his actions and decisions are shaping what is happening on the screen.

- Occasional disasters can be a good thing.

- If it is a real-time game, let the player vary the speed of events, and allow him to pause the game.

Overall, think of the game as a big sandbox for the gamer to play in. Give him maximum flexibility, and never tell him that he has failed. You can create missions for him if you like, but you also must let him set his own goals and make his own game. The closer you come to giving the player a definable goal, the more likely people will call it a strategy game.

Will Wright

Will Wright co-founded Maxis in 1987. His SimCity *was released in 1989 and has since won 24 domestic and international awards. Will co-designed* SimEarth *in 1990 and* SimAnt *in 1991.* SimCity 2000, SimCopter, SimCity 3000, *and* SimCity 4 *followed in quick succession. His ground-breaking game* The Sims *was released in February of 2000 and has since inspired six expansion packs. Will was included in* Entertainment Weekly's *1999 list of "the 100 most creative people in entertainment," as well as* Time Digital's *"Digital 50," a listing of "the most important people shaping technology today." He has been inducted into the Academy of Interactive Arts and Sciences' Hall of Fame, and has also received a Lifetime Achievement Award from the International Game Developers Association.*

I don't believe there is a hard boundary between games and toys. Toys invite open exploration. You can use a toy to make up lots of games, but the toy itself isn't a game. You can play a lot of games with a ball, for example.

Toys imply more creativity to me. With a toy, the player has creative freedom to explore the system and its state, whereas games typically have a more formalized state space. There's a big region that's the win condition, there's a big region that's the lose condition, and there's a big region that's the unfinished condition. So games can have a more formal topology in that sense.

I tend to like games where I can go in and think of my own goals, where I can play several different games within the environment. In *Grand Theft Auto*, for example, you can pursue very different goal structures. In some sense you can think of it as a toy—a little toy world.

One of my goals is to create a good system for the player to play with, one that is very malleable from the player's point of view, and that is also emergent and interesting, so they're encouraged to experiment with it—to press buttons over *here* and see what pops out over *there*.

On deciding where to put boundaries

Unfortunately, you can only build so much. What you're trying to do is maximize the amount of developer time to player enjoyment. An infinitely explorable world would come at a severe development cost. Your goal is to figure out the regions that players will want to explore most, and put the bulk of your development effort there.

Another way of looking at it is to ask, "How can we channel the player into the most dramatic, interesting regions of this space?" In the design of the environment, you can look for psychological attractors that will make players want to explore certain areas. It's better to wall them in with lights than to put a fence around them.

Player goals

There are goal states where the players want the computer to recognize their success, and there are goal states where they want other players to recognize their success. These latter goals exist in dimensions that are very hard for a computer to parse.

So, for example, it's easy for the computer to recognize if my army is beating yours, or if my city is doing well and my people are happy. It's much harder for it to recognize if you've created a cool avatar or an interesting house. These goals are based on a kind of aesthetic performance, which can only be self-recognized by the player, but they invite a much more open-ended exploration of the experience.

Designing for emergent behavior

The goal is to get a minimum number of agents to interact in a way that emerges to a higher level of organization. And at that next level, you're going to see other groupings, which are made up of the lower-level units, acting as agents themselves. Aesthetically, we want the minimum number at each level to allow the formation of the level above it. So if you look at one level of the game and realize you're not getting the amount of emergence you want, you solve the problem by going down maybe two or three levels and increasing the state space at that level.

Implementing the vision

The best tool I've found to bring the vision to life is prototyping.

On my current project, we've already built over 100 separate, executable prototypes that simulate various little aspects of dynamics, or interfaces, or whatever. We usually build them in a few days, and they become scaffolding for our imagination. I can see some playable little prototype with dots and lines moving around on the screen, and on top of that, I can imagine the graphics being nice, the UI being slick, and the game being more dramatic. Prototypes allow my imagination to build much more detailed constructs than if I'm just sitting there trying to visualize everything in my head.

I do start with a vision of what I want the game to be, of what I want the player to be feeling emotionally. Prototypes are all about finding the right combination of rule sets that will give us the emergence, or the interaction, or the behavior that will then evoke that kind of mindset. We have to go in and do an extremely detailed map of each area, figuring out its regions and boundaries, its shape and size. And that involves a very sensitive survey of all the related dynamic systems in that region. Prototypes show that it's a fairly rugged landscape, that very slight changes in rulesets can create totally different feelings.

Managing development while prototyping

The process is very organic. Different components will be on very different cycles, and the art lies in weaving them together smoothly. It takes a lot of experience to marry the creative process of exploring this dynamic space with the production process of managing project milestones, workflow, content, and tools development.

Development is a multithreaded tapestry, and prototyping is one of the major threads. In the early stages we spend a lot of time on it. Then we taper off, but well into the project, and even near the end, we'll still be building prototypes for various aspects, because it's a cheaper way to explore an idea than actually putting it into the production pipeline and then finding out it doesn't work. It's much cheaper to explore that space as a prototype.

The designer as filter

If the game designer is the one holding the creative vision, then you're the final arbiter of whether new features or ideas or directions are true to that vision. If there's a compelling thing that is pulling you away from the vision, you need to decide whether or not your vision is going to change.

Sometimes I find myself in that position, where something sounds really cool, but it's not within my original vision. So then I have to decide whether this is a cooler path than the one that I had planned, or whether it's worth it to stay with the original vision—despite the fact that the new idea is cool—because at the end of the day I think that current vision is going to build us a better game.

How to intuit when you're heading down a design path that's not useful

Usually on any task, I'll be pursuing at least two, maybe three alternative paths that we could be doing. At some point we'll have two or three alongside each other, and there's almost always one that stands out. So generally, it's not so much that I say one branch is dead, as that the other branch is clearly better.

Tips for designers in this genre

- The sooner you can be playing the game, the better. (Which is another argument for prototypes!)

- Simplify! The game generally wants to be simpler than most designers want it to be. Every day I come in and tell myself, "Simplify the game, simplify the game, simplify the game." In *The Sims*, we had twelve motives for the longest time. After pulling our hair out a lot, we got it down to ten. We finally shipped with eight. It's not hard to add stuff, it's hard to take it out!

- Iterate the interface, to ridiculous amounts. Keep scrapping it and starting over. Each time you'll learn a little bit, and each time it will get a little bit better.

- Each day I try to figure out what are the three most important things I have to balance that day. Is it the size of my art team vs. the testing budget? Is it the amount of effort on the UI vs. the simulation? Is it the attention I'm giving the music vs. the lighting or the camera? There are so many places you can put your money and put your people. So every day you should ask yourself, "Out of all the factors that I'm balancing right now, what level should I be looking at today, and at that level, what are the two or three areas where I should really be worried about balancing my resource expenditures?"

Tips for designers in general

- The first step is to get a basic grounding in design as a field. Game designers can learn huge amounts from design professionals in other fields, especially from disciplines like architecture, industrial design, and toy design. Other disciplines have hundreds of years of thinking about the design process and problems. They're just an incredible resource. And all this is available on the net, just a browser away from you, if you want to go look for it.

- Also, designers should have a high visibility into the world. They should have the most external focus of anybody on the team, in terms of all the things you can draw inspiration from. Most designers stay way too focused on the games industry and what other games are doing, when there are a million cool things happening elsewhere that we can learn from. A designer should be an obsessive learner across different subjects. And it's fun! Game design is one of the few fields where you can go off and spend time immersing yourself in these different areas and actually using it in your job.

Books to read

Information Anxiety by Richard Saul Wurman

Design Thinking by Peter G. Rowe

Understanding Comics by Scott McCloud

Envisioning Information by Edward Tufte

The Design of Everyday Things by Donald Norman

The Coolest Cross Sections Ever by Stephen Bietsy

Gaia: An Atlas of Planet Management by Norman Myers

A Pattern Language; Towns, Buildings, Construction by Christopher Alexander

Laws of the Game: How the Principles of Nature Govern Chance by Manfred Eigen and Ruthild Winkler

Micromotives and Macrobehavior by Thomas C. Schelling

Things that Make Us Smart: Defending Human Attributes in the Age of the Machine by Donald A. Norman

Educational Games

The goal of an educational game is to teach a specific body of knowledge.

You must have a clear idea of what this knowledge is from the start. You cannot create a game first and then tack on some educational value at the end. This usually means working with a subject matter expert and adhering to the following guidelines:

- Have a clear goal. "By the time the player is done, he will know *this*."

- Consult *state frameworks*, the documents published by state governments that contain the objectives for a given curriculum.

- Target age is important. Children develop rapidly and move quickly from one stage to another. For example, older kids like the element of mystery in a game, whereas younger kids need to feel safe.

- Interactivity, important in every genre, is even more vital in children's games. Every time the player does something, he wants to see something happen on the screen.

- Keep the interface simple. Don't clutter up the screen or give the player too many options at once. Make buttons large and easy to click. Young players might not yet have the motor skills to maneuver the cursor to a precise area on the screen.

- Engage the emotions, and wrap the educational content into goal-oriented behavior.

- Reward the player often, not necessarily with points but with responses that encourage him to carry on. Deemphasize failure with encouraging words and a hint to push him in the right direction.

- Don't shy away from conflict. It is as engaging to kids as it is to adults (witness Saturday morning cartoons). Do steer away from violence, however. It will never be accepted in a children's game.

Kenny Dinkin

Kenny Dinkin was Creative Director at Riverdeep—The Learning Company/Broderbund from 2000-2004. There he oversaw game design and story development for a large portfolio of interactive children's products, including Reader Rabbit, Where in the World is Carmen Sandiego?, Oregon Trail, The StarFlyers, Zoombinis, Scooby Doo, Powerpuff Girls, Batman, *and* Strawberry Shortcake. *Other career highlights include a year as*

Executive Producer of the Mattel Interactive Education Innovation Lab, and three years as Senior Producer and game designer on the award-winning CleeFinders *series, where he led the creative team developing the brand.*

Make sure you don't oversimplify the enormous differences in developmental stages that a child goes through. For example, a game for a preschooler will need to be completely different from a game for a third grader—their cognitive abilities and capacities for abstract thought are completely different. So starting out by understanding your content and your target audience are the principal keys to success.

Rules of thumb for designing learning games for kids

I. Content Drives Structure Drives Story.

1. **Content drives.** Depending on what material you want to convey and depending on which age group you are targeting, your content will change. The content itself needs to drive your design. This isn't to say that there can't be an elegant game structure or gripping story line in an educational game. The content however drives and determines the structure and story—if you are trying to teach math, you may need a particular kind of game structure which utilizes (and integrates) on-screen manipulatives and inventory. If you are trying to work with language arts you may need to integrate words and letters into your game or to involve keyboard use. These structural elements need to be determined by allowing the subject matter (or content) to drive. In an educational product where one sets out to teach curriculum-based content, teams are typically guided by a defined educational "scope and sequence" which says what topics to teach and in what sequential order to teach them. Typically, a subject matter expert in the curricular area you are targeting would be a key member of a design team for an educational game.

2. **Don't start with story.** A classic mistake in game design for educational adventure games is building a story world first, and only then delving into game structure and content. Starting with story is like cutting the fabric for a couch before you've determined the armature. Cut too much or too little fabric and you may need to start all over.

II. Know Your Audience

3. **Know your target age.** Approaches to content change as developmental stages progress. Because of changes in developmental phases and cognitive abilities, a game design for five-year-olds needs to be handled very differently than one for seven-year-olds, even if in both cases you are tackling addition.

4. **Test, test, test!** Usability is critical in kids' educational games. You need to get it right, and your audience's needs are very particular. As a designer, you want to be careful not to over-design or make it too complex, but you don't want to dumb it down or bore your audience because you oversimplified. Kids can have pretty sophisticated needs when playing a game, but they can't handle overly complex or overly sophisticated UIs. (Who can?) No product should feature a complex UI, but it's particularly cruel to put a kid down in front of a badly designed graphical interface. No matter how sure you are, *test!*

5. **Become a kid expert.** Bring kids from your target age group in. Talk to them. Get to know what they like and don't like. Play games with them. Invest time in immersing yourself in their world. Remember that developmentally, kids change enormously between five and seven. Sit down with your target audience and see that developmental shift for yourself.

6. **Ask.** Ask kids for their ideas. You won't believe how much that can pay off.

III. **Respect Your Audience**

7. **Kids are smarter than you think.** No need to write or talk down to kids. Kids appreciate gameplay elegance just like adults. Using story and inventory to drive a compelling game can be just as effective in a kid's learning game as it is in a game for adults.

8. **Everybody loves a story.** Kids love story and they appreciate having a reason to do a computer activity. In other words, games that just plop a kid in front of a math activity but don't make any effort to integrate the activity in a larger story context can often leave a child asking: Why am I playing this again?

9. **Seamless integration.** We often try to create an immersive story world in our games, taking care to build a seamless integration between the story and the interactivity. We strive to create or use compelling characters and to stay vigilant about not having them break the fourth wall—that is, not addressing the user directly. By creating a third-person world we often allow the characters to reveal gameplay, puzzle, and curricular hints by using in-game dialogue between the characters. (So in order to keep players immersed in the game world, in-game characters might say to each other: "Hey, maybe if we move that rock, we can balance out this rickety bridge." As opposed to speaking directly to the user: "Hey player, take the mouse and click on the rock" which takes you out of the experience.)

10. **Make the technology invisible.** The best game experiences make you forget you are using a PC or console. They put you in the experience. An educational game typically sets out to be a fun way to have a learning experience. There is no need to emphasize the medium itself—it's just a vehicle to deliver the experience.

IV. Leverage What a Computer Does Best

11. A solid foundational puzzle, like dominoes, or solitaire (or at its most complex, a sophisticated AI) will typically be much more engaging than a foundation of multiple choice or "bean and bucket" activities. Too often I see game designs with activities that are just dressed-up multiple choice or Concentration. Kids will be compelled by—and learn more from—learning activities where three layers have been thought through:

    Content (What are we teaching?)

    Context (What is the story context?)

    Concrete (What is the foundational puzzle upon which my activity is based?)

12. **Personalize it.** Use the PC to keep track of the player's progress. This is particularly important in an educational game where we often track the level and adjust it in accordance with the player's progress through the curriculum.

Games you should play

If I had to tell an aspiring educational game designer to play just four titles, they'd be:

- *Logical Journey of the Zoombinis*
- *ClueFinders 3rd Grade*
- *SimTunes*
- *Putt-Putt Saves the Zoo*

Below is a longer list of canonical games. (I'm sure I'm leaving out tons.) Designers should also familiarize themselves with learning toys like LeapFrog's *LeapPad* books and Fisher Price's *Pixter*.

- The Reader Rabbit series, especially *Reader Rabbit's Toddler* and *Reader Rabbit's Preschool (Star Sparkle Rescue)*
- The ClueFinders Series, especially *ClueFinders 3rd Grade Adventures (Mystery of Mathra)* and *ClueFinders 5th Grade Adventures (Secret of the Living Volcano)*

- *Where in the World Is Carmen Sandiego? (Treasure of Knowledge)*
- *Oregon Trail*
- The Edmark *House* series, especially *Bailey's Book House*, *Millie's Math House*, and *Thinking Things*
- The *StarFlyers* series
- *Kidpix*
- The *Adi* series
- *Pajama Sam: No Need to Hide When It's Dark Outside*
- *SimCity*
- The *Jump Start* series
- The *Blaster* series
- *Roller Coaster Tycoon*
- *Disney's Magic Artist*
- *Triazzles*

Books to read

Here's an eclectic mix of books I recommend to game designers working in the kids/learning field:

Life on the Screen by Sherry Turkle

Visual Communication by Paul Messaris

The Psychology of Television by John Condry

The Tipping Point by Malcom Gladwell

Game Design: The Secrets of the Sages by Marc Saltzman

Understanding Comics by Scott McCloud

The House of Make-Believe: Children's Play and the Developing Imagination by Dorothy G. Singer and Jerome L. Singer

Puzzle Games

Many games include puzzle elements, but some games consist *solely* of puzzles, presented on their own without surrounding story or action. The challenge in writing such a game lies not in designing a single brain teaser, but in creating enough puzzles to be interesting to a wide range of players and in sequencing those puzzles properly.

Design the kinds of puzzles that you yourself like to solve (verbal, visual, or both). Remember that what seems simple to you might be hard to the player. When you know the trick to a puzzle, it always seems trivial. However, when you're on the other side of the great divide from the "A-ha!" experience, even the simplest of problems can seem monumental.

Your goal is *not* to make the player feel stupid. Your goal is to allow him to challenge himself, and to help him win. Make a graded series of hints available, and always give him the option simply to learn the solution, especially if solving this puzzle stands in the way of gaining access to other puzzles.

Most puzzles should be presented without time pressure, and it is enormously important that the rules be clear. The interface should be simple and allow for trial and error without penalty, by making it easy to reset the problem or undo a particular move.

For the fanatic portion of your audience, go ahead and include some extraordinarily difficult puzzles, but make it clear to the player that he is entering "expert" territory. There is a real sense of accomplishment in solving very difficult puzzles, and every game should include at least a few.

Scott Kim

Scott Kim has been an independent designer of puzzles for magazines, physical toys, computer games, and the Web since 1990. Major works include the computer games Heaven & Earth, Obsidian, MetaSquares, *and* Scott Kim's Puzzle Box *on the JuniorNet kid's online service. He also contributed to* Jeopardy! Online, The Sims Online, *and* Law & Order: Dead on Target. *He writes a monthly puzzle page for* Discover *magazine and is the author of the book* Inversions. *He is currently developing daily puzzles for the Web and mobile phones. You can visit him online at www.scottkim.com.*

A puzzle is a problem that is fun to solve. Puzzle games are toys with the goal of finding a solution.

Most people have a strong preference for one of three types of puzzles: Word, Image or Logic. Each of these types of puzzle exercises a different type of thought. Some puzzles, however, combine more than one modality. For instance, the paper-and-pencil game Hangman is a logical word puzzle that uses the image of a hanged man. Games aimed at a wide audience, such as story-based adventure games, generally include a wide variety of puzzle types, so there is something to please everyone.

On the structure of puzzles

Just as a joke has a setup and a punchline, so puzzles have a predictable dramatic structure. Here are the major steps, in the order they occur:

- **Hook.** The hook gets you interested in playing a puzzle, even before you know how to play it. The hook can be a dramatic situation, such as a crime scene; an engaging and suggestive title, such as Lemmings; or a purely abstract graphic, such as falling Tetris pieces. The hook should be short and compelling—one sentence or a few seconds of animation should suffice. Note that the hook does not need to explain the goal of the puzzle, though it may hint at it.

- **Problem**. The problem statement establishes the goal of the puzzle and the rules of play. In some cases rules are stated explicitly, in other cases deciphering the rules is part of the puzzle itself. Since players hate to read instructions, problem statements are best kept short, with little or no text. Often it is best to reveal rules as they are needed, instead of all at once, in order to maintain pacing.

- **Choices**. Every puzzle involves making choices. In a maze, the choice is which turn to make. In a crossword puzzle, the choice is which letter to write in which square. A puzzle need not have many choices to be interesting. Some of the best puzzles have just one tricky decision.

- **Dead ends**. Some choices lead to dead ends. Too many unprofitable dead ends leads to frustration. Some dead ends should reward you with information that steers you toward the solution.

- **Insight**. The best puzzles have moments of insight when you suddenly understand a better way of thinking about the problem. Some puzzles, like creative brainteasers, have one big moment of insight that leads quickly to the solution, while others, like crossword puzzles, chug along with many little insights.

- **Solution**. The resolution of the problem is the solution. There should be a clear signal when the puzzle is solved, so the player feels emotional closure. Some puzzles have intermediate subproblems, each with its own solution. Longer puzzles need more subgoals to maintain player interest.

- **Payoff**. The payoff is the in-game reward for solving the puzzle. Ideally, the payoff should be set up in the hook. In a story game, for instance, unlocking a door lets you pass through to a new location. In abstract puzzle games, solving a puzzle may unlock other puzzles.

On puzzle types

There are five main genres of puzzle games:

- **Action-puzzle games** (*Tetris, Pipe Dream, Collapse!*). Puzzle-solving combined with time pressure. When designing these games, you must keep the controls simple and get the rhythm right.

- **Story-puzzle games** (*Myst, Metal Gear Solid*). Puzzle-solving combined with storytelling. For these games, your main challenge will be integrating the puzzles smoothly into the story.

- **Competitive puzzle games** (*Boggle, Wheel of Fortune, You Don't Know Jack*). Tips for designing these games include:

  Keep the question format simple.

  Maintain pace.

  Add secondary rhythms (such as using lifelines in *Who Wants to be a Millionaire*, or buying a vowel in *Wheel of Fortune*).

  Generate content efficiently.

  Design for the medium.

- **Construction puzzle games** (*The Incredible Machine, Lemmings, Pikmin*). Here, your main challenge is to create an economical set of pieces that combine with each other in rich, unexpected ways.

- **Pure puzzle games** (*Pandora's Box, Heaven and Earth*). These games are large collections of puzzles of the same type, sequenced to start easy and get progressively harder. For more variety, break your ramp into a series of smaller saw teeth that start easy, get gradually more difficult over the course of 5 to 10 puzzles, then start easy again.

On design

When you're designing a puzzle, the first step is to find an inspiration. This may come from anywhere—advances in technology, real-life stories, other games, etc. Once you've got the basic inspiration, the key design activity is to simplify the puzzle activity to its essence by identifying the core skill the player will need. Then you simplify further by eliminating irrelevant details, making all the pieces uniform, and creating easy-to-use controls.

Puzzles are miniature works of art, like songs or poems. They can be as disposable as advertising gimmicks, or as lasting as great works of art. Designing a puzzle is like composing a song or writing a poem. The craft can be taught, but the best work requires that you reach deep into your soul.

Online Games

Games from any genre can become online games when modified to be played over the Internet (see Figure 3.8).

Figure 3.8 *You Don't Know Jack* is a successful series of online trivia games. Used with permission of Sierra On-Line Inc.

The biggest influence on the design of these games is their profit model. If a publisher makes his money by selling advertisements, he wants your game to attract as many people ("eyeballs") as possible and keep them there for a long time. He will also want you to design in opportunities for the advertisements to be displayed, perhaps in the "lobby" while players wait for the next game to start, or even during the game itself. This will lead you to design a series of quick-to-learn, easy-to-play games that have short sessions with frequent pauses. You don't want to lose the player during these pauses, so insert them while compiling the scores, or by giving the player a quick break halfway through a session to rest his fingers and gather his wits.

Ad-supported games are likely to be located on the Web itself, rather than as a download to the player's computer. This makes updates quick and convenient (because you only have to update the master server to change the game), and you don't have to worry about different versions of the software residing on various players' machines. This also allows you to provide fresh content regularly, which is vital in encouraging casual players to visit your site again and again.

If a publisher makes his money via pay-per-play or hourly connect fees, he will want to maximize the number of players and the amount of time, but he won't want anything at all to interrupt the game. After the player enters the game, the publisher will want to keep him locked in for hours at a time. This should lead you to design longer play sessions where everyone wants to stay on board until the activity is complete. (This revenue model has almost completely disappeared, however.)

If your game is a single-player game with a multiplayer component, the publisher probably makes his money strictly from selling the box. In that case, online play will be free, but you still want to encourage it because the more people you can hook into playing online, the more boxes you will sell. In this case, you need to design an interface that makes it easy for players to go out and find each other. It is also a good idea to provide a master server that tracks all the host servers out there on the Internet.

Finally, if the publisher sells subscriptions, your design focus shifts to creating long-term commitments to the game and building a user community. Within this community, a player can create an identity that is very different from his real-world persona. No matter how low his status might be in the real word, he can achieve fame and recognition within this virtual world.

These products are likely to be persistent world games, and in them you should do the following:

- Enable chat capability during the game.
- Create a gathering area outside the game space where people can exchange conversation, strategies, and items of value within the game.
- Create identifiable status markers so that players have an incentive to play over a period of several months to attain them.
- Protect new players so that they can become established in the world before being preyed upon by more powerful opponents.
- Develop world rules that help build community and prevent a minority of idiots from spoiling the game for the majority of the users.
- Provide both competitive and cooperative opportunities for play.
- Continue to add to the design over time so that the game world keeps expanding and is never "done."

Beyond the profit model, other factors also influence online game design.

The primary technical challenge of online games is dealing with *lag time* (also known as *latency*), the amount of time it takes information to be transmitted over the wires. The issue is especially critical in multiplayer games, where you must keep the gamers' screens synchronized so that everyone sees the same thing at the same time. This can especially be a problem when some players have faster Internet connections than others.

This becomes a design issue when it affects gameplay. In some games, lag time is irrelevant. In Poker, for example, it doesn't matter whether everyone sees the cards dealt at precisely the same instant. Each person has plenty of time to make his decisions when his turn comes. In a first-person shooter, however, split-second timing matters a great deal because a player with a slow connection can find himself firing at an opponent who is no longer there.

For your game, decide which activities are time-crucial, and work with your tech lead to determine how to adjudicate the outcomes of player actions.

Your game design must also allow for dropouts. Players come and go suddenly in online games. Their connection can be broken, or they might be called to dinner. Either way, the game cannot grind to a halt for 20 players if one of them suddenly disappears.

Finally, you need to consider which back-end services to offer. Some games provide automatic updates for players who might not know that a later version is available. Others provide free matching services. Some companies maintain servers on both the East Coast and the West Coast, and even in selected countries overseas.

Regardless, it is always wise to think of your online game as a service instead of a product. A traditional box game is a product—you build it, ship it, support the customer in his effort to play and finish it, and then you're done. An online game is more of a service—when you build it and publish it, your main effort is just beginning. After it's out there, you must help your customers find it and one another, and you must constantly fix and upgrade the game, add new features and modules, and occasionally overhaul it entirely. The ideal box game is played to completion and makes the customer want to go out and buy another one. The ideal online game is never finished and makes the customer want to reenter the game again and again—forever.

Raph Koster

A professional game designer and frequent writer on issues of virtual world design, Raph Koster was the lead designer on the seminal online world Ultima Online, *which first brought online worlds to the mass market and has sold over one million copies. He is currently Chief Creative Officer for Sony Online Entertainment, makers of* EverQuest, *where he previously led the design of* Star Wars Galaxies. *His essays and writings on online world design include widely reprinted and influential pieces such as "Declaring the Rights of Avatars," "The Laws of Online World Design," and "A Story About a Tree." He is in demand as a speaker and lecturer on issues of online world design, particularly in the area of community building. He is a regular speaker at the Game Developers Conference and is the maintainer of the canonical history of virtual worlds at his Web site,* http://www.legendmud.org/raph/.

The entire modern puzzle game genre operates slightly differently than the models you cite—they are based on free online play, followed by downloads of shareware or crippleware versions that you pay for. Popcap in particular has been tremendously successful in this regard. The pay-per-play or hourly model has just about vanished.

Tips for designers

- Think about ranking services. The canonical example is probably ngWorld-Stats for *Unreal Tournament*.

- It is pretty much mandatory these days to supply tools for user-created content, at least in the boxed multiplayer space. Not just for FPS games either, but role-playing games as well.

- Dig up some good papers on prediction algorithms for latency handling, which are a basic part of any 3D online game.

- Read Bernd Kreimeier's paper on ratings systems, similar to ELO for chess, which is excellent for designing ladders (http://www.gamasutra.com/features/20000209/kreimeier_01.htm).

- For persistent world titles, read up on a variety of topics, such as architecture, sociology, psychology, etc. Running these games is much more like governing a small city than like making a game. Don't underestimate the need for customer service.

Other design considerations

Games that are based on player vs. player skill have classically had problems in attracting wider audiences than games where mere persistence can help you succeed (e.g. Compare PvP RPGs vs. cooperative ones, or the number of people playing FPSs online versus playing them at home). This is because people dislike getting crushed. We don't do leagues or handicaps very well yet.

Casual gamers are by far the largest audience in online gaming, and they primarily play puzzle games and skew heavily female. An important thing to keep in mind: Online games in general skew more female than single player games do, generally.

A "contemporary" perspective on the canonical online games

Puzzle games

> *Bejeweled/Diamond Mine* and other Popcap games, because of their massive popularity. There are also several online party games that are literally designed around live chat capability.

> Visit the Pogo or MSN websites to understand the social/online context, and the importance of classic card games.

Online multiplayer games

Counterstrike—The single most popular online shooter by far.

See also *Quake* and *Unreal Tournament*.

Look at other *Half-Life* or *Quake* mods to understand the modding community.

Diablo 2, *Starcraft*, or other Battle.net games, for their popularity and their lobby implementation.

Neverwinter Nights for user content in a non-shooter setting.

Massively multiplayer games

Gemstone III to understand the text-based roots of online worlds.

EverQuest as the basic template for the modern combat-centric MMORPG.

Ultima Online or *Star Wars Galaxies* are the canonical examples for "virtual world" sorts of MMOs.

There.com as the exemplar of social world.

LambdaMOO for user content (text-based). *Second Life* is the best graphical example.

Planetside for MMO shooters.

Lineage to understand Asia's different MMO emphasis.

On technical advances

Mostly, their effect has been confined to the ever-rising graphical bar. We have gained some CPU, but not a ton, so we haven't really been able to make tons more complex stuff. We just barely managed to get the stuff that worked in the 2D space, like player housing and decorating, in the 3D space. As CPUs rise, we'll be able to do more complex AI and behaviors, and as storage costs fall, we can push persistence further.

On broadband

The increase in broadband has allowed more latency-sensitive games to thrive (like shooters) but it's important to point out that broadband is a bit of a red herring, it's *not* the savior of all online gaming. We can't generate enough content to shove down the pipe, so it's mostly about speed, not bandwidth.

Designing for an international audience

It sure is different, but heck if I know the formula to lick it. Neither does anyone else. (Obviously, design all text in files with Unicode support, etc.) But the design challenges are tough, and no game has crossed over significantly except Blizzard games into Korea. No MMOs have crossed over significantly except *Ultima Online* into Japan.

The Asian market is heavily driven by play in Internet cafes, as opposed to at-home play. China is potentially an explosive market. Korea is a non-console country, so PC is huge there, and China is similar. The result has been a massive adoption of MMORPGs there—literally hundreds of them exist.

Books that designers should read

For MMOs, definitely Richard Bartle's *Designing Online Worlds* and Mulligan & Patrovsky's *Developing Online Games*.

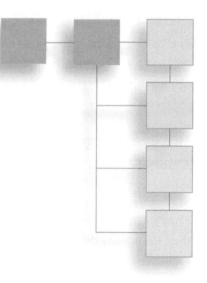

CHAPTER 4

STORYTELLING

W hen our industry was young, storytelling was the exclusive province of adventure games. Then role-playing games appeared on the scene, and they, too, had strong storytelling elements. Now we find storytelling in many genres, including action, real-time strategy, and sims (see Figure 4.1).

If you are going to tell a story with your game, it is important for you to understand the fundamentals of how tales are told. Traditional authors deal with plot, setting, and character. As game designers, so must we.

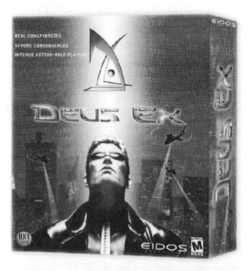

Figure 4.1 *Deus Ex* is a hybrid RPG/action game that features a strong storyline. Used with permission of Eidos Interactive Ltd.

Plot: The Three-Act Structure

The basic structure of a good plot was discovered a long time ago. It's called the *three-act structure*. Aristotle first identified it in his *Poetics*, which gives it the kind of halo that sometimes makes ideas seem unapproachable. But his point is very simple: A story must have a beginning, a middle, and an end (see Figure 4.2).

The Beginning

A story begins at the moment your hero has a problem, and that's the moment you should begin your game. Many writers make the mistake of starting their story *before* the beginning. They open with a long-winded introduction that sets up the game world. They recount events long past, fill in the details of the hero's ancestry, and finally, when they think that the player has seen enough to appreciate their special creation, they get around to kicking off the action.

This is all wrong.

If you pick up a best-selling book at the newsstand and turn to the first page, you will find yourself in the middle of an action scene. Chances are, the author will start with bullets flying and bombs exploding, and only later will he pause to catch his breath and explain who these people are and how they came to be in danger.

First, he gets your attention. Then, he fills in the backstory.

That's how you should begin your game. Start with a small piece of gameplay, where the player doesn't have to know much but has an easy task to perform. He'll pick up a lot on his own without any formal exposition from you. The mere look-and-feel of the environments will introduce the player to the world. By putting a simple obstacle in his path and forcing him to deal with it, you've already begun the process of storytelling.

In *Abe's Odyssey*, the true beginning of the story is when Abe learns that they're planning to make meat out of him. In *Unreal*, it is when the ship crashes and you have to get out.

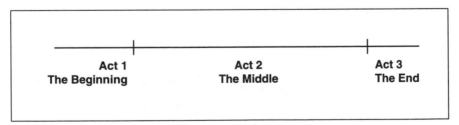

Figure 4.2 The three-act structure.

In *Half-Life*, it is when you learn that something has gone terribly wrong at the Black Mesa site.

Think about the opening scene of the movie *Raiders of the Lost Ark*. A mysterious figure in a hat emerges from a jungle to stand before a waterfall. He puts together two pieces of paper to form an old map. Without any dialogue, this instantly establishes character, setting, and goal. Here is an adventurer in a remote wilderness searching for treasure. This is the beginning. The hero has a problem. How does he get the treasure?

In the next few minutes, he flicks a gun away from a man with his bullwhip, enters a cave full of poisonous spiders, puts his hand in a shaft of light to set off a booby-trapped wall of pointed spikes, swings on his whip over a bottomless pit, uses a torch to spring a paving-stone trap, swaps a weighted bag of sand for the golden idol, and then runs for his life to outsprint that huge rolling boulder.

In each of these cases, the hero is presented with threats or obstacles that are appropriate to the exotic setting. In each case, he uses the material at hand to overcome the problem.

The job of the game designer is exactly that, to create threats and obstacles that are appropriate to the story and the setting, and to give the player the means to solve those problems in a way that makes sense within the story's genre. The best designers do this from the very start of the game.

The Middle

When Indiana Jones emerges from the cave and the bad guy takes the idol from him, you have the end of the first act and the beginning of the second. Now is the time to fill the player in on some of the hero's background and set his actions within a larger context. We learn that Indiana Jones is not just a fortune hunter—he is an archeologist, with much nobler motives.

If you map out the middle of the story on a piece of paper, it should look like a series of ascending arcs (see Figure 4.3). The player knows what his long-term goal is, and you let him make progress towards that goal. But every time he overcomes one obstacle, you put another in its place—not just any obstacle, though.

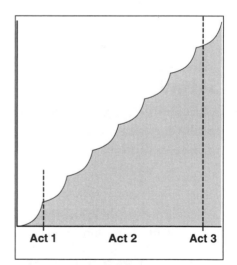

Figure 4.3 Every time your hero overcomes an obstacle, put a new (and harder) one in its place.

In the best stories, the hero has to work his way through inner conflicts and overcome them. Only when he has done so will he be ready to go on and achieve his final goal.

As a game maker, of the hundreds of obstacles you *could* design to put before your hero, you *should* pick the ones that reveal his inner workings. They should expose his faults and fears. In conquering these challenges, he is not only making progress towards his external goal, but also conquering his inner problems. He is experiencing character growth.

The End

The story ends when the hero solves his problem.

The third act of your game should be like the conclusion of a symphony, where the many musical themes introduced along the way are brought together in harmony at the end. After your hero overcomes his own problems, he is now ready to face the external embodiment of those problems, which usually appears in the form of the Ultimate Bad Guy.

In the best of games, it is revealed that this Ultimate Bad Guy is the source of many of the obstacles your hero has encountered in the course of the game. This only makes sense. For any story to be interesting, it must have conflict. There must be some*thing* or some*one* who does not want your hero to succeed. To face off against this adversary at the end of the story and whip his butt is a very satisfying experience.

A simple tip for remembering this three-act structure is an old writer's maxim: In the first act, you get your hero up a tree. In the second act, you throw rocks at him. In the third act, you get him down.

Setting

As an industry, setting is one of the things we do best, so we don't need to spend too much time examining it here. Game artists are constantly creating new and evocative images, and as tools and hardware improve, game graphics just keep getting better.

Remember, though, that setting is not just a physical location—it's the whole world you create to tell your story. For a fantasy game, this can include magical creatures who live in the natural world before the age of machinery. For a science fiction game, you can create a distant planet subject to unusual laws of physics.

In creating the basic rules of your universe, you should invent only one major "what if?" and everything else should follow logically from that. What if you discover a hidden organization that seeks world domination (*Deus Ex*)? What if government experiments at a secret facility have opened a transdimensional rift (*Half-Life*)?

After you've established this major premise, players will go along for the ride, but only if you make everything else as real as possible and avoid contradictions. John Gardner writes in *The Art of Fiction*, "Vivid detail is the life blood of fiction . . . moment by moment authenticating detail is the mainstay not only of realistic fiction but of all fiction." The artistic presentation of this "vivid detail" also establishes mood, which can be just as important a part of the setting as the physical location.

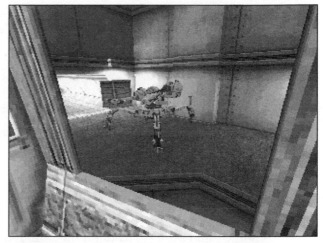

Figure 4.4 A denizen of the Black Mesa deeps, as seen during the opening tram ride. Used with permission of Sierra On-Line Inc.

One of the most celebrated sequences in recent games is the opening movie of *Half-Life* (see Figure 4.4). As you take the tram ride down into the belly of the Black Mesa facility, you are presented with a continuous stream of images and sounds that authoritatively place you in that time and space. Through the use of consistent and concrete detail, the game draws you into its fictional world, while the real world around you dissolves, unnoticed.

Choose a setting that will entertain the player visually. Let your artists supply a stream of fresh backgrounds and creatures. By making your setting vivid and consistent, you'll transport the player into the waking dream that's at the heart of all fiction.

Character Development

Characters are the most fascinating part of stories. Events themselves are interesting only insofar as they give us insights into people. That's why you always hear that there are only seven basic plots, yet millions of stories somehow are told. We're always interested in the *people* to whom those plots happen.

Plot without character is about as interesting as a shopping list—it is just one thing happening after another. The poet said, "Man is the measure of all things." Or, put a less elegant way, "What people are interested in is people."

Many designers don't want to create a strong central character, because they believe the player's own personality should take center stage. Beginning with the amorphous *you* of the Infocom games, these types of games sketch in the barest outline of the hero, and then leave it to the player to fill out that outline with his own idiosyncrasies.

This might not be wise. Successful games (from both a commercial and an artistic point of view) frequently have heroes with well-defined personalities. Players seem quite content to step into the shoes of characters such as Duke Nukem, Lara Croft, and James Bond without trying to impose their own personalities on the characters (see Figure 4.5). Just as movie audiences identify with action heroes on the screen, gameplayers revel in taking on the hero's personality for a few hours.

Creating one of these memorable characters from scratch is hard, but the rewards (again, both commercial and artistic) are great. One tip for designing such a hero lies in a quote from the Pulitzer Prize-winning biography of Lawrence of Arabia, *A Prince of Our Disorder*, in which author John E. Mack writes:

A vital ingredient in hero-making is the resonance that the follower finds between the conflicts and aspirations of his own and those he perceives in the person he chooses to idealize. . . . The hero needs to appear to have mastered his struggle to achieve his ideals in such a way that an identification with him seems to offer the possibility of similar mastery to the follower.

Figure 4.5 Action hero Duke Nukem. Used with permission of 3D Realms Entertainment.

This is great stuff. As you think about creating your hero character, try to find problems that we all have as individuals, and let us fantasize through your hero that we can actually solve them.

NPCs can also play an important role that's frequently filled by secondary characters in films. They can reveal emotions and reactions that the hero can't show. How often have we seen the overmatched, steely-eyed hero face down the evil villain without so much as a tremor, while off to the side, the locals cower with knuckles between teeth and eyes wide in horror? This technique allows you, the storyteller, to instill in the game player emotions that you might not otherwise be able to create. Steven Spielberg is the master at this, and it is something to keep in mind when creating secondary characters.

Character Growth

In traditional literature, the worth of a story is often measured by character growth. What changes are wrought on the hero by the misfortunes that fall his way? What does he learn? How does his approach to life alter? How does what happened to him turn him into a different person?

However, in some stories, the hero doesn't change at all. He remains the same throughout, bending events to his will. James Bond is a perfect example. He's the same suave, debonair secret agent at the end of the movie that he was when it began. We can count on him to be the same way in the next movie as well. In fact, if he were not, we'd be disappointed!

In today's games, what little character growth we have is generally accomplished through statistics. Our avatars acquire more strength, experience, skill, and so on as they move through the game. Seldom do we have the opportunity to move beyond such trivialities.

This is so because of our medium. Character development in linear media is accomplished by putting people in stressful situations and showing who they truly are by the choices they make. In a game, the choices lie in the hands of the player! This brings us to the problems created by interactivity.

Interactivity

The demands of interactivity present a special challenge to any game designer who wants to be a storyteller. In traditional media, the author controls the story, and the audience passively absorbs the choices he has made. In games, there's a direct conflict between the freedom we must allow the player and the linearity necessary to any well-constructed story.

The solution is to create areas in which the player has freedom, and then to string these areas together in a linear series. In RPGs, such a series is organized into geographical areas or missions. In adventure games, it means giving the player more than one set of puzzles to work on at a time. In action games, it translates into levels.

The idea is to present the player with a limited challenge that somehow fits into the larger story. How this challenge is met will vary wildly from player to player, depending on his particular abilities and wits. What the storyteller *can* detect is the moment when all the tasks have been completed and the challenge has been met. That's the moment to slip in some more storytelling—perhaps through a new set of mission instructions, or maybe through a cutscene that shows the results of the level's action and pushes the player toward his next challenge.

As a limited example, think of an area in which the player must reach an inn by sundown, but to do so, he must cross a well-guarded river. The player can succeed by swimming across, swinging on a vine, or defeating the troll guarding the bridge, but the important thing is that he triumph over adversity and live to the end of the day. The player has filled in certain details of the story, but the main threads have stayed in the hands of the author, who says, "Yes, it was your individual ingenuity that got you to the inn, but now a new set of monsters is preparing to attack you tomorrow, and meanwhile, here's what has been happening back at the castle."

This technique is applicable across many game genres. With this linear series of open environments, the player interacts with the game in meaningful ways, yet the author retains control of the story.

The Tools of the Trade

In the past, we've looked to books as the model for our storytelling. These days, game design bears a much closer resemblance to screenwriting, and it is the filmmaker's tools that we must master. This is especially true when we present cutscenes and scripted events, or anytime we use dialogue.

The only things a screenwriter has to work with are the same tools we have—pictures and spoken words. All he's allowed to do in a screenplay is identify the setting, put words in an actor's mouth, and define his actions and movements. He's not like a novelist, who can go on at length about a character's inner conflict. If he wants us to know what a character is feeling inside, he has to *show* it up there on the screen, through either dialogue or action. We have the same task.

This is not a skill that comes naturally, but it can be learned.

Cutscenes

Cutscenes are mini-movies. As the game designer, you get to be screenwriter, director, and cameraman all rolled into one. With those roles come responsibilities. Everyone who plays your game has grown up watching television and movies, and each player will have internal quality benchmarks for dialogue, camera placement, acting, and action. If you don't deliver professional-quality work, the player will roll his eyes and the reviewers will skewer you.

Each cutscene should have specific goals, whether it is to develop character, introduce a new environment, advance the plot, or set out mission goals for the section to come. Design the scene in collaboration with professionals (usually writers and artists) who can help you accomplish your goals with the most economy. This has two benefits. Not only will the player appreciate your professionalism in moving the story along, but you'll also help your budget by avoiding long-winded scenes that ramble along at great expense and even greater boredom.

Scripted Events

Scripted events are brief sequences within levels that are usually triggered by something the player does (although they can be time-based as well). Whether they're snippets of dialogue or small bits of action, they can be very effective in imparting a backstory, building a character, or redirecting the player towards new goals. Prime examples of scripted events in an action game are *Medal of Honor* and *Halo*.

Dialogue

Good dialogue sounds nothing like regular speech. In real life, we pause and stumble and repeat ourselves. In a movie or a game, dialogue has to be better than that. It has to be crisp and to the point. You can't waste the player's time with a single extra word. Furthermore, every line of dialogue must do double duty. It must both advance the story and develop character.

Here are a few quick tips for writing dialogue:

> Never have a character say in dialogue something that the player already knows. It is a waste of the player's time.

> More subtly, never give information to the player by having one character tell another something the other character already knows. Nothing reveals the amateur status of a writer as much as a line such as, "Well, as you already know, Lord Veldran, the spell can only work if all three of the magical stones are in place . . ."

> Remember, when writing dialogue, less is more. Keep it short.

The Hero's Journey

In the end, your game should be your hero's story. Sure, gameplay comes first, but you can almost always make gameplay better by wrapping a good story around it.

Each genre is restrictive. We have conventions we must observe, and it might seem that there's little room for creativity. But our genres are certainly less hidebound than the requirements of the Elizabethan "Revenge Tragedy," which is what Shakespeare was faced with when his producer told him to sit down and bat out the play he eventually called *Hamlet*.

Joseph Campbell's Heroes

In his groundbreaking work *The Hero with a Thousand Faces*, Joseph Campbell revealed the hidden structure underlying civilization's most powerful myths and legends. Many authors, most notably Christopher Vogler, have further refined this work, identifying crucial elements that are present in most stories. The following summary of the structure is vastly compressed. For a complete exploration of the theme, see Vogler's excellent *The Writer's Journey*.

As you review these elements, remember that they're not a straightjacket within which your story must be confined. Rather, they serve as a useful set of guidelines to ponder when it seems your story has stumbled off course.

The Ordinary World

Act One. The player is introduced to the hero and learns about his world.

Call to Adventure

Something happens to disrupt the hero's world, to threaten life as he knows it.

Refusal of the Call (The Reluctant Hero)

Few people casually abandon their way of life to go out and do battle. The hero tries to bury his head in the sand and hopes the problem will go away.

The Mentor

A wise person appears to put things in perspective, explaining why the hero should take up the adventure. Frequently, this person eases the way by giving the hero a talisman.

Crossing the Threshold

The end of Act One. The hero realizes he must answer the call, and he takes an irrevocable step across a boundary to enter the dangerous land where the adventure will take place.

Tests, Allies, and Enemies

Act Two. We've got the hero up a tree. Now we throw rocks at him.

The Inmost Cave

After many trials and tribulations (the bulk of the game), the hero approaches the lair of the ultimate evil.

The Supreme Ordeal

The hero comes face-to-face with the ultimate evil, fights it, and triumphs.

The Hero's Prize

As a reward for his epic struggle, the hero acquires the magical item that will solve the problem that disrupted his world in the first place.

The Road Back

Act Three. We get the hero down from the tree. He's got the prize, but he must escape the dangerous land and battle his way back home.

Return with the Elixir

Resolution. The hero's world is saved or transformed through his efforts.

The Designer's Journey

It is not good enough to understand *how* to tell a story; you also need to have a story worth telling. Where do you start?

You are an author. Your job is to have a vision, a purpose, a greater truth. You have the job of any artist. You need to think of yourself as a hero—not a "Lawrence of Arabia" kind of hero, but a "Joseph Campbell" kind of hero. Every author and every artist must himself make the Hero's Journey. You must step outside conventional society or philosophy and look back at the way things really are, or perhaps the way you think they *should* be. You must go beyond the boundaries of the known and accepted, in search of something new and important.

What you acquire on your journey is the Hero's Prize. It is that thing which only *you* know. Many of you have probably already taken this journey. You have a vision of your own, a personal slice of reality, something that you know in your heart is true, even though the rest of the world doesn't believe it. When you find it, you must bring it back to us so that we will all benefit from it. That's what a hero does. That's what you must do.

If you take that journey, this piece of knowledge will become imbedded in your story. Not in a preachy way—it will just be there.

Before you sit down to write a story game, think hard about that thing which only *you* know. If you do, it will subtly inform all the design decisions you make in your game. It will be the thing that sustains your interest across the 18 to 24 months you will be working on the project. Eventually, it will become the thing that your game is about.

That story will be a game worth playing.

CHAPTER 5

LEVEL DESIGN

When the design document is done, teams of specialists swarm over it to bring the words to life. Engine programmers figure out graphics pipelines and how to detect when objects in the world collide. Modelers build complex creatures and hand them off to the animators, who give them movement. AI programmers tell the creatures how to behave. Texture artists clothe the creatures and paint the world in which they live. Composers dream up atmospheric music. Audio technicians twist everyday sounds until they emerge anew from the player's speakers as echoes of a wholly imagined world.

It is the level designer ("LD") who takes all these pieces and stitches them together to make a game. How well you do this determines whether you're a Dr. Frankenstein creating a monster or a Pygmalion breathing life into a beautiful Galatea.

This chapter deals mostly with level design as it applies to action games. However, many of these principles apply to other genres, whether you are creating tracks for a racing game, missions for a strategy game or sim, or dungeons for an RPG.

Concept Work

As a level designer, you must align yourself with the main premise and flow of the game. You are creating a piece of the puzzle, a part of the greater whole. When you begin to think about your level, you must consider why it is there in the first place. What function does it fulfill in the grander scheme of things? Is it meant to introduce a new character, weapon, or monster? How does it move the story along? Does it come early in the game, or late? Is it part of the single-player game, or is it a multiplayer level, such as a DeathMatch or Capture the Flag scenario that will stand on its own?

With these considerations in place, it is time to select a single idea as the focus of your level. This can be a *gameplay* idea, such as holding off a series of invaders for a specific length of time, husbanding a limited resource through the level, or learning how to use a particular weapon. It can be a *visual* idea, such as building everything around a series of fire images. It can be a *gimmick*, such as low gravity or clever use of portals. Whatever the idea, it becomes the unifying theme for the level. When too many ideas are at work in a level, it loses focus and the player becomes confused.

Although each level has a single focus, be sure to provide variety from level to level. One mission can be an all-out firefight; the next can involve stealth and avoiding detection; the next can focus on a single, very powerful enemy; and the next can be all about avoiding traps. Each of these levels has a single focus, but taken together, they provide variety and work together to move the story along.

Sketch out your level ahead of time (see Figures 5.1 and 5.2). Experiment with different ways to make the core idea work. Do this on paper, rather than on the computer, so you

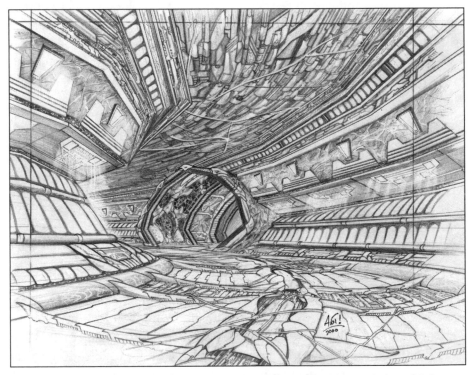

Figure 5.1 Concept sketch of a hallway in *Unreal2.* Used with permission of Epic Games Inc.

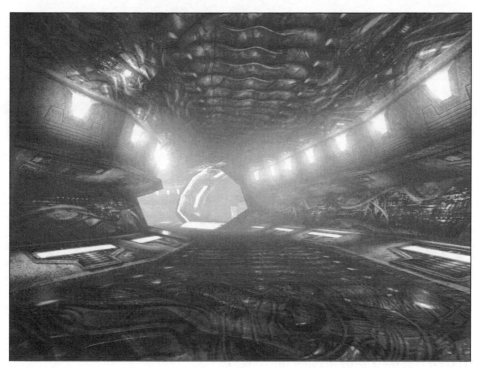

Figure 5.2 That same sketch, as implemented in the game. Used with permission of Epic Games Inc.

can cycle through more iterations. By sketching out and then discarding a series of ideas, you can quickly hone in on the layout that will bring your core idea to life. Do not fire up the level editor and start to create the space until you have a really good idea of what you are going to build.

With sketch in hand, you are just about ready to start . . . but not quite. To do a professional job, you need specialized tools. At the very least, you need a level editor that goes beyond off-the-shelf packages (see Figure 5.3). Your editor should provide multiple views, including the player view. It should allow you to tweak geometry while you place creatures in the world and toggle hidden elements on and off, and it should let you navigate through a level as you are building it. A good scripting language lets you operate somewhat independently of the programmers, and it lets you experiment more rapidly and safely with new ideas.

Figure 5.3 The Unreal Editor. Used with permission of Epic Games Inc.

Building the Level

The physical layout of your map will be heavily influenced by its gameplay type.

Single-player levels tend to be linear. If the level is too open, the player doesn't know which way to go and can become lost. You should design these levels with a flow that leads the player along until he has reached his goal.

DeathMatch levels tend to be circular. The architecture should be simple and easy to navigate. The player should be able to learn the map quickly and thereafter never be confused about where he is. These levels should have no safe territory where a player can hide out indefinitely. They should have several ways players can double back on each other, along with the requisite hard-to-reach places where expert players can snipe at unsuspecting novices below.

Capture the Flag levels should be balanced, with each team's home base equally easy to attack and defend. Give special thought to color schemes to help the players know when they are entering enemy territory.

In all cases, the look of the level should be internally consistent. Don't mix graphical styles within a level, particularly if it is a small map. Although larger maps can contain a series of smaller locations that look different, the style should be consistent within the boundaries of each location. This constant supply of convincing, coherent detail helps sustain the player's waking dream as he travels your landscape, totally immersed in the world you have created.

You should also create visually distinctive landmarks that help orient the player as he navigates through the world. It is easy for players to become lost, and it's part of your job to make sure that they always know where they are.

The most memorable levels are designed toward one defining moment. Whether it is the player's first view of a spectacular monster or the instant he rounds the corner on some incredible vista, the artful designer builds the entire level with that one moment in mind.

Gameplay

Each *level* is the larger game writ small. Everything you learned in Chapter 2, "Principles of Game Design," applies here as well.

Goals

Give the player a goal.

In too many levels, the player knows only that he needs to keep moving and shooting until the magic word *Loading* appears, signaling that he has somehow accomplished whatever the level designer had in mind.

Make sure that the player knows what his objectives are for each level. You can do this either in a cutscene prior to the level, or within gameplay when the mission gets under way. It is also a good idea to create a screen the player can always access to get his current status and a simple restatement of his mission.

Have you ever read a strategy guide that seems to be explaining a different game than the one you are playing? It is usually because the author has consulted with the level designers and learned what they *intended* to do, instead of what they actually presented in the game. Do not let this happen to you.

Mission briefings can be presented in whatever manner fits your fiction. In a fantasy game, a ghostly apparition of a wizard can give the player a quest. In a military game, the commanding officer can issue a set of orders and objectives. Just make sure that when the player enters the level, he knows his goal. Do not let him stumble along saving, shooting, dying, and restoring, until he walks through a door that looks like any other and learns that he is done (see Figure 5.4).

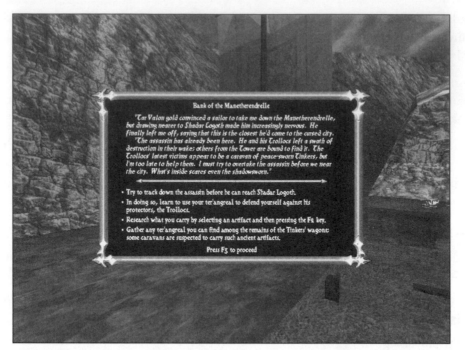

Figure 5.4 A mission briefing screen from the fantasy game *Wheel of Time*, which is based on Robert Jordan's best-selling series of novels. Used with permission of Infogames, Inc.

Also, let the player know where he stands in relation to his goal. If his success depends on preventing the enemy from reaching some target, tell him how his opponent is doing. You can't just let 20 minutes go by and announce, "The enemy has succeeded. You have failed." Instead, give him progress reports, or give him a view of the enemy forces that allows him to judge for himself how they're getting on.

Structure and Progression

Ease the player into the level, and build up the difficulty as you go along. Do not make the hardest part of the level the first thing the player has to do.

The structure and progression of a level mirrors that of the game itself. Thus, you should build conflict in a series of ascending arcs until you reach the climax. Give hints and teases of what is to come. Create a sequence of ever-tougher challenges, interspaced with bits of humor, and include breaks in the action so that the player can collect his wits before moving to the next challenge.

Do not just keep throwing things at the player. Vary the pace. There should be times when he's frantically trying to stay alive, other times when he's warily exploring, and still other times when he's safe and able to absorb the information he's gathered.

Also, make sure that there's enough for the player to *do*. A level can be pretty to look at, but if all the player can do is wander around, he'll get bored in a big hurry. Make sure that there are enough challenges to keep him occupied.

Flow Control

Two hidden problems of single-player level design are how to contain the player in a given area of a level until he has accomplished what you want him to and how to prevent him from returning to that area after he's done.

The first problem is especially prevalent in open-air levels, where there are no natural barriers to keep the player from moving around. In these levels, the player can sometimes simply run past his opponents, rather than engage them in battle. This will effectively "break" the game, because the player either arrives at the end of the level with a host of bad guys on his tail who are sure to kill him or reaches the end with no challenges and wonders why the game is so short.

There are many solutions here; the key is to be aware of the problem. You can create natural barriers that are destroyed as a byproduct of the player making progress in the level. Or you can provide naturally occurring choke-points in the level geometry that are guarded by mini-boss monsters. The point is to ensure that the player doesn't get too far too fast.

The second flow control problem is how to close off an area after the player is done with it. There are many reasons for doing this, including better memory management and prevention of player paranoia. If a player cannot return to a given area of the level, he knows that he's making progress and doesn't wonder whether he left any tasks unfinished back there. Of course, closing off the area also means that the programmers can free up the memory associated with making everything there work.

Again, there are many ways to accomplish this after you become aware that it needs to be done. The simplest solution is to create a one-way barrier that blocks the player from going back after he has crossed it. This barrier can be anything—a door that locks when the player goes through it, a waterfall that the player goes over but cannot climb back up, or perhaps a narrow pass that is blocked by an avalanche after the player passes through.

As you are designing your levels, think about ways the player can break the game by doing the unexpected. Try to control the flow by keeping him where you want him while he faces the challenges you've created, and then channel him to new areas after he's met those challenges.

Degree of Difficulty

A single-player level should never be so hard that the player keeps dying again and again. Challenge is good—even a little frustration is good—but do not make it so tough that only experts can survive. It is fine to design for the hardcore gamer market, but if the average player can't have fun, you won't stay in business long.

Suppose, for example, that the player rounds a corner where a sniper is waiting to kill him the instant he appears. If he has no warning of the assassin's presence—no sound, no shadow, no bodies of previous victims—the only way to find out is to walk around the corner and get shot. The oh-so-clever level designer says, "Okay. Now he should know enough to throw a grenade through the door first." How can the player know that ahead of time? "Bang, you're dead" is a very bad kind of challenge.

Even worse, however, is a level where the designer forces the player to find the single hidden weakness of an overwhelmingly powerful foe. That structure is all right if the player has a way to safely scout out his opponent's capabilities. More often, though, the player is killed every ten seconds and has to restart again and again, ad nauseum, until he wants to throw his machine out the window. Experts thrive on these kinds of challenges. Average gamers regard them as frustrating and unfair.

How do you satisfy both the expert and the novice? Build multiple types of challenges into the level.

Think of your level as an amusement park. Everyone goes into a theme park through the same gate. Everyone walks along the same main path and sees the same rides and attractions. Some of the rides are too wild for some of the visitors, and some are too tame. No one is offended by the presence of the rides that do not suit them, just as long as there are enough of the kinds of rides *they* want to go on.

As a level designer, bring everyone through the same front door of your level, ensure that there's enough of each kind of challenge, provide good signposts so that no one gets lost, and make certain that everyone finds his way to the exit when the day is done.

At some parks, the triple-loop Death Drop roller coaster has a special line for those who want to sit in the very first car. The people who wait longer for that experience are the aficionados (expert players). This doesn't mean that other riders (average players) can't have a good time. Some wave their hands over their heads and scream, whereas others close their eyes and hang on to the bar for dear life. They all enjoy the ride. Nor does it mean that the person standing on the ground (the novice) isn't having a good time as he eats an ice cream cone and wonders how the others got the nerve to get on board in the first place.

(As a side note, the roller coaster itself has the same structure and progression as your level. It starts off easy, with hints and teases of what's to come. Then it builds in a series of dramatic arcs to a climax, and finally gives the rider a few seconds to catch his breath as it glides to a halt and dumps him out to wobble, weak-kneed, to the next ride.)

Applying this amusement park model to the business of designing levels means creating multiple challenges in each of your maps. If you put a powerful, tantalizing, but unnecessary, power-up in a hard-to-reach spot, the expert will accept it as a personal challenge and keep trying different strategies until he acquires it. The average player will take a few swipes at it but then move on with the meat of the mission. The below-average player might not even notice it.

You should also design multiple ways for the player to beat your level. There shouldn't be just one strategy the player must follow to succeed. The expert can choose a high-risk, high-reward strategy, and the novice can plod along on a safer path, but each player will succeed in his own way and be satisfied.

Like the amusement park designer, you should not be upset if every single "visitor" doesn't see every single feature of your "park". In fact, you should try to create nooks and crannies (secret areas) that only the dedicated few will find. Remember that the point is never to show off, or to make yourself happy—the point is always the visitor. The goal is to make *him* happy. If you do so, and if you have built in enough depth, he will come back to your park over and over again.

Balance

There should be neither too many nor too few resources in a level. The player should be concerned about running out of ammo or nervous that his health is running low, but there shouldn't be so little of either that he spends all his time hunting for them. Ideally, the resource should appear just before he starts to panic. Divining when that moment occurs is part of the art of the level designer.

Balance risk and reward. The more dangerous the weapon or valuable the armor, the harder you should make it for the player to acquire. In multiplayer games, the more powerful a location, the harder it should be to get there. The best weapons should spawn in places where other players have a shot at whoever tries to go for them.

In multiplayer games such as Capture the Flag, each team should have a roughly equal chance of prevailing. The weapons should be evenly distributed, the bases should be equally defensible, and the most powerful weapons and power-ups should be equidistant from the bases so that each team has the same opportunity to get at them.

Puzzles

The single biggest problem of puzzles in action games is that players often do not know where they are. Sometimes a player will slay all the monsters on a level, yet still be left wandering around wondering why he's not done. After a while, he'll either give up in disgust or reluctantly reach for the strategy guide. Only then will he learn that the ledge that looked too narrow can actually be traversed, the jump he tried five times can really be made, or the wall he tried to climb in six places can be scaled from a seventh.

This problem arises from the wealth of realistic graphical detail we can now put in our levels. If we can make the entire level look interesting and beautiful, how do we draw the player's attention to the spots that are actually important?

The answer is to give the player clues, to leave a trail of breadcrumbs that he can follow, instead of bashing his head against the level in an orgy of trial and error. The size of the breadcrumbs determines the difficulty of the puzzle. The clue can be a trail of blood leading to a certain spot, a glimpse of an adversary making a jump from one ledge to another, or even a blatant message over the radio that tells the player where to go and what to do.

Other Design Tips

Here are some other tips to keep in mind as you design your level.

- Avoid head fakes. If you have something in a level that looks important, and the player expends considerable effort on it, if you put in a big red door with tough guards on either side and gun turrets along the passage that leads to it, the player had better find something of value on the other side of that door, not just an empty room. If you make the player work to cross the rainbow, you must put a pot of gold on the other side. The harder he works, the bigger the pot.

- AI. Work with your AI programmers to learn the capabilities of the AI. Design your levels to take advantage of the AIs' strengths and hide their weaknesses.

- Asset sequencing. Your level is part of an overall progression. You need to know which resources the player has when he begins your level, and which new assets you will be allowed to introduce. Do not break this asset sequence. If you give the player something he shouldn't have, you will screw up the other level designers who are working on later missions.

- If you need to deprive the player of a tool or weapon he's previously acquired but that will break your level, go ahead and take it away from him, but make sure that you have a good game reason for doing so. A common example of this is when a player is captured and stripped of all his weapons, and his goal in the level is to escape.

- Do not design a level where the player has to use every weapon in the game to get through it.

- Accommodate different playing styles. Some people are cautious. They take two steps and then pause to look around in all directions before proceeding two more steps. They're fearful of missing something and fearful of failing. Others speed ahead, figuring that they can deal with anything that shows up. The sooner they land in a nest of bad guys, the sooner they can have some fun!

- Provide eye candy, but do not reveal everything all at once. Hold things back so that the player continually has new and interesting things to look at throughout the level.

Evaluation

Level design is an iterative process. No one conceives a level in his head, builds it once, and then walks away. A level must be honed and balanced constantly, from the moment you start working on it to the moment the producer rips it out of your hands.

The evaluation process begins with you. You yourself must play your level as you build it, not only to find bugs but also to create new gameplay. As you come at what you have created from the point of view of a player, you say to yourself, "Okay, what if I tried *this*?" Then you get the fun of answering yourself. If you enjoy yourself in this fashion, the player will too.

Be knowledgeable and competitive. Keep track of what other LDs within your company are doing, and go on the Internet to find out what LDs at other companies are doing. Keep playing other designers' levels, extract the principles that make them appealing, and apply those principles to your own work. This is not to say that you should steal or otherwise plagiarize the work of others; just that you must continue to learn.

After you have the rough level in place, let others come in and look at it before you try to polish it. Listen to their comments about the basic ideas. Accept suggestions that solve problems and amplify the theme. Reject suggestions, even if they are interesting, that confuse the player, detract from the theme, or upset the balance.

A common problem at this stage is when someone says, "Hey, that so-and-so reminds me of something I saw in Game X." Unless you discover that you have ripped off Game

X completely, the correct response is to shrug your shoulders and continue. Remember, there's nothing new under the sun, and anything you create could remind *someone* of *something*. If you let this get to you, you will be paralyzed. Ignore it. Go ahead and create. Draw on the work of others for inspiration, but process everything through your own filter. Be as original as you can, but remember that even Sir Isaac Newton said, "If I have seen further, it is by standing upon the shoulders of giants."

After others have agreed that the basic idea of the level is fun, it is time to start polishing. Fix the door that has an awkward trigger. Change the geometry in the tight spot where the player's collision cylinder becomes trapped. Make sure that all the holes have been eliminated. Find the places where the frame rate is bogging down, and analyze your engine's capabilities to eliminate the cause of the slowdown.

After you've polished the level, open it up to the testers again. Watch others play your levels, but put some tape over your mouth. Your job is to observe and learn. If you tell someone to turn left instead of right, you have robbed yourself of seeing how thousands of people will play your game. Never assume that what one tester tries is unique. Instead, for every move a tester makes, think of 10,000 other people doing the same thing. *Then* you can decide whether that action is worth handling.

Remember that early on, you will lose perspective on how easy or hard your level is. For that, you can rely only on the word of fresh testers who have never seen the level before.

Know when to walk away. Levels are never perfect. You can always tweak something to make it better. You must develop an internal barometer that tells you when you are done, and you must be able to listen to outsiders as well.

Above all, work with the other level designers on your project, not only to review one another's levels for quality and new ideas, but also to ensure a qualitative consistency (consistent look-and-feel) and to ensure that no one introduces something in one level that will somehow break another. For these reasons, many level designers like to work in a large open area where they all have easy access to one another.

As a builder of levels, you are a jack of all trades and a master of *one*. You must be part artist, part architect, and part programmer. But when you combine these skills in the service of gameplay, you become all designer.

CHAPTER 6

DESIGNING THE PUZZLE

This chapter deals with puzzles in action games, action adventures, and RPGs. You will look at the different types of puzzles, what distinguishes good design from bad, how to adjust the level of difficulty, and how to use puzzles to enhance your story.

After you create a hero and give him a goal, if you don't put obstacles in his path, you won't have a game.

This is a requirement we have inherited from storytelling.

You never read a story in which the bad guy is coming to town and the hero goes out to meet him at noon, slays him with one bullet, and gets home for lunch at 12:05. No. There's not just one bad guy—there's a whole gang of 'em. And the hero's favorite gun has just been stolen, so he has to use an old pistol that doesn't always fire. And he has one fewer bullet than there are bad guys. And he had his appendix out yesterday, so he can hardly walk. And just as the bad guys show up at one end of town, he learns that some dynamite is set to go off at the other end of town. And the dynamite is under his daughter's house. And his daughter is pregnant.

In traditional media, these are problems the hero must solve. How he does so becomes the story. In our business, the player becomes the hero, and the obstacles become puzzles.

Good puzzles contribute to plot, character, and story development. Good puzzles draw the player into the fictional world. Good puzzles make a game great. Bad puzzles, however, do none of those things. They are intrusive and obstructionist. Like bad writing, they draw attention to themselves and divert the player's attention from the game, destroying the magical experience you are trying to create.

A good puzzle fits into its setting and presents an obstacle that makes sense. When the player solves it, he knows why what he did worked.

Types of Puzzles

The art of puzzle design lies in creating an original set of problems and solutions that are appropriate to your world. Behind the details that make each puzzle unique are structures that fall into recognizable categories. Knowing these structures will give you a toolbox for getting your hero into and out of trouble.

Let's examine them now and apply theory to practice by exploring a simple problem every designer faces again and again in his career: How to get a player through a door.

Ordinary Use of an Object

Ordinary use is the simplest puzzle of all. The player enters a dark room and discovers an empty light socket. He checks his inventory and discovers a light bulb. He screws in the light bulb, turns on the switch, and now he has light. This is the most straightforward kind of activity you can ask a player to perform.

Door example: The player finds a door with a golden lock. He has a golden key. He unlocks the door with the key, and everyone is happy. The player's challenge with these puzzles usually comes from finding the object, rather than figuring out that it is needed. Normally, the designer puts it in a location that is geographically separate from where it is used, or he hides it in a container that also requires a puzzle to open.

Unusual Use of an Object

Unusual use takes advantage of objects' secondary characteristics. It requires the player to recognize that things can be used in ways other than what their creator intended. Diamonds make pretty rings, but they can also cut glass. A candle can light up a dark room, but its wax can also be collected to make an impression of a key, it can light a fire that will set off a smoke alarm, or the heat from its flame can be used to expose secret writing on a piece of paper.

Door example: The player finds a door that has no key but is barred from the other side. It's one of a series of doors he has encountered, and each of the others had a guard who pulled on a rope that passed through the wall to raise the bar on the other side. This door has a similar rope about five feet away from the door, but no guard. The player can step over to the rope, pull it, and hear the bar go up on the other side. But when he releases the rope and runs back to the door, he hears the bar fall back into place. Earlier in the game, you gave him a 20-pound sledgehammer to drive a tent spike into the ground. He could quite reasonably try to use the hammer to smash the door, and you may or may not let this work (see "Alternative Solutions" later in this chapter). The real solution here is to tie the hammer to the rope, which raises the bar and keeps it raised while he goes over to open the door.

"Building" Puzzles

Sometimes you can require the player to create a new object out of raw material that is available in the game. He can do this either by converting one object into another or by combining two or more objects to create something totally new.

An example of the first: If there is a crevasse to cross and a tree growing next to it, you give the player an ax to cut down the tree and create a bridge. An example of the second (courtesy of designer Ken Rolston): A baby is crying in a cradle, and the player needs to calm her down. He can take a few strips of kindling, tie them together with thread, attach a few brightly colored trinkets, and hang the resulting mobile over her bed.

The most common danger with building a puzzle is when the designer assumes that players will automatically jump to the solution he has in mind. Perhaps the player thinks that the baby is crying because she is hungry or cold or she wants to be rocked or just held? Building a mobile is far down on the list of things a player might think of to calm a baby. What you must do is give the player the information he needs in order to nudge him toward the solution. In this case, you can have the infant's father tell the player that the baby is well rested and fed, but that he left her favorite toy—a mobile— back home.

Door example: In *Eric the Unready* (a comedy game), there is a door with a key on a chain hanging next to it. However, the chain is too short for the key to reach the lock. A proclamation with a wax seal is posted on the door. The solution is for the player to melt the seal, use the wax to take an impression of the key, and bring it to the locksmith at the Cross Keys Tavern. The locksmith turns the wax impression into a real key, and the player uses that to unlock the door.

Information Puzzles

In information puzzles, the player has to supply a missing piece of information. It could be as simple as supplying a password, or as complex as deducing the correct sequence of numbers that will defuse a bomb.

Door example: It is common for a guard stationed outside a door to request a password before allowing the player to enter. Usually (if the guard cannot be bribed or distracted), the player must search other areas of the game for the keyword. Finding it can involve talking to other characters, searching through documents, or deducing what the password might be, based on what you have told the player about the character who created it.

Codes, Cryptograms, and Other "Word" Puzzles

Puzzles such as these make up a subset of the information puzzle, defining the boundaries of the kind of information for which the player is looking. It is important that the designer let the player know when he is trying to solve a word puzzle, because generally these puzzles are unrelated to the game's mood and setting. One way to do this is to establish the character who's demanding the information as someone who relishes wordplay. In the case of cryptograms, anything more complex than a single-letter substitution should probably be considered out of bounds.

These word-related puzzles have become rare not only because they are difficult, but also because of the problems translating them into the many languages accompanying a worldwide release.

Door example: The door to a mad scientist's lab has an access panel covered with pictograms. You tell the player that the scientist is fond of rebuses. The player has to press the symbols in an order that will spell out a word or phrase that he knows is important to the scientist.

Excluded Middle Puzzles

The excluded middle is one of the hardest types of puzzles, both to design and to solve. It involves creating reliable cause-and-effect relationships and then requiring the player to recognize that a particular action will kick off a chain of events that culminate in the desired action. Stated in terms of logic, *a* always causes *b*, and *c* always causes *d*. When the player finds himself in a situation that requires *d*, in a location where he has reason to believe that *b* and *c* would be linked, he will perform *a* (you hope).

Fortunately, the following example is much easier to understand than the preceding explanation.

Door example: Tell the player that rubbing a magic lamp (a) always summons an enormous bull (b). Also, say that any time the bull sees something red (c), he charges at it (d). Now put the player in front of a locked door that happens to be red. With luck (and a few nudges from the designer), the player will realize that if he rubs the lamp, the bull will come, see the door, and charge at it to knock it down.

Preparing the Way

A wrinkle on the excluded middle that makes it even more difficult is to require the player to *create* the condition that will cause the final link in the chain to occur. The longer the logical chain and the more conditions the player has to create, the harder the puzzle becomes. Be careful of this, however, because it can quickly become a case of asking the player to read the designer's mind (see "What Makes a Bad Puzzle?" later in this chapter).

Door example: In the preceding example, let's say that the door is green but that the player has a bucket of red paint. When he first encounters the door, he tries rubbing the lamp, but when the bull comes, it just ambles around and eventually leaves. The solution is to paint the door red *before* summoning the bull.

People Puzzles

The most satisfying puzzles are those that involve people. This is because while trying to solve them, the player inevitably learns more about the game's characters, and good characters are the backbone of good stories. These puzzles usually involve a person who is blocking the player's progress or is holding a piece of information the player needs. To progress in the story, the player has to learn the key to that person's desires. If he is a guard, perhaps he can be bribed. If he is a spy, perhaps the player can uncover the secret piece of information he has been seeking. If he is a megalomaniac, perhaps the hero can find something to stroke his ego. If he is a child, perhaps the player can find a toy.

Door example: In *Eric the Unready*, an interior tower door is guarded by a soldier described as "very alert." The more you talk with him, the more you learn that he can't be bribed, distracted, or outfought. Outside, however, is a bard who sings songs, tells jokes, and if paid enough, recites the *Epic of Baldur*, an excruciatingly boring story that instantly puts all who hear it to sleep. The player has to lure the bard into the hall and (after donning earmuffs that prevent him from hearing the story) pay the bard to launch into the epic. As soon as he does so, the guard falls asleep, and the player gains access to the tower.

Timing Puzzles

This is a difficult class of puzzle that requires the player to recognize he must take an action that does not yield an instant effect, but instead will cause something to happen at a particular point in the future. This becomes even harder if more than one location is involved.

Door example: The classic diversion. If the player has seen that a guard will always leave his post to investigate a noise, he can go to a different location and set up a noise-making device there. Setting it off immediately, however, would cause the guard to come and discover him. Instead, he puts it on a timer and returns to the original location. When it goes off, the guard disappears to investigate, and the player slips through the door.

Sequence Puzzles

Sequence puzzles rely on performing a series of actions in just the right order. Mostly, they are comedic, as in the Babel Fish puzzle in *Hitchhiker's Guide to the Galaxy* by Steve Meretzky. Usually, the player is presented with a simple means of achieving a simple goal. When he performs that action, however, something suddenly pops up to prevent his achieving that goal. The situation then resets, and the player must put something in place to solve the *new* problem before kicking off the sequence again. This can become quite elaborate.

Door example: The player finds a door with a huge St. Bernard lazing in front of it. He puts down a piece of meat to lure the dog away, but a smaller dog suddenly races in through a pet door, snatches the meat, and disappears. The player nails shut the pet door and puts down another piece of meat. This time, the little dog jumps in through the open window and grabs the meat again. The player shuts the window. This goes on until the player has hermetically sealed the room so that the little dog can't get in, and the St. Bernard finally lumbers over to get the meat, unblocking the door so that the player can go through.

Logic Puzzles

In logic puzzles, the player must deduce a particular bit of information by examining a series of statements and ferreting out a hidden implication. They most commonly take the form, "If Mr. Robinson is a dentist, and Mr. Smith drives a brown car, and Mr. Jones only opens doors on Wednesdays . . ." and so on.

Door example: The player is following a character but momentarily loses sight of him and then rounds the corner to find himself in a room with three doors. There is no sign of his quarry, but fortunately, there's a leprechaun who offers, for a fee, to tell him which door the character used. The player pays up, and because no leprechaun can ever just play it straight, he gives the player a set of elaborate rules by which the player can deduce the correct door. The leprechaun then disappears in a puff of green smoke.

Classic Game Puzzles

Classic game puzzles aren't true action or adventure game puzzles, but they seem to find their way into many games anyway. Examples include magic square puzzles, move-the-matchstick puzzles, or jump-the-peg-and-leave-the-last-one-in-the-middle puzzles. The thing to remember about them is that there should be an easy way to reset them so that the player can return quickly to the opening position if he gets hopelessly tangled. The designer should also provide either a help system or an alternative to completing the puzzle so that players who are not adept at them don't become stalled.

Door example: In a science-fiction game, it would not be unreasonable to have a mechanical contrivance built in to the wall that requires the player physically to manipulate its elements into a certain configuration before the door will open. In *Death Gate*, a fantasy game by Glen Dahlgren, the entrance to a cave is controlled by just such a device, created by clever dwarves.

Riddles

The riddle is one of the least satisfying kinds of puzzles because if the player doesn't get it, he just doesn't get it. If you're going to do a riddle puzzle, be sure to include plenty of hints in nearby locations.

Door example: The player is standing outside a door guarded by an impish creature who demands that the player guess his name before he can pass. The creature provides a clue in the form of the following riddle:

> *My first name comes before a duck,*
>
> *My last name's found in fences.*
>
> *Some days I have to bring a truck,*
>
> *To take home all my pences.*

If the player can't figure out the answer (Bill Gates), he is stalled.

Dialogue Puzzles

A byproduct of dialogue trees, dialogue puzzles require the player to follow a conversation down the correct path until a character says or does the right thing. The advantage of dialogue puzzles is that nothing brings out character like the way people talk. The disadvantage is that these aren't really puzzles—all the player has to do is pursue every option of every dialogue. This is tedious at best and promotes a feeling of player paranoia.

("Gee, I wonder whether I missed some crucial piece of information because I didn't go down every path of the dialogue tree. Maybe I'd better restore and go back and do that.") The best solution to this problem is to acknowledge that you're not *really* presenting a puzzle here, and to manage things so that the player cannot exit until he has acquired whatever crucial piece of information he needs in order to proceed.

Door example: A guard mentions to the player that he's a big fan of horse racing. Later in the dialogue, the player gives him a hot tip on Seabiscuit in the Fifth at Belmont. The guard becomes so excited that he leaves his post for a few minutes to put down a bet.

Trial-and-Error Puzzles

A player is confronted with an array of choices, and with no information to go on, he must try each one until suddenly one of them clicks. Designers who do this should be defrocked and run out of town.

Door example: The player must choose from fifty doors with nothing to distinguish them from each other. He tries door #1. It won't open and provides no clue as to why. He tries door #2. Same result. When he gets up to door #34, it suddenly opens. This isn't puzzle-solving. It's hard labor. Ideally, a player should be able to solve a puzzle the first time he encounters it, just by looking at it and thinking hard.

Machinery Puzzles

In machinery puzzles, the player must figure out how to operate the controls of a machine. Sometimes it involves minor trial and error, sometimes logic. In *Mission Critical* by Mike Verdu, there's a rupture in the pipes that supply coolant fluid to a spaceship's nuclear reactor. The player has to manipulate the controls of the machine that pumps the fluid through the pipes, to reroute the fluid past the rupture and prevent a meltdown.

Door example: In *Companions of Xanth* by Michael Lindner, the door that controls access to the magician's castle is operated from a panel with several levers. The player has to learn how to manipulate the levers, and when he does so correctly, the door opens.

Alternative Interfaces

Alternative interfaces can be anything from machinery puzzles to maps. You remove the normal game interface and replace it with a screen that the player has to manipulate to reach a predefined condition. The coolant fluid puzzle mentioned in the preceding section provides an excellent opportunity to create an alternative interface.

Door example: In *Callahan's Crosstime Saloon* by Josh Mandel, the entrance to an ancient Mayan temple is blocked by a massive stone door. Above the entrance is a mosaic. When the player examines a nearby pedestal, an alternative interface appears that allows him to move colored stones around according to certain rules. When he has manipulated the stones to duplicate the picture in the mosaic, the huge door slides open.

Mazes

"You are in a maze of twisty passages, all alike." Mazes used to be a staple of adventure games. Players mapped them using pencil and paper. Over time, they have become clichéd. You should create a maze only if you have developed an interesting, unique twist to mapping or navigating.

Gestalt Puzzles

Sometimes a puzzle comes not from performing a specific action, but from recognizing a general condition. One of the best examples is the sundial puzzle in *Trinity* by Brian Moriarty. At the beginning of the game, the player is standing next to a sundial in London's Kensington Gardens. After a sequence of extraordinary events, he finds himself transported to a completely bizarre world. As he explores this world, he finds some parts of it shrouded in darkness. Later, those same areas are bathed in light. After a while, the player realizes that this new world exists on the face of the sundial, and the darkness is the shadow cast by the gnomon as time passes.

The interesting thing about a gestalt puzzle is that the author never actually states the condition. Instead, he provides evidence that builds up over time. Some players will solve it quickly, and some will take longer. The hardest part for the designer is to create an action for the player to take that definitively shows that he's figured out what's going on.

What Makes a Bad Puzzle?

The key to the reasonableness of puzzles is to make their circumstances fit the world you have created. You wouldn't have malfunctioning nuclear plants in a sword-and-sorcery fantasy game, nor would you try to summon a magical wizard in a hard science fiction game. Good puzzle design involves looking around the world you have created and using obstacles, objects, and characters that would naturally occur in that environment. Bad puzzles violate this rule, and they frequently break other rules as well.

Restore Puzzles

It's unfair to kill off a player for not solving a puzzle and only *then* provide him with the information he needed to solve it. For example, let's say a player innocently opens an unmarked door and walks into a room. The door locks behind him, and the room fills with poisonous gas. As he chokes and dies, he sees someone else entering the room wearing a gas mask.

It is reasonable enough to have a gas-filled room. It certainly is easy enough for the player to restore (or undo) to the point before he entered the room and to find a gas mask. However, it is not fair. You gave him no reason to think ahead of time that opening the door was dangerous. Ideally, a player should be able to complete a game without ever having to restore. In this case, you could put a warning sign outside the door, show tendrils of smoke escaping from under the door, or arrange any of a thousand other ways to avoid putting the player in a position where you say without warning, "Bang! You're dead."

Arbitrary Puzzles

Effects should always be linked to causes. Events shouldn't happen just because the designer decided that it's time for them to happen. This occurs most frequently when the designer doesn't want to let the player leave an area until he has solved all the puzzles there. The designer traps the player there until the last of the puzzles has been solved, and then magically allows the player to proceed, without explaining how solving that set of puzzles logically led to his new capability.

Designer Puzzles

Avoid, too, those puzzles that make sense only to you, the designer. Just because the connections are clear in your head doesn't mean that they will make sense to the player. The best defense against designing these kinds of puzzles is a good testing team. Bounce your ideas off people. If you have to explain how (or why) the puzzle works more than twice, you should either simplify or abandon it.

Problems also arise when the designer sets out to prove that he is smarter than the player. Perhaps you know some arcane bit of information or are aware of a little-known relationship between two people or events. It is tempting to make this the core of a puzzle and only reveal the information after the player fails to solve it. Resist this temptation. You're as much the player's partner as his adversary. He's relying on you to give him the information he needs to play the game. He will admire you more for playing fair than for showing off your storehouse of unusual knowledge.

Binary Puzzles

Avoid binary puzzles. These are puzzles with yes or no answers that yield instant success or failure. If the player opens door #1, he dies; if he opens door #2, he wins. It becomes but the work of a moment to try door #1, fail, restore, and open door #2. This is one of the most common errors that inexperienced designers make. They create "the lady or the tiger" puzzles, and gamers blow right by them without expending more than two seconds of creative thought. Whenever you give the player choices, give him *lots* of choices, and make it difficult for him to simply choose, fail, and restore.

Hunt-the-Pixel Puzzles

With the increased richness of today's game graphics, another trap has been set for designers who don't work closely enough with their artists—the *hunt-the-pixel* problem. Sometimes an important object on the screen is so small that it's easy to overlook. This is usually created by problems of scale. If the room is large and the object is small, the player might overlook it.

Solutions to this problem are to (a) make the object stand out against the background through contrasting color or animation, (b) move the object into the foreground, or, as a last resort, (c) make the "hot spot" of the object larger than the object itself. Thus, when the player is *scanning* the screen (running the mouse back and forth across the picture to see which object names light up), he has a better chance of stumbling across the item. This will also help reduce player paranoia. It is very unsettling for a player to worry that the reason he can't solve a particular puzzle is that he has overlooked some tiny area of the screen. If he discovers that this is true, he will be mad at you.

What Makes a Good Puzzle?

Many of these design problems yield puzzles a player not only fails to solve but also could *never* solve (he eventually learns). This leads to a "poisoning of the well"—an unhealthy skepticism in players' minds that the designer isn't playing fair. It is essential to learn the elements of good puzzle design so that players will learn to trust you.

Fairness

In a fair game, the answer to every puzzle is contained within the game. In addition, a player should theoretically be able to solve it the first time he encounters it simply by thinking hard enough (assuming that he has been presented with all the information). Like a good mystery novel, it isn't fair to wait until the last page only to have the author reveal previously withheld information that identifies the murderer.

Appropriate to the Environment

Plopping a logic or mathematical puzzle into the middle of a story is *not* a good way to move a narrative along. The best puzzles fit naturally into the story and give the player the opportunity to learn more about the people, the setting, and the world they are exploring.

If the player enters a room and the first thing he encounters is a magic-square puzzle that seems to have dropped out of nowhere, all suspension of disbelief is gone. The magic of the environment evaporates. The player might as well be reading *Games Magazine.*

Instead, imagine that he enters a room and discovers a door blocked by a woman whose head is bent in sorrow, tears falling from her eyes. To get through the door, he must dislodge the woman, but she is so distraught that he cannot get past. *Now* you have something. Who is this woman? Why is she crying? What will it take to make her stop crying? To find the answers, he will have to talk with her or someone else, learn a little about her background, or look around in other spots to find something that might mollify her grief. All these activities draw him into the story. They make him explore the setting and the motivations of the characters who populate this world. If the backbone of good fiction is character, the backbone of good interactive fiction is a puzzle that involves those characters.

Amplifying the Theme

Ideally, a puzzle should amplify the theme of the game, if it has one. You shouldn't have the player taking actions contrary to the character you have set up. The actions must be reasonable things for his character to do. You wouldn't expect an animal rights activist to gain access to a high-security compound by shooting the guard dog.

The V-8 Response

The sign of a great puzzle is the V-8 response. When the player finally gets the answer, he slaps his forehead and says, "A-*ha!* Of *course!!* How could it have taken me so long to figure it out?" The sign of a bad puzzle is when he says, "There's no way I could *ever* have solved that. I don't even understand it now! Why does this work? Oh well, either I'm just stupid or this game is really unfair."

Levels of Difficulty

In the early days, games were difficult. Now games are easier. Whether it's because of the advent of the mass market, the poisoning of the well, or players' shortened attention span, you have to be very aware of how difficult your puzzles are. Fortunately, one of the simplest parts of designing a puzzle is adjusting its level of difficulty.

Bread Crumbs

One of the easiest ways to adjust the level of difficulty is to change the amount or directness of information you give the player. Remember the story of Hansel and Gretel walking through the forest, dropping bread crumbs behind them so they could find their way back? The bigger and more numerous the bread crumbs, the easier it is for the player to find his way through the woods.

For example, suppose you've created a wall safe that the player knows contains vital information. If you tape the combination on the wall next to the safe, it's scarcely a puzzle at all. The player can just read the combination and use it to open the safe. If you hide the combination under the rug in that room, the puzzle becomes more difficult because the player has to lift the rug to find it. It's still not all that difficult, however.

Now, rather than write out the combination, you put a picture of a smiling older couple, with the inscription *Happy Anniversary: 6-9-93*, on the desk in the room. It would be more difficult for the player to make the jump that the date on the picture is the combination of the safe. Now, change the inscription to *Happy 50th Anniversary, June 9, 1993*. It requires even more thought for the player to realize that the person owning the safe might consider the wedding day more memorable than the anniversary of it and, therefore, that he should subtract 50 from the 93 to get a combination of 6-9-43. The next step would be to put the picture not on the desk but in the owner's wallet, which the player discovers in a trash can on the other side of the city. Finally, if you *really* want to be cruel, you could make the man British, so the combination would be 9-6-43 because the English order their dates by day/month/year rather than month/day/year. (If you don't mention this idiosyncrasy elsewhere in the game, however, you are falling victim to the designer puzzle trap mentioned earlier.)

The Solution's Proximity to the Puzzle

Although, in a fair game, the answer to every puzzle is contained within the game, how close the designer puts the answer to the problem determines how easy the puzzle is. This is true both psychologically and geographically. If it's late in the game and the answer involves remembering an arcane bit of information you supplied in a side comment back at the beginning of the game and half the world geography away, that puzzle will be difficult. The more attention you draw to that side comment, the easier the puzzle will be. When the player is confronted with the puzzle near the end of the game, if another character pipes up and reminds him of that side comment, the puzzle becomes easier.

Alternative Solutions

Another way to make a game easier is to provide alternative solutions to puzzles. The problem with these is that they can be expensive to implement because of the increased graphic requirements, and they can make the game *too* easy. Also, it's hard enough for the designer to handle *one* solution robustly, much less two.

Red Herrings

One way to make a game harder is to include red herrings. Generally, it's not necessary to do this. Players spend so much time generating their own false theories that it becomes completely superfluous for you to do so as well.

Steering the Player

This brings us to responding to player inputs that don't actually solve puzzles. You should constantly be steering the player toward the right answers to the puzzles by providing little (or big) clues in the responses you make to his inputs.

Responses should contain little nuggets of information so that the longer a player sticks to it and the more things he tries, the more knowledge he accumulates about what might work. You should help him circle in on the solution, never being entirely obvious but providing enough bits of data that eventually a critical mass is reached and he realizes what he is supposed to do, all without feeling he has cheated by going off and looking for a hint.

How to Design the Puzzle

Having learned about various puzzle types, good and bad design, and adjusting levels of difficulty, how do you go about actually creating the puzzles?

In any story, the author creates a character and gives him a goal. In a good yarn, the path to the goal is never easy. Myriad opponents stand in the way—bad guys, nature, internal conflicts, fate—all these conspire to litter the hero's path with obstacles. If the path were easy, the tale would be dull. The same is true of games. If the player can click through a game in two hours, he is not making significant choices, and he is not getting his money's worth.

Creating the Puzzle

You begin where any author begins, with your story and characters. You create a setting and populate it with interesting characters. Then you create the role of the player and give him an overall goal. As you break down the story into scenes, you establish a subgoal for each scene that fits into the overall story. Within the scene, you create obstacles that hinder the player from reaching the subgoal. Those obstacles are the puzzles.

In Chapter 4, "Storytelling," we looked at the opening sequence of *Raiders of the Lost Ark*. That sequence is a great example of a storyteller dreaming up exotic threats that are appropriate to a particular situation, and then giving his hero reasonable tools to overcome those obstacles. Puzzle designers do the same thing. We create problems for the player that are appropriate to the story and the setting, and we give him reasonable ways to solve those problems.

As you approach the problem of puzzle design, think of the character you have created. Think about where he is trying to go and what he is trying to do. Then think about reasonable obstacles to place in his path. Finally, using the principles of good design to make the task fair and reasonable, give the player the means to get past those obstacles.

The Villain

Probably the single most useful piece of advice about designing puzzles is to think about the villain. Something is there that does *not* want your hero to succeed. Whether it is a person, the gods, the government, or the ultimate bad guy—whatever that thing is, that's the villain.

The villain is in active opposition to your hero. He's the one creating the obstacles. He says to himself, "I do not want the hero to succeed, and I will stop him by doing *this*." The material he uses is material from the environment. His purpose is clear, and it's up to the hero to overcome the obstacles.

When you're designing a puzzle, ask yourself why it should be there. Who would have put it there? Why? Who is this bad guy, and why is he threatening your hero?

Player Empathy

To determine what is "fair and reasonable," you need to be able to put yourself in the player's shoes. You need to develop *player empathy*. This is the ability to look at the game from the player's point of view, even though the game might still be nothing more than a swirling design in your head. You must, as the potential player, be able to say, "This is the situation I'm in, and here is what I've been told. I know my long-term goal, and I know my short-term goal within this scene, but right now I'm being blocked by these two problems. Now, how am I going to solve them?"

When you can look at the game from the player's point of view, you can anticipate the kinds of things he will want to try. When you learn to anticipate his moves, you can give him a better game experience by creating interesting reactions to them.

Another part of player empathy is letting the player know where the puzzles *are*. In a game, anything the player can't do is likely to be perceived by him as a puzzle. It's up to the designer to let him know when this is true and when it's not. Players have enough trouble solving the real puzzles in the game that you don't need them chasing off to solve puzzles that aren't really there.

For that reason, it is sometimes useful to let the architecture of the game show through. "You can't go that way" used to be a response that would annoy game players because they wanted a *reason*. However, when the player has bumped up against the limits of the world, it is important to let him know so that he doesn't perceive this limit as just another obstacle to be circumvented. If you had said instead, "A large boulder blocks your path," it is reasonable for the player to think that his next task is to move that boulder. If this isn't a puzzle you want him to be solving, you must say so in the most unambiguous language you can muster.

This idea of player empathy is so important that some consider it the single greatest indicator of whether a person can be a successful game designer. If you cannot learn to put yourself inside the player's head, you will never be able to design a game that captures and holds someone's attention. You must learn to "play the movie in your head" and anticipate what the player is going to try. Only then can you steer him towards the right answers, respond to his off-the-wall actions, and ensure at every turn that he is having fun.

Summary

As a puzzle designer, make sure that your puzzles enhance the game rather than detract from it. Use puzzles to draw the player into your story so that he learns more about your characters. Don't withhold the information he needs in order to solve the puzzle. Develop player empathy, and strive for that perfect level of frustration that drives a player forward rather than turns him away. Above all—*play fair!*

CHAPTER 7

FRANCHISES, BRANDS, AND LICENSES

We live in a brand-driven world.

Companies such as Coke and Perrier can charge more for a basic commodity than their competition, because they have a recognized brand. Why does this work? Because the brand creates a safe choice for the consumer. He knows what he's buying before he opens the package. He's confident that he'll receive value for his money.

A brand or a franchise also represents safety to a game company executive. It means risk reduction. To most finance people, game development is a black box. They put money in one end, something mysterious happens, and eventually money comes out the other end. (More money, they hope, than if they had put the same amount in a bank account and drawn interest for two years.) Over time, these financial folks have noticed that when they feed a franchise into the front end of the box, larger amounts of money tend to come out the back end.

In an ideal world, this wouldn't cost anything. However, a franchise is free only if you already own it, which means that you have to develop it internally. This is why some companies constantly seek to build their own brands. Internal franchises like *Pokemon* and *Tomb Raider* are like gold. When you own the brand, not only can you build your own product line around it, but you can also license it out to other companies for products such as books, action figures, and even movies. Money for nothing!

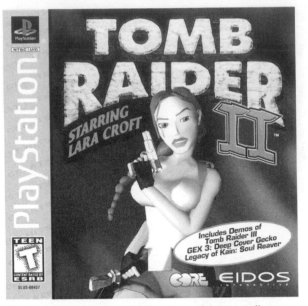

Figure 7.1 *Tomb Raider* is a powerful, internally developed franchise. Used with permission of Eidos Interactive Ltd.

Establishing a brand carries its own cost and risk, however, which is why game companies sometimes prefer to pay a fee to use an external franchise (see Figure 7.1). The intellectual property (IP) they license can be a movie (*Mission Impossible*, *Blade Runner*), a sport (*Major League Baseball*, *NHL Hockey*), or even the endorsement of an individual (Jack Nicklaus, Tony Hawk). In these cases, the executive hopes that the additional money he spends to buy name recognition will deliver higher sales and bigger profits, and reduce his overall risk (see Figures 7.2 and 7.3).

This chapter discusses how to develop original IPs for your company, and also how to work with franchises you license from others.

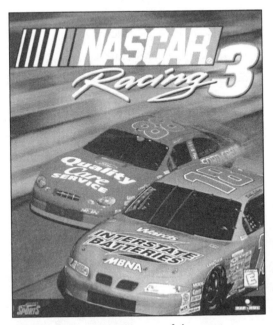

Figure 7.2 NASCAR is one of the most recognized names in sports. Used with permission of Sierra On-Line Inc.

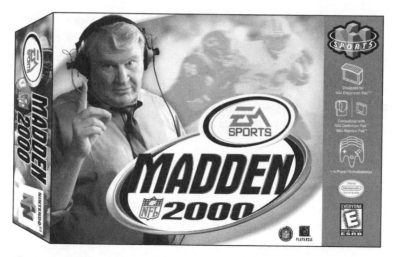

Figure 7.3 The *John Madden Football* franchise has been going strong for over ten years. ©1999 Electronic Arts Inc. All rights reserved.

Creating an Internal Franchise

Hit games tend to be about interesting people in interesting places doing interesting things. There are exceptions (*Pac-Man*, *Tetris*), but the rule generally holds true.

When you look at some of the best, established "franchises" in literary history, you can see all these elements at work. King Arthur has a vivid cast of supporting characters: Guinevere, Lancelot, Merlin, the Knights of the Round Table, the Lady of the Lake, and the powerful villain Mordred. The settings are fabulous: Camelot, Avalon, and Joyous Gard. The activities are likewise fascinating: slaying dragons, jousting, and questing for the Holy Grail.

Sherlock Holmes, one of the most fascinating characters ever, also has a strong supporting cast in Dr. Watson, Inspector Lestrade, the Baker Street Irregulars, and the criminal mastermind Professor Moriarty. The stories are set in the drawing rooms and back alleys of Victorian London, mysterious old country manors, and the howling mists of Dartmoor. We eagerly follow along as Holmes cuts through the Gordian knots of mystery using relentless logic as his sword.

Robin Hood has Little John, Maid Marian, Friar Tuck, and the villainous Sheriff of Nottingham. Sherwood Forest is an ideal setting, and Robin's call to action resonates to this day: "Steal from the rich to give to the poor."

The trend continues in modern times. James Bond has Miss Moneypenny, M, Q, and a series of great villains who are always considerate enough to stock their lairs with high explosives so James can blow them to smithereens in the final scene.

As you set out to create a franchise, keep these examples in mind. Try to develop a franchise character who has interesting companions and is opposed by a powerful villain. Put your character in a series of unusual places, and give him or her lots of interesting things to do.

Inside the Character

A hero who will endure from game to game, and possibly break out into other media, must have a strong personality. He cannot be an amorphous character that the player fills out with his own personality.

To create this franchise character, start with a single vivid stroke—one defining statement that sums up who your hero is. You'll add shading later, but at the beginning you need to find the core of the character, the single trait that best defines his personality. This core will be reflected in his visual look (which we'll get to in a minute), in his attitude, his actions, and his dialogue.

Next, add to this core as a sculptor adds clay to a statue. Establish your character's attitude toward life, which governs how he responds to the problems he faces. Decide what he cares about most. Perhaps introduce an internal paradox to create complexity, an interesting flaw such as a phobia, arrogance, or lack of compassion.

A good character is like an iceberg—only ten percent is visible above the water. His background, the ninety percent that lurks below, is the hidden foundation that drives him to be who he is. These are elements the player might never see but which you must know. Where was your hero born? What are his hopes and dreams? What is the worst thing that could happen to him? The best?

This is not meant to be a checklist of items you must complete. The point is that to be a fully rounded character, your hero must have a history. He must have emotions, attitudes, and values. Otherwise, he will become a cardboard cutout, a stereotype with whom no one will want to spend time.

A larger-than-life character often has a mysterious past that you can keep hidden from the player. He needs enough specific detail to come across as a real person, and yet he should have an air of mystery about him. If you do this right, your hero can come to represent more than just himself—he can become a symbol.

As you create your hero, consider the kinds of villain he will face. It is a writer's axiom that the strength of your villain is the strength of your story. Just as Holmes needs Moriarty and Superman needs Lex Luthor, your hero needs a powerful nemesis.

This villain should *not* simply be a one-dimensional, mustache-twirling bad guy. He should be a complex character in his own right, who believes passionately that his goals are reasonable and good and who has a realistic chance of succeeding (were it not for the brilliance of the hero you have created to oppose him). For extra points, you add greater depth to your story if you can make the villain the external embodiment of an internal conflict the hero must resolve. Even if you can't, the important thing to remember is that great heroes need great villains.

When you create the villain, have him threaten the thing the hero cares about most. Sharpen this threat until the hero can't take it any more and feels compelled to fight. This compulsion to take action in pursuit of a specific goal becomes the driving force of the game.

Here are a few other thoughts to keep in mind when creating a franchise character:

- The character's name is important. It should be distinctive and easy to remember. Double entendres, puns, and names that suggest the hero's core character trait are all common, such as Superman, Duke Nukem, Luke Skywalker, and Max Payne (see Figure 7.4).

Figure 7.4 Duke Nukem's name is a perfect fit for his character. Used with permission of 3D Realms Entertainment.

- Consider giving your character a catchphrase. We have seen this work in other media (The Terminator: "I'll be back," Austin Powers: "Yeah, baby!"), and it can be effective in games too, as long as it's not overdone. Remember that a movie scriptwriter can definitely control how often a phrase is spoken, whereas a game writer never knows how often a player will play through a given sequence. Even the cleverest phrase will start to grate if it's endlessly repeated.

- Give your character a prop, a physical object that becomes identified with him. Arthur has Excalibur. Robin Hood has a longbow. Sherlock Holmes has his pipe. John Steed has his bowler and umbrella. Indy has his whip.

- Create a hero who fulfills a fantasy. Superman can see through walls and fly. Robin Hood is the best marksman in the world. James Bond is cool under pressure. Rocky Balboa can fight. People want heroes and stories that let them shuck off their own limitations for a while and imagine that they can succeed at anything.

The Visual Look

If you're out to create a franchise character, start working with a concept artist as soon as possible. A useful technique is to think not of the tiny pixel character you will eventually see on the screen but of the 8-foot-tall stand-up you would like to see promoting your game in the aisle at the computer superstore. What will your character look like when he is literally larger than life? What are the dramatic features that will draw and hold a player's attention?

Select one or two important traits, and accentuate them so that they become the visual "hook." Superman, for example has the red and blue suit and a big *S* on his chest. Batman has the dark cape and the mask with the pointy ears. Indiana Jones has his hat and whip. Duke has his muscles. Lara has her chest. To this, you add a color scheme that echoes the character's personality. This color scheme must stay consistent wherever you present the character. You rarely see Superman in black, and you never see Batman in red and blue.

Next, consider a characteristic pose or stance. One way to focus on this is to consider the character's silhouette. You can often recognize characters just from their outline and the way they stand, even though their face can't be seen and their costume is obscured. No one would ever mistake the silhouette of Spiderman for that of James Bond.

After you've settled on the static poster presentation of the character, you still have opportunities within the game to continue to give him a unique look, primarily through animation. Give your character signature moves that set him apart. Even habitual mannerisms such as tugging on an ear or adjusting a pair of glasses can help to establish personality.

Revealing Character

Creating an interesting personality and a distinctive look for your hero isn't sufficient—the player must *see* them.

In third-person games, displaying the look is easy—the hero is always on the screen right in front of the player (although it would be nice if we didn't have to watch the back of his head for ninety percent of the game). Through the hero's physique, costume, and idiosyncratic animations, it's easy for the player to form a mental image of him.

In first-person games, however, gameplay demands that the character *not* be seen. This makes it much more difficult for the player to form a mental image of the hero. Because he sees the world from inside the character's head looking out, the player rarely sees the hero on the screen.

The answer to the visual portion of this problem is to create cutscenes and in-game scripted sequences, during which the program momentarily takes control of the game and moves the camera outside the character's POV for a brief bit of action or dialogue. This allows the player to see the hero in action, and it helps fix his image in the player's mind.

It's good to remember, however, that you don't need to rely solely on in-game graphics to accomplish this mission. Posters, magazine ads, and your box art will also help establish the image of your franchise character. For these, don't use low-poly, game-rendered art. Instead, hire a great character artist to create highly detailed paintings of your character, and use those images wherever possible.

The nonvisual part of your character is harder to reveal. How do you show on the screen that someone is honest, brave, or superstitious?

One answer is through dialogue. Whether in conversation with other characters or through interior monologue, the hero's voice and the words he speaks will give the player tremendous insight into his character.

Another answer lies in how other characters react to your hero. If someone asks your hero to hold his wallet, it reinforces the impression that he is honest. If someone turns to him for help in times of danger, it shows that he is brave. If someone hides his black cat whenever your character enters the room, it shows that he thinks your hero is superstitious.

The best way to reveal character, however, is through action. For many writers, character *is* action. You must design game scenarios specifically to bring out the personality traits of your hero. If you want to show that your character abhors prejudice, put him in a situation in which someone is being discriminated against, and give him the means to stop it. If you want to show that he is suave and sophisticated, put him in a high-class environment where he must successfully navigate encounters with the social elite.

World-Based Franchises

In some games, the setting is the star. There is no hero. What draws people to games such as *Everquest* and *Starcraft* are the fascinating worlds that the designers have created and the subtle interplay of rules that make achieving goals challenging.

These worlds can arise from a single idea. What if there were life inside a black hole? What if there were a parallel universe where our myths are their realities? What if there were magic users living among us today? Starting with any one of these ideas, you could create a gameworld no one has seen before.

Next, you must develop the background of your world. How have the people and creatures evolved or adapted to its physical laws and limitations? What conflicts have been generated in their fight for survival? What societies have developed, and what are their customs? Who must cooperate with whom, and which groups are fighting for the same resources?

For the game writer, these decisions are vital because they generate the game's conflict. Whether it's a colony fighting the elements, commanders facing each other across a battlefield, or civilizations competing for growth and survival, conflict is what drives the game forward.

The world can have a deep, complex society or be a place where unusual physical elements have driven unique adaptations. From a gameplay point of view, it is these rules and restrictions that make the place interesting—if everything were possible, you would have no game. It is only when you give the player a set of limitations and some obstacles to overcome that the game comes to life.

If you are creating a science fiction or fantasy world, don't make the mistake of thinking that anything goes. In science fiction worlds, you must obey the laws of physics or provide plausible explanations of how you are bending those laws. In fantasy worlds, you must obey the laws of the magic you create. The world must be consistent. Indeed, one of the biggest problems in writing a fantasy game lies in developing spells that work consistently throughout the environment, rather than just when it's convenient for the designer.

For one of these worlds to become the basis of a franchise, it must be complex and rich. Relationships must be well thought out. History is important. The Star Wars universe isn't something George Lucas sketched on the back of an envelope. The political factions of Robert Jordan's *Wheel of Time* or the racial interactions of Terry Brooks' *Shannara* can't be explained in a paragraph.

These complexities will also help determine the look of the game. The physical (or magical) laws of the game world will drive the appearance and capabilities of the creatures. The uniqueness of the world can be expressed in its geography, its climate, or a peculiar set of natural resources. If the world is one that is topographically similar to ours, the look can be driven by the technological and social advancement of its people, or lack thereof.

Working with an External License

There are many valid reasons to work with an already existing franchise rather than try to create one of your own. Primary among these is risk—it's *hard* to create a compelling new character or world, and luck plays a big role in determining which ones break through and which languish in obscurity.

Purely financial considerations also can drive you to an external license. Nothing is so expensive in the consumer world as establishing a brand. If your product can hit the shelves with a brand already in place, you might be able to increase sales while decreasing overall expenses.

Finding a license or franchise that will work in the gaming world is not easy, though. Ideas that work well in one medium might not succeed in another. Experienced executives will consider more than just name recognition when evaluating licenses, including the following factors:

- Do the demographics of the property align with the demographics of the hardware platform for which the game is intended?
- Does the genre cross over to the game market?
- Does the license suggest gameplay?
- Is the licensor easy to work with?
- What kinds of rights come with the license?

Acquiring the License

If you haven't negotiated one of these deals before, it's a good idea to bring in someone with experience to help you cover all the bases. How many games can you make using the franchise? If several games are contemplated, are they cross-collateralized (that is, are their finances linked, or will the accounting for each be separate)? Is the deal exclusive to your company, or will there be others? For how long can you make the games? What happens to your inventory when the term is up? (Usually, there's a *sell-down* period, during which you can't manufacture more but can sell what you have.) Which hardware platforms can you produce? What about online rights?

However, to the designer, the single most important issue is which rights have actually been acquired with the license. If the licensor is a book author, do you have rights to a single book he has written or the entire series? Can you use characters from other books? Will the author write new material for your game, or something new to put in your game box? Do you have to adhere strictly to the books, or can you create new material of your own?

If you're dealing with a sports license, the rights are likely to be even more of a headache. Even if you get the rights to use the logo of a major sports league, for example, you might not get the rights to use the likenesses of the individual players within that league, the stadiums or other venues in which the events are held, or even the equipment used in the sport.

If your deal is with an individual star, you should consider how willing he is to get involved with the game. People want a personal connection with celebrities, and the better you are able to establish that connection, the better off you'll be. Will he give you some time in a motion-capture studio to record his signature moves? Will he share his strategies with the game designers? Or does he just want to sign the contract, take the money, and run?

Working with the Licensor

Acquiring the license is only the beginning of the struggle. After the deal is signed, you and the licensor must build a partnership that will continue until the game is published, and beyond. Some licensors are completely hands-off, whereas others want to be involved down to the smallest detail.

Some authors are just happy to receive the advance check. They say, in effect, "Take the world with my blessing, and I hope that something interesting comes of it." This is especially true when you are licensing a world in which an author no longer intends to be active.

In most cases, however, you'll be working with an author or corporation who has a huge vested interest in protecting the value of their license. Invariably, your deal will cover only a few years, and the licensor will want to ensure that the value of his property is enhanced (or at least isn't sullied). That way, when you exit the picture, he can turn around and license it to someone else.

In the practical world, this translates into permissions and approvals. These are very tricky and may be negotiated before you ever get to the project. If you have any say in it, though, try to get the licensor to approve or disapprove your work as early in the production cycle as possible, and try to prevent him from interfering with it thereafter. The nightmare scenario is that your company spends millions of dollars developing a game, only to have the licensor step in at the last minute with his complete approval rights and say, "No, I don't think so."

Because this is the touchiest of points, it's a battle you can very well lose. (Or it might have been lost already, before you came onto the project.) A useful compromise is to give the licensor *approval* rights at the end of concept development, or even as late as alpha, but thereafter to grant him only *consultation* rights. This means that you acknowledge the licensor's interests in protecting his property, but you're also protecting your company's investment. Granting consultation rights means that you'll show the work to the licensor and work in good faith to integrate his comments into your game. If those comments are unworkable or too expensive, however, you reserve the right not to implement them.

It's also important to structure the approvals in tiers. After the licensor has agreed to a certain element, he shouldn't have the right to change his mind. In explaining this to licensors, it's sometimes effective to compare developing a game to building a pyramid. When you've just laid the bottom course of stones, it's easy to replace one of them. When you're halfway up the pyramid, however, if someone says, "I don't like that stone on the bottom layer," you have to tear down an enormous amount of work to replace it. Licensors usually understand this idea and are reasonable about it. Of course, the higher the profile of the license, the less likely you are to get this reasonable reaction.

Another thing you want is a fast turnaround time for approvals. If you are dealing with a large corporation with many layers of bureaucracy, your team could sit idle for a month or more while waiting for various go-aheads. Try to get a turnaround of less than two weeks, and try for a clause in the contract saying that material you submit is automatically approved should they not respond within the specified time frame.

Try, too, for a single point of contact. This avoids the nightmare of dealing with conflicting instructions from different departments within the organization.

If you are the game designer, try to get a copy of the actual contract rather than asking your producer for a summary of what's in it. There may be important restrictions that will affect your design. Projects take a long time, and memories become fuzzy. There's no substitute for having the restrictions available to you in black and white at all times.

Regardless of the words in the contract, it's always a good idea to keep your licensor well fed and cared for as the project progresses. As soon as you have some work you're proud of, show it to the licensor. If you have material that you think might present a problem, bring the licensor in on it as soon as you can. It's always easier and less expensive to fix something in the design phase than after the game has gone into production.

These words hold true across the entire project, and they apply to your development partners both within and outside your organization. As soon as you have a problem, let all concerned parties know about it! Problems seldom become better after sitting around. If someone feels that you have concealed something, you've just added a whole new set of issues to deal with—and you *still* need to solve the problem you tried to conceal in the first place.

When you encounter a problem—a schedule slip, discovering that you can't include a feature you were planning on, or whatever—your first reaction might be to cover it up. Resist that impulse, and bring your partners in on it to help you solve the problem.

Creating the Material

Just because you are working in an already existing world doesn't mean that you can't be creative in your own right. Even Shakespeare based many of his plays on well-known plot stereotypes. Just as he transformed the original material with his genius, so you, too, can create something fresh and original within the franchise you have been given.

The biggest advantage of working with a franchise is that a lot of the hard work has already been done. If it is a book license for a story game, the author has already created compelling characters and an interesting environment. If it is a sports license, the rules of the sport have already been determined, and the player is likely to be familiar with most of them.

The biggest disadvantage of a franchise, however, is that because the fans know a lot before they ever open the box, they might have specific expectations that you may or may not fulfill. This is especially true when you have to adapt or make changes to a world in order to make a game out of it.

Another difficulty of working with a license is to explain the world to novices without boring the die-hard fans. A good way to handle this is to create an introduction and practice levels that help the newcomers but can be bypassed by the experts.

If you are adapting a book or set of books to the game world, there are several ways to go about it: a straight adaptation of an existing work, a summary treatment of a series, a new game based on an existing world, or a new game set in a universe that doesn't exist yet.

A Straight Adaptation of an Existing Work

The challenge here is to create a game that follows the events of a known storyline while still making the experience fresh for the player.

One game that does this well is *GoldenEye 007*, which duplicates the settings of the film and converts the problems that Bond encountered in the movie into goals for the various levels. As the player plays the missions, they are familiar yet new. The placement of the soldiers, turrets, and traps cannot be derived from watching the movie. A player who has seen the movie has no advantage over a player who hasn't. Yet, the experience is enhanced for the player who has seen the film, because he has more context for what's going on than his counterpart.

A Summary Treatment of a Series

In this type of game, your goal is to condense the action of a series of books or movies into one comprehensible plot. Here, you must focus on the main story arc and ruthlessly discard characters and places that, although they might be personal favorites, do not add to the overall story.

The *Death Gate Cycle* is a series of books that has an extended plot involving a single hero battling a single villain, but spread over a series of seven books. Glen Dahlgren's *Death Gate* effectively collapses the plot of that series into a single game (see Figure 7.5).

A New Game Based on an Existing Universe

The universes of popular fiction are generally well thought out. They are fascinating places created by imaginative writers, populated by interesting people or creatures who live in interesting physical environments or are subject to unusual circumstances. Setting a new game in such an existing universe is a treat for the game designer. Consider the following worlds:

Figure 7.5 *Death Gate* condenses the plot of seven books into a single game. Used with permission of Infogrames, Inc.

- *Star Wars*
- *Star Trek*
- *Wheel of Time*
- *Dune*
- *Shannara*

Each of these immediately conjures up images in the minds of those who are familiar with them. Each feels like a real place, full of concrete detail that bolsters the fiction. Also, each has played host to top-selling games, where the action and story are something wholly created by the designer.

A New Game in a Universe That Doesn't Exist Yet

On rare occasions, you might get the opportunity to work with an established writer to create a brand-new world. *John Saul's Blackstone Chronicles* came about in just this way (see Figure 7.6).

Figure 7.6 The plot of *John Saul's Blackstone Chronicles* was developed at the same time as the book series. Used with permission of The Learning Company.

It began with a game proposal from best-selling author John Saul. His idea was to create a story set in a beleaguered town in New Hampshire that is dominated by an abandoned insane asylum on the hill overlooking the town. In his original four-page concept document, he laid out a scenario in which people who live in the town are going mad. However, each person's problems are somehow connected to an ancestor who had been incarcerated in the old asylum on the hill.

At that time, John had no clue about what the sicknesses were or what the connections were. Nevertheless, it was an interesting idea. John was a rare author who was also a gamer, and Legend Entertainment agreed to collaborate on the game.

John decided to write a serial novel based on the idea and "split the turf" with Legend. The book series is set in the present day and deals with the inhabitants of the houses and the horrors they suffer. Legend's game is set several years after the events of the books, when the asylum has been converted into a museum. Most of the characters in the game are the spirits of the ancestors of John's characters, inmates of the asylum who reveal to the player why their descendants have gone mad. The books and the game stand on their own, but each contributes to the other in a rare case of true synergy between linear and interactive media.

Extending franchises in this fashion through different media will soon become commonplace, with the same world represented in books, movies, plays, TV, comic books, board games, episodic Web sites, and so on. In each case, the basic material must be adapted to the peculiar demands of the particular medium, which in the case of games, means making sure to give players a way to participate in the action.

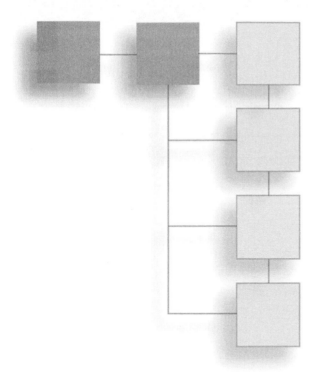

PART II

TEAMS

CHAPTER 8

THE DEVELOPMENT TEAM

I n Hollywood, each job has a name, and specific duties come with it. Everyone involved in making a movie knows the exact scope of his responsibilities, and no one is in doubt about what he's supposed to do.

The game industry is different.

Every company divides the subtasks of making a game in its own peculiar way. The work itself doesn't vary, but what each job is called and how it's done can change greatly from one company to the next. No matter where you work, though, the tasks stay the same. Each game must be managed, designed, and programmed, it needs art, sound, and music, and it must be tested. This chapter examines those tasks and how the people who perform them contribute to game design.

There are two caveats to keep in mind.

The first is that, although the tasks may seem to separate neatly into one-job-per-person classifications, in reality everything is much sloppier. On some teams, a job can be divided among several individuals. It's not uncommon for a game to have two coproducers, or for a pair of artists to share the duties of the art lead. On other teams, a single person can take on more than one project role. The tech lead, for example, can double as the producer, or the art lead can also be the game designer.

The important thing is to take a practical approach. Don't get hung up on formalities. Instead, look at the talent you have available for each project, and divide the tasks among the individuals in whatever way makes the most sense.

The second caveat is to remember a central theme of this book: *Everyone who touches a game participates in its design*. Although design is singled out as a separate role in this chapter, it is a task that is ultimately shared by all.

Vision

Every project has one person who is the keeper of the vision. This isn't a job title you'll find on any organizational chart. It's a function that usually falls to the game designer, but the slot is sometimes filled by the producer, tech lead, or art director. In very rare cases, the vision can be shared by two individuals working closely together, but that's a tricky proposition and should be approached with caution.

The *vision guy* is the person who, throughout the chaos of development, knows how all the pieces will eventually come together and how the player will experience the game. Although not an expert in any of the disciplines, he must have a working understanding of all of them. He need not be a programmer, but he must understand how technical issues affect and constrain the project. He need not be an artist, but he must understand the complex subdivision of tasks that go into creating images on the screen. He need not be a game designer, but he must have a feel for what's fun. He need not be a psychologist, but he'd better be a good "people person," someone who can smooth ruffled feathers and get people with different interests and agendas to pull together toward a common goal.

The vision guy is the game's internal "compass." He's the gatekeeper, through whom all new ideas must pass. He's the final arbiter of what stays in and what doesn't.

If you are the vision guy for your project, you must have a firm understanding of the core elements that will make your game successful. This is the irreducible feature set that must be in the game before you can ship. During development, thousands of ideas will appear and beg to be included in the game. At the same time, schedule pressure and production problems will put enormous pressure on these and other features to be dropped. It is up to you to decide whether a new idea contributes to, is neutral to, or detracts from the core of the game.

It may be easier to resist new features when you realize that the best games aren't loaded down with bells and whistles, but instead focus like a laser on what they do best. As Eric Bethke puts it in *Game Development and Production*, "If you want your game to sell, study how narrow the feature sets of *Mario64*, *Half-Life*, and *Diablo* really are, and how well and deep these few features are executed."

As you evaluate these ideas and features, remember that "the game's the thing." The parentage of an idea is unimportant. If it contributes to the game, you should accept it, whether it comes from a tester, your nephew, or the head of the company. Be open to different ways of doing things. If someone argues passionately to eliminate or change a feature that doesn't affect the core of the game, be flexible. Odds are that the game will be better for your respecting the opinions and honoring the vision of those who are building it. But if a crucial feature comes under attack, be prepared to dig in your heels and defend against all comers.

Production

Two separate jobs commonly bear the title of *producer*. The first is the *external producer*, who works for a publisher and oversees the efforts of an external development house. The second is the *internal producer* at a development house, who manages the team itself and represents it to the outside world (including the publisher's management, as well as the marketing, PR, and sales departments). Some companies call this person the *project manager*, *project lead*, or *director*.

Whether internal or external, the producer is the game's champion to the rest of the company. He explains the game's highlights and selling points to PR, marketing, and sales. He understands how the game aligns with the company's goals and can explain to "the suits" why it's a good idea to keep the product in development. He sticks up for the team. He demonstrates the game at project review meetings and explains where the team is, whether they're ahead of or behind schedule, the problems that have cropped up, and what's being done about them.

The producer is also management's champion back to the development team. He explains to them how the game fits into the company's plans. He keeps the team up-to-date on the PR and marketing efforts being made on behalf of the game. He gets the team the resources they need to perform well, whether it's software, hardware, or other equipment. He keeps the team informed about the company's overall health.

Another crucial part of the producer's job is risk management. Games never run smoothly. There are always problems, and they come from both inside and outside the project. A competitor can come out with a new feature; the team's office space can be too cramped; the lead programmer can be carrying on a romance with a tester. Literally thousands of things can go wrong, and inevitably, some of them do. It is not the job of the producer to ensure that no problems arise, because that is impossible. Instead, his job is to deal intelligently with the risks that threaten his game and to manage them so that they cause minimum damage.

Therefore, on a regular basis, the producer should make a list of the worst things that could happen to the project, try to figure out how to prevent those things from happening, and make contingency plans for dealing with them in case they do (see Appendix A). The risk list includes possibilities such as

- What if the devkits for the next-gen system don't arrive on schedule?
- What if the engine developer is late with a key feature?
- What if a key hire cannot be found in time?
- What if the AI programming takes longer than scheduled?

The list should *not* include possibilities such as

- What if a meteor hits the building?
- What if the publisher goes out of business?
- What if the power goes out during the last week of development?

These last three are not risks that can be managed. The producer can take no steps to minimize the probability that they will occur, nor should he create a contingency plan for dealing with them. In short, he shouldn't worry about them.

The External Producer

As an external producer, you are the person in a publisher's organization who is responsible for getting the developer to deliver the game on time, on budget, and with great features. You (and your assistant or associate producers) track milestones, approve payments, handle hardware requests, and ensure that the developer is well fed and cared for in general.

Typically you'll be responsible for more than one project at a time. If so, try to have the projects in different stages of development so that they don't enter crunch mode at the same time. The last few weeks of a game's development require an enormous amount of time and attention. Managing two games simultaneously would not only be a nightmare for you personally but would also cause each game to suffer because you couldn't do justice to either of them.

Although you might not be the vision guy for the game itself, you are definitely responsible for making sure that the game meets the goals your company has set out for it. If the day comes when there has to be a trade-off of money against time or features, you have to be in the thick of the discussion. You need to know which features are essential to the game's success and which are "nice-to-haves." You need to know whether it's more important to your company to have the game be great or on time.

At the beginning of the project, you will probably be involved with the evaluation and selection of the external developer. Try to learn as much as you can about the staff. How long have they been together? What games have they produced? How well have their games sold? Is this new game similar to anything they've done before? Do they have prior experience on the hardware platform? Do they have engine code or tools they can apply to your project? What is their track record for being on time and on budget? How many teams do they have? How many other projects will be running simultaneously with yours?

In general, you don't want to be a development team's sole source of income. You might think that you'll have more clout with them, but the reverse is true. If they get into financial trouble three-quarters of the way through your game, often your only realistic option is to bail them out with more advances. The alternative is to watch them shut down and to see all the money you've spent on the project go to waste. However, if they have multiple products, that's a sign that they do good work and have diverse sources of income. Just make sure they don't "borrow" resources from your project to help out another one that has fallen behind.

After you've selected the developer and started to work with the staff, you need to get to know them even better. There's no substitute for getting on an airplane and visiting them regularly. Get to know the team members. Find out whether they're passionate about this product or are just using it as filler when they're not working on their "real" project at other times. Do they believe in the schedule, or do they look at it as something their management agreed to, but doesn't have a prayer of working out? Do they establish internal mini-milestones that will help them meet the larger contract milestones? Is the company living milestone to milestone, dependent on each payment to stay alive, or does it have a financial buffer?

You also need to ensure that your own organization is treating them well. This means acknowledging receipt of milestones, responding promptly to questions, taking quick action on requests, and above all, making sure that they are paid. You want to keep them in a comfort zone, where they are focused on the work and not distracted by extraneous issues.

In short, your job is to be the oil that reduces friction between the publisher and the developer. Without you, the machine seizes up and bad things happen. You must be honest, and you must build up a storehouse of goodwill between the organizations so that they have reserves to draw on when disagreements arise. Consider setting up an early series of small commitments that each side can easily fulfill for the other. If difficulties arise later, those early successes will help each company accept that the other is dealing in good faith.

You also have enormous contributions to make to game design. You give guidance to the team about your publisher's principles and whether certain elements are acceptable. You steer them towards creating a project that fulfills your company's goals in funding the project—whether those goals are to create a blockbuster hit or just to build something that fills out the fiscal quarter. However, your biggest contribution comes as you constantly juggle features, money, and schedule. It is this balancing act that determines what the game will finally look like.

As you work with the developer, be very aware of the effect your comments have on them. If you casually mention that it would be nice to add a particular feature, they might interpret that as a mandate that it *must* be included.

On the other hand, if your style is habitually low-key and something comes up that you feel strongly about, be sure that you're direct and firm about it. Otherwise, your comment may be interpreted only as a friendly suggestion that the developer is free to ignore.

You must also *listen* well to the developer. Often, casual comments carry deeper significance, and what one person says might not be what the other person hears. Because of this, following up conversations with written summaries is always a good idea, and it is never a mistake to be explicit. Having a detailed paper trail is a boon to both the developer and the producer, so each can say with confidence, "This is what we agreed to, and here is when it happened."

When changes are made (and trade-offs are constant), e-mail is fine for small items, but larger issues should be noted as amendments to the contract. In particular, any redefinition of what constitutes a milestone, a change in the delivery schedule, or an alteration to the payment schedule is important enough to update the contract. Turnover in our business is constant, and projects run for a long time. No one wants to be in a position where obligations are murky because of verbal agreements made between people who are no longer around.

Finally, as the person to whom the developer must turn for money, you have an enormous amount of power. Don't abuse it, and don't let it go to your head. Your job is to be a facilitator, and your goal is simply to help them create the best game they can.

The Internal Producer

As an internal producer, you manage the development team directly and report on their status to the funding organization, whether it's the company for which you work or an external publisher.

One of your first tasks at the beginning of the project is to work with the art lead and tech lead to determine the right staffing for the game. If your company doesn't have enough resources, you must either create a hiring plan to bring in new people, or survey outside resources to see whether they can be used effectively on a contract basis. (This is more easily done with art than with programming, but make sure that your department heads support whatever plan you develop.)

If you're short on resources, an alternative to staffing up or contracting out is to go back to the designer and alter the game concept to fit the people you have. This might not require a complete overhaul; it might just mean cutting back the scope. However, it is folly to go into a project without sufficient resources to pull it off. In particular, don't plan on everyone working 60-hour weeks. All your planning should be based on 40-hour weeks, with sufficient time allocated for overhead (those pesky meetings!), for demos (miniprojects unto themselves), and for holidays and vacations. Crunch time always comes, but responsible producers ensure that their product never turns into a "death march."

During development, your contribution to game design comes mainly in the day-to-day running of the project. A game design isn't a static document, and a project team is rarely stable. The military has a saying that no battle plan survives the firing of the first bullet, and that the genius of the field commander is how he responds to the chaos around him. The same is true of the producer. After development begins, your goal is to guide the team through the fog of war, keeping everyone together and moving toward the same goal so that when the smoke clears, you've achieved your objective.

With each new idea that is generated, you help determine its specific effect on the game's design, but also the more global effect on the project: Who does this affect? How many schedules will have to be altered? Does it bring the game closer to the publisher's goals? The answers to these questions will determine whether the idea is accepted or rejected.

This process is easier if you're the vision guy. If you're not, you must work closely with him to ensure that the suggested changes are compatible with his vision. Either way, you will constantly be forging compromises among the working groups. No matter what the game design looked like on paper, the game that winds up in the hands of the consumer will be the result of those compromises.

Throughout development, you manage the schedule and make adjustments to stay on track. See Chapter 11, "Managing Development," for more on handling this process.

At the end of the cycle, you work with the test lead and lead programmer to manage down the bug list. You evaluate the seriousness of each bug, determine the level of effort required to fix it, and assess the risk of the "fix" itself creating other bugs. You will sometimes find yourself playing referee between testing and programming. As pressure mounts, tempers can flare. It is you who must stay cool and arbitrate disputes, keeping in mind at all times that "the game's the thing."

Finally, you are the one who must decide whether the game is ready to ship. No game is ever bug-free. You need input from all the departments to help you decide whether any of the remaining problems should be considered showstoppers. In the end, though, you're the one who declares the release candidate good enough.

The Assistant and Associate Producers

If you are an assistant or associate producer (an AP), your duties will vary, depending on the strengths and weaknesses of the producer and the development team. You might find yourself in a pure management role, in a hands-on position on some portion of the project, or handling a variety of general support tasks. In general, you will find yourself hip deep in the minutiae of the development process, and you must be prepared to be more detail oriented than you ever thought possible.

Some common tasks for APs include the following:

- **Managing assets**. As projects and teams grow larger, the amount of data generated during development explodes. The typical high-end program has hundreds of thousands or even more than a million files to manage. The asset manager (or *data wrangler*) has the formidable task of keeping track of every one of these files. Which is the latest version? Where is it on the server? Can someone overwrite it with a version from his or her local machine or otherwise accidentally delete it? What if someone makes an update to it, and it doesn't get recorded? If the file is no longer useful, is it included in the final build "just in case"? Most companies have rudimentary tools for addressing these problems, but ensuring the safety and usability of data will nevertheless be an almost full-time job for someone on the team.

- **Supervising the daily build and the backup**. When a project is well under way, generally it falls to an AP to ensure that a current playable version is always on the network. He's also usually responsible for ensuring that a solid daily, weekly, and monthly backup plan is in place and implemented.

- **Maintaining the design Web site**. Teams are rapidly moving away from the "telephone book design document" and toward designs that live solely on an internal Web site. This is a great advance, because everyone can see what everyone else is working on. It doesn't appear magically, however, and someone (usually the AP) must collect, organize, and post the information, while archiving off old information as well.

- **Generating screenshots and supporting PR**. When a project is announced, an immediate—almost insatiable—demand for screenshots springs up. Generating interesting shots is an art unto itself, and it takes time to produce pictures that show off the game at its best. In addition, the team always needs a knowledgeable "demo guy" who is available to sit down with visiting journalists and take them through the latest version of the game.

- **Reviewing milestones.** When a milestone is submitted, the material must meet specific requirements before it can be accepted. It usually falls to the AP to do the actual examination of the game or the materials to ensure that all the requirements have been fulfilled.
- **Paperwork.** The AP often generates most of the management paperwork associated with the project, including submissions to console manufacturers to satisfy their approvals process.
- **"Other duties as assigned."** Hundreds of small, ad hoc tasks crop up in the course of development. Generally, it falls to the AP to deal with them. These tasks can be almost anything: making an emergency run to the airport FedEx dropoff, ordering carry-out food for a late-night work session, or packing up machines to take to E3.

Your opportunity to influence game design comes from your being so involved with the minutiae of all aspects of the project. Your contribution will probably not take the form of grand, sweeping decisions. Rather, you will contribute to the thousands of smaller, informal decisions that are made every day. As programmers, artists, and level designers build each small piece of the game, you will be one of the early sounding boards against which they test their ideas. If your opinion is respected, this constant, informal exchange will be the forum in which the game takes its shape.

Design

The formal design team is made up of the game designer, the level designers, and the writer. Although everyone on the project will influence the design before it's done, this is the group that establishes the game's original blueprint.

The game designer (who often doubles as the writer) creates the design document and updates it throughout the course of development. He designs the basic gameplay mechanics, and he's also likely to be the vision guy who evaluates new ideas to determine whether they help or hurt the overall game.

The designer works with a storyboard artist to design the introduction, extro (end movie), and cutscenes. If he's doubling as the writer, he creates all the game dialogue and also probably does the first draft of the manual. If he doesn't do the writing himself, he hires and directs a professional writer to do the job instead.

The designer usually directs the level design (LD) team, if there is one. He creates the flow of the game and then directs the LDs in creating the smaller units that fit into that flow.

The designer also collaborates with the PR department as it builds the Web site, the marketing department as it creates advertisements and the game box, and the sales group as it generates sell sheets and other sales materials. He designs demos for all three groups so that they can promote the game, and he makes himself available for press interviews as well.

The Game Designer

If you're a producer putting together a development team, get a designer who loves what he's working on. The first section of this book addresses a multitude of design traps and pitfalls, but you will never avoid them unless you find a designer with a passion for his job.

If you're the game designer, you're the one who must figure out what the player will actually *do*. You're the source of the *fun*. You're responsible for entertaining the player from moment to moment.

Usually (but not always) you are the vision guy, the one who can play the movie in his head. It's rare that a game design can be written down and then simply implemented. In the course of development, thousands of decisions are made by all the team members. You're the filter through which those decisions must pass. You compare each idea against the vision of the game and decide whether the two match.

During this process, you must stay flexible. Your vision cannot be some unassailable monolith that must be implemented no matter what. Game design always involves compromise. Each hardware platform has limitations, no budget is bottomless, and no schedule stretches to infinity. You will constantly be asked whether something can be done this way rather than that. You must always be practical and ready to adapt the vision so that it can be implemented by the rest of the team.

Don't make snap decisions. If someone asks you to change a given feature, take the time to think through why you put it there in the first place. A game is a complex web of interdependencies. Some are casual, but some are crucial. You don't want to approve a request only to realize, months later, that a large portion of the game no longer makes sense because that one element was changed.

If the change is benign, however, try to say yes. Often, a small design change results in huge programming savings and reduction of risk. Other changes may save man-months of modeling and animation time. Listen carefully to the requests of other team members.

Although some ideas might be suggestions born of different sensibilities, others are prompted by sound technical reasons for doing things a slightly different way.

If your game has a scripting language, you should learn it. In the days of the one-man team, the designer was the programmer and vice versa. As specialization has split up the roles, it's now common for a designer to have no programming skills whatsoever. This removes the opportunity for you to get in there and noodle around, which is an essential part of the game design process. This is why scripting languages have arisen. They enable nontechnical designers to input their ideas directly into the game and see how they work out. A robust scripting language also enables artists and level designers to do the same.

Ironically, one of the hardest parts of being a game designer is playing other games. Like any professional, you have to stay current with the state of your art. This might seem like an easy, even enviable task, but it's not. Thousands of games are published each year. Of these, only a few hundred are good enough to merit close examination. Playing today's typical computer game takes anywhere from 20 to 100 hours, so you can see the problem right away. You simply don't have enough time to play all these games while designing one of your own.

There's no perfect solution to this problem, but there are some useful ways to attack it.

The first is to weed out unimportant games by reading reviews. Magazine reviewers spend thousands of hours playing games so that you don't have to. If you subscribe to one or two of the top monthlies, this will help you stay on top of which games are relevant to your own work (see Figure 8.1).

The second is to play demos. Every month, game magazines enclose CDs that are chock-full of game demos. Downloadable demos are also common on the Web. These demos frequently distill a game's essence into a much tighter experience than you get in the full product. That's just what you're looking for—a concentrated knowledge dump that doesn't take forever. If you have developed a new feature and want to know whether anyone else has thought of it, a quick scan of previews and demos can reveal the answer.

Figure 8.1 Reading reviews will help you decide which games you need to play. Used with permission of *PC Gamer Magazine*.

A third way to keep up is simply to look around the office. If you work for a game company, it's likely that your coworkers play games every day. Some play during lunch, some during work breaks, and almost everyone plays at the end of the day. This is a golden opportunity for you, because someone else has already gone to the time and trouble of installing the game and climbing the learning curve. Go look over his shoulder. Ask him about what he's playing and why. What does he like about the game? What does he dislike? Is it worth your time to play it?

The result of all this filtering is that eventually you'll come up with a short list of games that you *do* need to play. The final step is not to feel guilty about doing so. It's part of your job as a game designer to know what's fun, and if you stop playing games altogether, your fun-detecting muscles will atrophy. Fire up the games you need to know about, and develop a thick hide about the jabs and barbs that will come your way for playing games during office hours.

Another task of being a game designer is handling the outside attention that comes your way. For good or ill, the designer is more likely than anyone else to be identified with the product. This is enormously misleading, because the game results from the work of the entire team. You can help redress this imbalance during interviews by constantly giving credit for specific features to the person or group who worked on them. Don't just mention the people in passing—take the time to spell out their names, and make it clear to the reviewer that you think it's important he get them right. This simple tactic makes a difference. When a reviewer is on deadline and he has the correct spelling of someone's name, he'll use it. If he has to make another phone call, he'll drop the mention altogether.

Another tactic is to encourage your team to maintain plan files on the Web. This allows other personalities than your own to emerge, and anyone who is curious about the game will quickly see that the game is the work of more than just a single designer.

The Level Designer

If you're a professional level designer, you're in one of the newest fields in our business, so not many guidelines have been established to help you along. A few years ago, your position didn't exist. Then it was the province of the talented amateur. Now it's a key position on many teams.

Chapter 5, "Level Design," contains a lot of information on designing levels. This section is more about what your day-to-day life is like.

First of all, you are likely to work in a bullpen rather than in an individual office. This encourages a more rapid exchange of ideas and helps keep everyone on the same page. It also results in a much less formal atmosphere, which has advantages and disadvantages. Try to enjoy and take advantage of the former and develop techniques to overcome the latter. The biggest problems you will probably face in this regard are the distractions that come with working so near other people. A good pair of headphones is a smart investment.

Another oddity of your position is that you will somehow acquire the responsibility to demo the game at various points during its development. This is not a casual task, and you should practice and prepare for it. On any given day, you could find yourself suddenly showing off the game to the chairman of the company, prospective investors, magazine reviewers, or a crowd at a trade show (in which may lurk some influential person of whom you're not even aware).

Even if you are basically shy and would like nothing better than to be locked in a room twenty hours a day alone with your computer, you have to develop speaking skills that at least enable you to summarize the key features of a game and show off what's cool. This doesn't mean that you have to take a public speaking course, but you should have a basic patter for the game and have a general plan for five-minute, twenty-minute, and in-depth demos.

Speaking of those 20-hour days, try to pace yourself. Level designers today are in somewhat the same spot as lone-wolf programmers in the early days of our industry. Strings of all-nighters, gallons of caffeine, and uninterrupted coding binges were badges of honor and became the stuff of legend. Although it's true that there's nothing like being "in the zone" and riding those bursts of creativity while they are flowing, you also must give your body time to refresh itself so you can avoid burnout. Despite the myths, study after study has shown that programmers are more productive when they put in regular eight-hour days than when they go into Superman mode and load up on the overtime. The same is true for level designers.

If you remain unconvinced, think of it this way: Having a life outside the office can help your work. The more interests you have, the more influences you can bring to your levels. Whether it's art or architecture, literature or sports, movies or music, the more well-rounded you are, the better your work will be.

The Writer

If you are a freelancer or a staff writer who is not the designer, you probably won't be on the project full-time. Instead, you will be brought in from time to time to work on various parts of the game. This work can include character dialogue, sports commentary, cutscene narratives, journals, an instruction manual, a hint system, or any other portion of the game where words are needed.

When you first come on board, it's important to sit down with the designer and get a comprehensive overview of the game. Read all the design documents, and talk with various team members to ensure that you understand what the team is trying to accomplish. Later, when you reenter the project after having been away for some time, repeat this process to see what has changed, because something always does. Omitting this step is dangerous, because the people involved with the game every day might not be conscious of how the concepts and goals have drifted. If you launch in without getting back in sync, suddenly you'll be writing stuff they don't like, and they might assume that the problem is one of incompetence instead of miscommunication.

If you come from linear media, take the time to understand the special requirements of interactivity:

- A player can go through the same section of a game multiple times. This means that he can encounter your words not just once but many times. Don't annoy him. Something that is fresh when first encountered can be annoying the tenth time through. Write with repetition in mind, and work with the programmers to introduce variations.

- Different players take different paths through the game, so not everyone will encounter information in the same order. Where possible, write modular segments that make sense in whichever order they are read.

- Keep dialogue short. Write in snippets rather than in screeds. If players wanted to listen to speeches, they'd go to a movie. They want to be *doing* something.

- Keep exposition short. Distribute background information across an environment rather than in one big text dump. If players wanted to read a book, they'd go to the library. Again, they want to be *doing* something.

- Every line of dialogue has to do double duty. It must establish character and provide information.

- If dialogue is to be spoken, accents and colloquialisms are okay. However, if the words appear in text on the screen, don't write in dialect.

- If the project is a story game and the designer hasn't done a good structural job (see Chapter 4, "Storytelling"), sit down with him and see whether you can fix the story without ruining the gameplay.

- Tone is important. Within the game, match tone to character or environment. When writing materials associated with the game (for example, manuals), use an informal, nonthreatening tone.

- Use vocabulary appropriate to the target market.

- In an action/adventure game, as much as 90% of your writing will be in response to player inputs that are not effective. You must still entertain the player with these responses. Otherwise, the player ends up encountering something like this: *Nope. Nope. Nope. Nope. Nope. Nope. Nope. Nope. Nope. BINGO!* Instead, for each of those *Nopes*, you should write something interesting, and perhaps something that will allow the player to get to *BINGO* earlier. This is part of entertaining the player from moment to moment. Instead of forcing the player to trek across a desert of uninteresting responses until he stumbles on an oasis of interest, make the entire game a garden of feedback delights.

Programming

This is not a technical book, and there are more aspects to game programming than could possibly fit in a single volume. (Shameless plug: That's why you should look for the other books in Course Technology's *Game Programming* series.)

Instead, this section looks at the role the tech lead and other programmers play on the development team, and how coders influence game design.

The Tech Lead

As the technical lead, you should be on the project from the very start, alongside the producer, designer, and art lead. One of your earliest tasks is to inform and inspire this group as to what is technically achievable, holding down unrealistic expectations on the one hand while identifying exciting areas of innovation on the other. Try to pick no more than two areas of major technical risk per project. You can shoot for the moon and attempt more, but you will probably end up missing the moon (and your schedule, budget, and market window as well).

Evaluate your delivery platform, and create an architecture that will maximize its strengths and compensate for its weaknesses. If you have a multiplatform game, plan special features for each of the various hardware versions to take advantage of the peculiarities of that system's internal structure.

During preproduction, you create a technical plan that enumerates all the knowable tasks on the project and estimates the manpower and schedule required to complete them. When you deliver these estimates, it is important to identify them as a bell curve of probabilities, which should help manage expectations about their accuracy. (For more on estimating and scheduling, see Chapter 11.)

Preproduction is also the time when you build your team, either hiring them from outside or selecting them from internally available resources. Assembling a great team is one of the most consistently underestimated tasks in game development. It's *hard* to get good people, and it costs both time and money. Much of your time will be spent prequalifying applicants with tests and phone interviews. More time and money will be spent flying them in for face-to-face interviews. Even after you hire them, still more time will be lost as they give notice at their old companies and move themselves and their families to your location. When you're putting together your technical plan, make sure that you're extremely conservative in any estimates that rely on resources you don't already have in-house.

As you build the team, be sure to equip them properly. Your developers should always have the most powerful machines you can lay your hands on. Never buy anything less than the fastest CPU, the most RAM, and the biggest hard drive you can afford. Halfway through the project, they'll already seem woefully inadequate, and you can be sure that everyone will need at least one equipment upgrade during the course of the project. Also, make sure that you have or can build an infrastructure that will support your development: a high-speed network, huge amounts of storage, and the capability to back up everything.

Every copy of every piece of software you use should be legal. It would be the height of hypocrisy to ask consumers to pay for the software you develop while using pirated software to make your product.

Try to get offices with closable doors for your programmers. Studies show that a one-minute distraction can cost fifteen minutes of productivity. This is because it takes that long for a programmer get back into a "flow state" after he has been disturbed. Interruptions also introduce bugs: While a programmer is writing one piece of code, he makes mental notes of other bits that need to be modified. If he is interrupted, those mental notes are erased, the modifications are not made, and the unchanged code emerges later as a bug.

If separate offices are impractical, try to design the programmers' area so that they experience a minimum number of distractions.

Still another task during preproduction is evaluating the technology necessary for the game and recommending whether it should be built internally or acquired from outside the company. This applies not only to the game engine, but also to the suite of tools your team will use during production. Be wary of the not-invented-here syndrome, and be amenable to purchasing ready-made tools that will speed development. Base these decisions on the key competencies your team members already have. For applications within their specialties, let them do the development. This will put your team's unique stamp on the final product. For areas in which you have no expertise, bring in an off-the-shelf tool and modify it to suit your needs if necessary.

As the lead, it's your job to set coding standards, encourage "best practices," establish version control procedures, and implement a regular data backup plan in case of catastrophic failures.

During production, you manage the programmers' tasks and schedules. However, there's a difference between assigning tasks and scheduling them. Although you decide who does what, the actual schedule should be a roll-up of the coders' own estimates of how long it will take to complete these tasks. As the project continues, track each developer's estimates against actual results so that you can help them learn how to get better at estimating. Then, as you close in on the final third of the project, these estimates will become a useful tool to help you load-balance and to decide which features you can deliver and which you must cut.

Because the technical world is such foreign territory to nonprogrammers, you must become adept at explaining technical issues. Demystify them as much as possible. Don't take the "high priest" approach and claim that you're the only one qualified to make technical decisions. Instead, share your knowledge with the team so that you can all make intelligent choices together.

In particular, you should be able to explain technical trade-offs to the producer. A project can be optimized for schedule, cost, quality (lack of bugs), or user satisfaction (great gameplay), but not all four at once. There are choices that must be made every day of the project's life, and you're the one who must explain those choices well enough for everyone to understand them.

Perhaps the most frustrating part of being a lead programmer is that, having built your career on acquiring technical proficiency and becoming an expert coder, now the majority of your time will be spent in administration. This is an issue for all department heads. The larger the team, the more time you'll spend in administration, planning, scheduling, load balancing, code reviews, and other management activities, and the less time you'll spend writing your own code. If you're leading a small team, you can retain coding responsibilities, but if the team grows to more than about five developers, it's probably a mistake to assign any major systems of the game to yourself.

One solution to this problem is to reserve for yourself some of the nice-to-have Research & Development-type features. These are elements that aren't vital to the game but keep you engaged. If you can pull them off, they'll give you an enormous amount of personal satisfaction.

In the end, your ability to estimate, schedule, inform, inspire, compromise, and lead will determine the final design—the game that actually appears on the screen.

Programmers

Programming is where game design is accomplished. If you are a programmer, you're the one who must make real what a designer can only imagine.

Game designers frequently don't understand the technical implications of what they've written. When you come across problematic areas, you must work with the designer and explain to him what you'll have to do to implement the design. In particular, you should point out any places where minor changes can result in major savings, whether these improvements are internal to the code (for example, reduced complexity and increased efficiency) or directly affect what the player sees (better game speed and loading times, or fewer potential bugs).

On any given project, you'll find yourself working on one of the following subcomponents:

- The rendering engine
- AI
- Physics
- Tools
- The database
- Network and multiplayer code
- Graphics effects
- Sound effects
- Scripting languages
- Weapons
- Game logic
- The interface and I/O
- Asset integration

On a large team, separate individuals can work on each of these modules. However, the smaller your team is, the more likely you'll be asked to take on several of them. As you build a career in game programming, it's a good idea to maintain general skills *and* to pick a specialty.

The most common difficulty you'll have is that no one understands your job as well as you do, yet many people make decisions that affect it. In post mortem after post mortem, we read about unrealistic schedules, conflicting directives from management, and problems that were obvious to some people within the team but not others.

When the team doesn't communicate well among themselves and with management, when fantasy schedules go unchallenged, when problems are known but not discussed, morale sinks lower and lower. It doesn't have to be this way, and the way you can change it is to *talk!*

This will be especially hard for you if people don't want to hear what you have to say, which will generally be the case if you are the bearer of bad news. Don't be discouraged. Speak up anyway, and keep doing so until the message gets across.

This runs counter to some of our most basic social training. Many people are raised on the motto, "If you can't say something nice, don't say anything at all," which puts you in an awkward spot when you see a problem that should be pointed out. The result is that half the programmers retreat into their shells and say nothing at all, and the other half speak up repeatedly, only to gain a reputation for negativity.

One way to address this is to teach those around you what they need to know about your work. To many of them, you're a black box whose workings are unknown and mysterious. Many programmers like it that way because it gives them a sense of power and (they joke) job security.

However, the more people know about your work, the better off everyone is. When answering questions, take the time to explain trade-offs and gray areas. Generally speaking, most things are possible, given enough resources and time. What you want to avoid is answering yes or no to a request without letting people know what the hidden costs are.

If you're a manager, you must *listen* to these trade-offs, caveats, and warnings. You might never understand all the intricacies of what your developers do, but you must come to terms with the decisions they have to make. When you ask a question, give a programmer time to consider and get back to you with a reasoned answer, and then listen to the *conditions* he puts on it. One of the most pervasive problems across our industry is that people constantly hear the positive part of an answer and not the negative part. If a developer says that feature B can be included only if condition A is met, you can't walk away thinking that feature B is a done deal. Instead, you must keep your eye on condition A and be ready to deal with the consequences should it not fall into place.

It is this lack of listening that causes so many programmers' morale to tank. "Suits never learn" is the mantra one hears. "They live in a dream world."

If you are that programmer, help those around you to listen well. Keep them posted on the dependencies that affect your work. As critical dates approach, remind them of what's at stake, and discuss potential alternatives if the dependency isn't met.

Here are some other tips for game programmers:

- Read post mortems on other projects to see what went wrong. Think about how their problems apply to your own, and be vocal about bringing up these issues. Don't bury your head in the sand and say, "That could never happen to us." Or worse, "That's exactly what's happening to us, but I guess there's nothing we can do about it."

- Keep up with the state of the art in your specialty. Stay in a constant state of self-education. If you don't keep up in the game business, you will be left behind.

- Avoid the temptation to make the superhuman effort. It is truly necessary from time to time but not nearly as often as people seem to think. Remember, there is always a cost to making that push, either in reduced efficiency while in the middle of it or in required recovery time afterwards.

- Be open to peer review.

- Be honest about your work, both with yourself and with others.

- Take the time to plan.

- Reach out to other members of the team. Many positions now require technical proficiency from people who haven't had your training (such as artists and writers). Be kind to them and help them along.

- Beware of feature creep. The reason you're in this business in the first place is to do work that's *cool*, but don't get carried away. Work within the priorities set by the team.

- Remember, there's no such thing as a two-hour task. Everything you do must be integrated, tested, and debugged. Even the most innocent features can have unforeseen consequences that ripple through the rest of the project.

An important way you contribute to game design is by working with the designer on all the things he forgot in his original specification. The very structure of the code you write brings these things to your attention: For every *if* there is an *else*. The designer will always plan for the *if*s of a successful path through the game. He'll write something like, "If the player mixes the potion at midnight in the chapel, the ghost will appear." What he might not consider thoroughly are the *else*s. What you must ask him are questions such as "Does the player have to start at midnight, or be finished by midnight? Does he actually have to be in the chapel when he makes the potion, or can he come in with it already mixed? If he makes the potion sometime after midnight, will the ghost appear anyway? Does the order in which he adds ingredients to the potion matter?"

The earlier you identify these issues, the more robust the design will be. Addressing them with the designer before you start to write code is much more efficient than having to paper over them when the testers start tagging them as bugs. This is another argument in favor of scripting languages, which help train designers to consider not only the *if*s but also the *else*s of their designs.

Artwork

Great artwork has become one of the benchmarks by which games are judged. It's been said that you can't judge a book by its cover, yet millions of people do it every day. The same is true of games. People make their purchasing decisions based on what they see— after all, they can't evaluate gameplay while they're standing in the store. However, a quick visual demo and some sock-knocking screenshots on the box can propel the game from the shelf to the shopping cart.

Artists now affect every aspect of game design—from the user interface to the representation of the gameworld on the screen, to the special effects. Creating that art has become increasingly complex through the years, as have the content creation tools. Many companies who previously farmed out their art needs have now come to recognize great art as a competitive advantage and are building art departments of their own.

The Art Lead

As the art lead, you're responsible for the "look" of the game. Frequently, you will be the production designer or concept artist, but if not, you'll direct the people in those positions to create artwork that represents your vision.

You live at the crossroads of design, programming, and management. You need to analyze what the designer wants, work with the tech lead to establish the production path, and then determine the scope of the art tasks, how many people you'll need, what kinds of people they are, and how long it will take to bring it all together.

When you work with the designer, one of your goals should be to develop a consistent style that extends throughout all elements of the game, from the splash screen to the characters and environments, and even to the menu interfaces. After you've established the look, you should codify it in a style guide (frequently called *the bible*), the visual resource to which all the artists refer.

As you work with the tech lead, try to create a production path that gets assets from the artists' generating tools into the game as quickly as possible (see Figures 8.2 and 8.3). Ideally, an artist should be able to test his work in the game within minutes after he has created it, without the intercession of the programming team. See whether you can get the tech lead to agree to a scripting language or some other tool that will allow your artists to cut and paste their work directly into the current build and receive immediate feedback on how it looks.

Figure 8.2 3DSMax is one of the leading art packages on the market. Used with permission of Discreet.

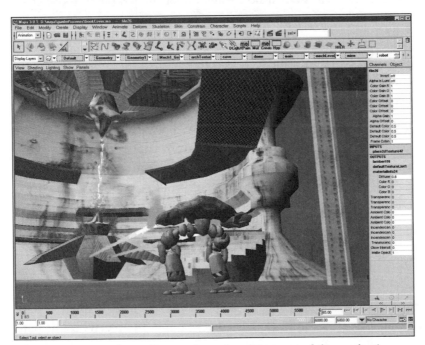

Figure 8.3 Maya from Alias can be an important part of the production path. ©2001 Alias Wavefront

This will avoid long turnaround times when artists create backgrounds or animations and then hand them off to someone else to put into the game, hoping that they'll look all right. Under that system, the next time they see their work might be months later, and if it isn't up to snuff, they'll have to exhume the original materials and have another go. Allowing the artists themselves to integrate the assets is much faster and more efficient for the team, and it results in superior work.

As a manager, you have to hire and coordinate the team, schedule the tasks, evaluate competing technologies, select tools, and decide which artwork should be developed internally and which should be shopped out to specialists.

Like any department head, you might find that your administrative duties leave little time for exercising the art skills that got you the job in the first place. Nevertheless, you'll always find areas where you can fill in, and when you mentor younger team members, you'll find that your work comes through in the final product more than you imagined.

Artists

No area of game development is evolving more rapidly than artwork. If you're an artist, you must constantly keep up with your craft and be ready to adapt or die. You cannot afford to be a technophobe. Not only do you need high-end computers and sophisticated software to create your images, but you also must have a working understanding of the limitations of your target hardware platform so that you can tailor your work to its strengths and avoid its weaknesses.

Your contribution to game design is there on the screen for all to see. Ninety percent of the feedback in a game is visual, and if something can't be drawn, most likely it will be dropped.

Your work on a game probably falls into one of the following specialties: concept, character modeling, animation, background modeling, or textures.

Concept

Concept artists work with the designer to create the look of the game. You make multiple sketches of characters and settings, trying to bring the designer's vision to life (see Figures 8.4 and 8.5). The final versions of these sketches become part of the game's bible, guiding other members of the art team so that the game has a cohesive feel instead of a jumble of conflicting styles.

You can also work with the designer to storyboard cutscenes so that when actual production begins, everyone is on the same page, and no time is wasted creating unnecessary material.

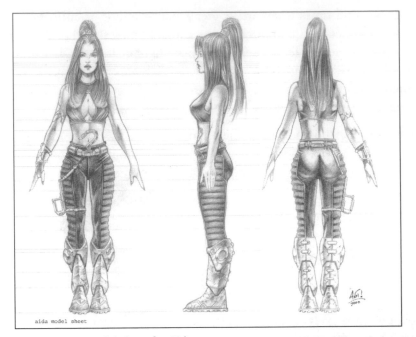

Figure 8.4 Model sheet for Aida, a character in *Unreal 2.* Used with permission of Epic Games, Inc.

Figure 8.5 Aida in the flesh. Used with permission of Epic Games, Inc.

Character Modeling

Character artists design and create people, creatures, and objects using sophisticated 3D imaging packages such as 3D Studio MAX and Maya. Working from the concept art, you make a 3D wire mesh (see Figure 8.6) and then apply textures to that mesh (although this "skinning" is sometimes a separate subspecialty). You can start entirely from scratch, or you can create a real-world 3D model in clay, scan it in, and work from there.

Animation

Animators give life to the creatures by making them move. You receive a list of all the activities the creature will perform in the game, and you have to create a series of movements for each. It's especially difficult to design smooth transitions from one activity into another, although the high-end graphics packages now include "blending" animation features that make this task easier.

A good knowledge of anatomy is vital to this job—especially understanding how muscles and bones interact. With the advent of skeletal animation, characters now move more naturally than ever before, and animators no longer have to hand-render every detail of every movement.

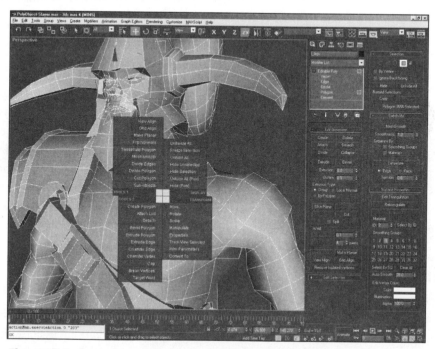

Figure 8.6 A monster mesh. Image courtesy of Andrew Gilmour; used with permission of Discreet.

Animation is more than having a good eye for natural movement, however. A lot of character development can take place in animation. When a character walks from one side of the room to the other, does he swagger? Stagger? Strut? Stroll? Dart? Slink? To a good animator, movement reveals character.

One way to achieve very natural movement is through motion capture. This is especially useful in capturing the signature moves of athletes, which are so complex that it might not be possible to duplicate them completely by hand.

In a motion capture studio, the director places sensors on key spots on the actor's body. The actor goes through the desired movement, and his skeletal information is captured, imported into a graphics package, and then manipulated from there by the animator. This is an expensive process, but it results in the most accurate depiction of the human body in motion yet to hit the computer screen. This technique is widely used for sports games and is growing in popularity for fighting and action games.

Background Modeling

Background modelers build the worlds the player moves through. You usually start with basic geometric shapes (called *primitives*) and then combine and deform them to create the rooms and objects that make up the game's environment. After the mesh is completed, you add flat shading, then textures, and finally lights so that the world comes to life.

Textures

Texture artists create the "skins" that fit over the modeler's wire meshes. For background textures, generally you work in 2D, painting surfaces that are then stretched over the geometry so that a wall looks like brick, stone, or metal. Sometimes you create these textures from scratch, building them up layer by layer. However, sometimes it's more effective to photograph an existing surface, scan it in, and then touch it up. For character textures, 3D painting packages are gaining in popularity. These allow you to paint in a WYSIWYG environment, instead of constantly switching between 2D and 3D, tweaking as you go.

Testing

Testing isn't just a quick check for bugs before the game goes out the door. Testers begin to play a vital role in the development team as soon as the first code is written. At the very end, it's the testers as much as anyone who determine when the game will actually ship.

The Test Lead

The role of the test lead is one of the least understood and most underappreciated jobs in development.

Your main responsibility is to ensure that the game not only works, but is also fun to play.

Early in the project, your team will be small, and its goal will be to provide a tight feedback loop to the developers. On a day-to-day basis, the programmers will implement a bit of code, take a quick look to see whether it works, and then ask you to bang on it to discover any hidden ramifications. It is during these cycles that you can have your biggest influence on game design because you can give feedback on all these features while they are still fluid.

As the project approaches *alpha* (the stage where the game is more or less playable from start to finish), you bring on the rest of your team and write your test plan. (See Appendix A for a sample test plan.) At this stage, your job goes far beyond merely reporting game crashes. You must be in sync with the designer and programmers, because you must know from moment to moment whether the game is behaving as they intended.

You can use the design document (assuming that it's current) as a starting point for your test plan, but a written document can never capture all the thousands of small choices made in the course of development. To supplement the design document, you must have as complete an understanding as possible of what the vision guy has in his head.

When other testers are on the project, you'll find that you have to mediate between them and the implementers. Remember that neither team can read the other's minds, and because the conversation will always concern problems with the game, everyone is likely to be sensitive.

When a tester sees something unusual on the screen, he often won't know whether it is supposed to be there. Is it a bug or a feature? He must err on the side of the bug and write up a report. This can exasperate the programmer, who is told that a problem exists with his code only to realize that the game is running exactly as intended.

Another common problem is that a programmer will report that he has fixed a bug only to receive another report a few days later about the same problem. At that point, it is difficult for him to tell whether the report originated before or after the fix. It is part of your job to stay current with bugs and fixes, to weed out multiple reports of the same problem, and to let coders know when their attempt to fix a bug didn't succeed.

Throughout, the best test leads are dispassionate and can defuse problem situations before temperatures start to rise. You should edit out inflammatory language from bug reports, and send vague or incomplete reports back to your testers until they contain enough details to be useful to the programmers. Coming the other way, you must defend your testers against the rants of programmers whose pride has been injured. Remember that it's the job of the testers to express their opinions, but it's the job of the producer or designer to decide what (if anything) to do about what your testers report.

A good bug-reporting system will help you immensely. If a bug report has an automatic version stamp, a programmer can quickly check whether it was reported before or after a given fix. A system that lets you sort bugs by developer is also helpful because it is far less psychologically devastating for a programmer to be handed a few pages that contain his own bugs than a large sheaf that contains the bugs for the entire team. (This also saves time because he doesn't have to weed through the larger document to ferret out which bugs are his.)

When the project hits beta, your team will be larger, and you will establish daily tasks, telling each tester specifically what to look for on that day. Your feedback to the development team at this point is vital, because everyone is trying to make the final decisions concerning feature trade-offs. Don't be afraid to stand up for features that you think are essential to the game, but also be honest about the ones that won't be missed if they're cut.

Cycle fresh testers onto the project if you can. These new eyes can spot a different set of bugs, or they can give a fresh perspective on problems that have been around so long that everyone else is used to them.

If you work for an external developer, you will now start coordinating with the publisher's team of internal testers. If this is a console game, you will also send builds to the console company and coordinate with their testers. If the game is multiplayer, you can also set up an external beta test involving hundreds of volunteers.

As you come down to the end, most of your time will be spent managing the bug list that results from all these activities.

At most companies, bugs are ranked according to your estimate of their importance. The A bugs are crash bugs or other bugs that are serious enough to prevent the game from being shipped. B bugs are quality problems that really should be fixed, but if the game absolutely has to go out the door for other reasons, they won't be considered showstoppers. (Enough B bugs, however, generally equal an A bug.) C bugs are usually nice-to-haves or obscure problems that arise only on rare occasions. The C list is also the grave-yard where tester recommendations that the rest of the team don't like go to die.

At the end of development, when pressure is mounting to get the game out the door, you'll probably have a better idea whether the project is ready to ship than either the designer or the tech lead. You'll meet daily with the department heads and the producer to discuss outstanding problems, and to decide which will be addressed and which will be left by the wayside. However, at many companies, the game won't be allowed to go gold unless you give it your personal approval.

Testers

It's no accident that many game designers get their start in the testing department. Here is where you see firsthand all the mistakes that can be made and how they can be fixed. There is probably no better training a designer could get than to spend a year in test.

When you are testing a game, you are on the lookout for several things at the same time:

- **Is it fun?** Early in a game's life, this is a question to ask again and again. Are the basic gameplay mechanisms enjoyable? Even though the game isn't balanced or tuned yet, can you see where the fun is going to come from? Your feedback to the designers and programmers during this pre-alpha development will have an enormous influence on game design.

- **Is it easy to use?** Are the controls awkward? Is the interface well laid out? Is the manual accurate? Has the designer "taken care" of the player? Go back to the principles of game design laid out in Chapter 2 and see how well the game measures up.

- **Does it make sense?** If the player follows along, will he get the experience the designer wants him to get?

- **Is it fun? (Part 2)** As you come up to alpha, this question emerges again. Earlier, you were examining the basic ideas to see whether they are enjoyable. Now, you are testing the game itself to see whether the fun has survived the implementation. Is it too hard? Too easy? Are there places where the player will be lost or won't understand what he's supposed to do?

- **Does it work?** This is the task most people think of when they think of game testing. If you play through the game, doing what the player is supposed to do, can you get to the end? If you do things the player *isn't* supposed to do, does it work anyway? Does it perform according to spec? Can you make it crash?

As you approach this job, do things differently each time you play the game. Your goal is to think of yourself as 5,000 gamers, each of whom plays the game in a slightly different way. Try not to fall into patterns, performing tasks in the same order or always taking the same path through an environment. Mix things up. Try things that no sane person would ever attempt. Playing through a game again and again becomes tedious, so you'll be doing yourself a favor (and doing your job better) if you introduce variety into your daily gameplay.

Writing a good bug report is an art. Your goal is to be specific. The more you can tell the programmer about the bug, the faster he'll be able to find and fix it. You should not only report exactly what went wrong but also supply as much information as possible about the circumstances that led up to it. You should also record any error messages that appear.

Repeatability is the Holy Grail of the bug report. If you can reliably reproduce a bug on demand, the programmer will be 90% of the way toward fixing it.

Throughout, don't be shy about providing your opinions, but don't be sensitive about the reactions they provoke. It's *your* job to tell people what you think—it's *their* job to decide what to do about it. However, be professional at all times, and be aware of where you are in the game's development cycle. Broad-impact suggestions that are appropriate in pre-alpha will *not* be welcomed two days before the game is due to ship.

The Cabal Approach

On very large games, a new approach is emerging whereby a small, focused group takes responsibility for various tasks instead of a single individual. Popularized by Valve's work on *Half-Life*, the cabal method brings the expertise of various departments to bear on areas of the game that cross traditional boundary lines (see Figure 8.7).

Take, for example, the user interface. This cannot be designed just by an artist to look good, nor can it just be designed by a game designer to be functional, nor can it come into existence without programming. However, a small group with representatives from all three disciplines can come together and make decisions, with the result that the end product is much stronger than if any one person had attempted it.

This process has two advantages: It gets input from people with appropriate expertise, and it gets buy-in from their departments as well. When the work feels as though it belongs to everyone, people are less likely to snipe at it.

This approach isn't without its dangers. Committees aren't generally known for their efficiency or design prowess. However, by including only those people who have a passion for getting it right and who acknowledge the importance of everyone's input, you have a shot at creating a whole that is greater than the sum of its parts.

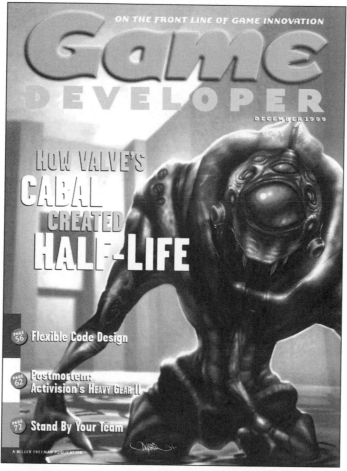

Figure 8.7 Valve's cabal approach to design has attracted a lot of attention. Used with permission of Game Developer magazine.

Here are a few tips for managing the cabal process:

- Try it on a small portion of the game first. This will let you see whether your team operates well in this kind of environment. It will also let you adapt the process to your group's personalities.
- If you decide to go ahead with this approach, keep the meetings focused. Publish agendas in advance, and stick to them.
- Make sure that all the disciplines relevant to a task are included in its cabal, including testing and (where appropriate) management.
- Take good notes.

- Try a reverse-hourglass approach. At the first few meetings of the cabal, accept any and all input (just as you do in brainstorming sessions) in order to get as many ideas as possible on the table. At later meetings, winnow those ideas down to the important few.

- Remember that the goal of the cabal is to deliver not suggestions but decisions. What comes out of the group should not be the fodder for more discussions. It should be ready for implementation.

CHAPTER 9

EXTERNAL RESOURCES

F ew companies have enough in-house talent to create everything that goes into a game. Voice acting, music, sound effects, and video are all important game elements that are routinely handled by outside professionals. Writing the manual and translating the game into foreign languages (*localization*) are also tasks that can be done by external teams.

This chapter deals with managing those external resources, giving them creative direction, and ensuring that your company obtains the rights to their work.

Administrative Issues

Generally, the administrative side of the relationship with an outside contractor is handled by your team's producer or associate producer. The creative direction comes from one of the department heads (the designer, art director, or tech lead). Tight coordination between these two members of your team is necessary, to find the best external people for the job and to get the best work from them after they've been hired.

Here are some tips for evaluating potential contractors:

- Look over samples. How closely do they match the style you need for your game? If the task is large, will the contractor do a piece "on spec" to demonstrate that he can work in the style you want? Consider starting with a mini-contract to test both the quality of his work and your ability to get along well with him.

- Be wary, however, of people who show you material they have developed for another company but which hasn't yet been published. Not only do you want to avoid the hassle of being exposed to another company's trade secrets, but it is also a sign they might show off *your* work before it becomes public.

- Get references. Find out who the contractor has worked for in the past, and call those people to learn whether they are happy with his work. Was he on time? Was he easy to work with? Were there contract disputes? How much management did he require?

- Find out whether the contractor is financially stable. Is his business model sound? Does he have enough clients to support him, but not so many that he's overwhelmed? Try to ascertain whether he has enough resources to pay attention to you, and that he won't disappear halfway through your project.

- Compare bids. Is the contractor quoting you a reasonable cost? Is he trying to charge you too much? Is he trying to lowball the bid to get the job, and planning to either deliver substandard work or raise the price later? The only way to find out is to get quotes from more than one supplier, and to talk with them about what you will get for the money.

After you've found a contractor, the key to managing him well is a good contract, backed by good communication. Not only does the contract cover the transfer of rights (see the legal section later in this chapter), but it also explicitly defines what the contractor will do for you, when he'll do it, and how he'll be paid for it.

When negotiating this contract, remember that your goal is to build a mutually beneficial relationship rather than to gouge anyone. It is in your best interest to build long-term relationships with quality suppliers so that you don't have to go through the interview-and-hire cycle on *every* project you do. This means paying professional rates so that the contractor feels well compensated for his work. If you are a good client and treat your contractor with respect, the prospect of getting future jobs from you will give him a huge incentive to do his best work on *this* one.

The agreement should establish milestones, define deliverables, and set out a method of resolving disputes should any arise. Remember that no development project ever goes exactly according to plan. If your requirements change, the contract should change as well. Small issues can be negotiated and tracked through e-mails. Larger issues should be reflected in amendments to the contract. These include redefining deliverables, changing dates, renegotiating payments, and so on.

The contract should have a clear statement of work that describes in detail each of the tasks the contractor will perform. It should also define the specific criteria that will be used to govern "acceptance."

Finally, try to schedule the contractor's work so that this never becomes the critical path to getting your game out the door. It is very difficult to see your ship date approaching while you are missing vital pieces of the game that are overdue from a resource you can't control.

Voice

The first rule of including voice in your game is to get professional talent. Don't use your friends or people in the office. Gamers have all grown up listening to professional actors on television and radio, and they expect the same quality of voice work in the games they play. Amateurish line readings instantly destroy the believability of your characters.

The quickest path to finding this professional talent is to hire a voice director. This director—with your help—should do the casting and direct the recording sessions. Ideally, you want someone who has worked with games before, who has a working relationship with a few of the local sound studios, and who is tapped into the local talent pool of voice actors.

To conduct auditions, the director will need an overview of the game and a list of the speaking parts, along with several lines of sample dialogue for each. Try to make these lines meaningful instead of throwaways. A paragraph-long speech that reveals character is ideal. The voice director should come back to you with tapes of at least three actors for each part.

As you select the actors, give weight not only to whether they sound right for the part, but also to their professional credentials. Try to hire members of AFTRA (The American Federation of Television and Radio Artists). They know their way around a recording studio. They come ready to work and don't waste time. They know how to take direction. They also avoid problems such as mouth noise and extraneous sounds, which you might miss during the session but can result in lines you can't use.

Also consider the future availability of the actors. If the game design changes, you might have to come back months after the recording session to rework some of the dialogue. If an actor has moved out of the area or is unreachable, you will have to rerecord his entire role.

Some designers and writers leave the recording sessions to the voice director. Most, however, prefer to be present. Because the actors have little context for the lines they are given, it is very helpful to have someone present who knows the big picture, someone who can explain the nuances of a line and, for example, say whether it should be read with sarcasm, irony, or despair.

Generally, the recording session will consist of you, the voice director, and the sound engineer in the booth, while the actor sits alone on the other side of the glass (see Figure 9.1). Any professional studio setup will allow the three of you in the booth to converse without the actor's hearing you. Actors are used to this, but it is a good idea not to leave them hanging for long. Actors tend to be insecure, so if you're just going over a technical problem, let them know that you're not talking about how lousy they are.

When you arrive at the studio, you should have at least four copies of the prepared script—one for the actor (also known as the "talent"), one for the voice director, one for the engineer, and one for you.

When you are preparing a script for recording, work with the programmer who will be integrating the voice into the game to assign a separate filename to each line of dialogue.

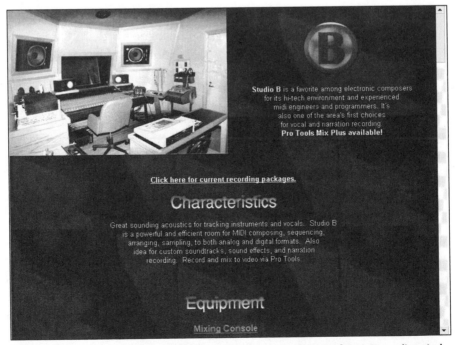

Figure 9.1 A typical voice recording studio. Image courtesy of Cue Recording, Ltd.

Decide on an order that sorts well, and then record the lines in that order. During the session, decide which take of each line you prefer, and have the engineer mark it on his log. When you send it to postprocessing, you will get back a set of files that you can drop right into the game. Then, when it is time to localize, you can swap out the files with a minimum amount of work or breakage. (Make sure, however, that someone listens to all of them to ensure that there are no mistakes. With thousands of files floating around, it is easy to transpose two of them or use the same one twice.)

When you meet each actor, take a few minutes at the beginning of the session to prepare him for the part he's playing. Give him a quick overview of the game and his character's place in it. Tell him as much as you can about the character's background, age, ethnicity, and so on. The more he understands his character, the better the audio picture he will paint for you.

If the actor has many lines and you're asking him to imitate an accent or create some other special vocal effect, start by making a few recordings where he gets it exactly as you want it. Later during the session, keep referring back to those benchmarks to keep him from drifting, and to make sure that the voice is consistent throughout.

Don't let the actor run the session. You're in charge, and studio time is money. After you have the take you want, move on (even if the actor wants another shot at it).

You and your director should decide ahead of time who will be giving instructions to the actor from the booth. Generally, because the director is the person with the relationship with the actor and because he has much more experience than you at getting different reads, it is best to leave the direction to him. What you are there for is to provide context and to listen until you hear in the headphones exactly what you were hoping for. You should be listening for effect, while the director and the engineer (who are both likely to be more attuned to sound than you) should be listening for extraneous sounds, such as voice pops, the rustle of clothing, page turns, and so on.

Having said that, however, listen with an open mind. Actors and voice directors bring a lot to the table. You will frequently be surprised at the different readings an actor will come up with, and you should be prepared to say, "That's not what I had in mind, but it is better, and it will work, so let's go with it."

Plan your studio time well. Union actors have a four-hour minimum, so you don't want to call them in for just a few lines. If you find yourself in that situation, prepare a wish list of alternative lines for an actor to record that you might find some use for. On the other hand, if you have an actor with hundreds of lines and you're worried about getting them all in one session, limit the number of takes for each line, and save any nice-to-haves for the end in case you run out of time.

Another way you can save money on actor and studio time is to have the talent double up on voices. Many actors can do multiple accents. If you can get one actor to do two or three voices in a single four-hour session, you will save yourself several hundred dollars.

When each actor is finished, you will have to sign some AFTRA paperwork that includes a timesheet and a description of the work. Make it a habit to get the actor to sign *your* paperwork at the same time. Some actors lead a nomadic life, and trying to track them down later to get releases may be next to impossible.

Respect the rules of the studio. Many of them don't allow food or drink inside the control room. Many are also nonsmoking. Also, spare a thought for your engineer. He's probably a hardworking guy, and he might think that games are cool. See whether you can get him a finished copy of the game when it is done. Not only is this good manners, but it can also benefit you in the long run. The more he knows about games, the better he can help you if your paths cross again.

Music

Have you ever watched a movie without its musical score? Even the action scenes can seem flat and disjointed. Music is a way of telling the viewer how he should be reacting to the visual images on the screen.

The same is true in games. Music can heighten the thrill of action, tell the player when danger lurks around the corner, or set a lighter tone for comedic moments.

Generally, a game composer's work is done at a keyboard, using special synthesizers that put an entire orchestra at his fingertips. He can go for a hi-tech soundtrack for a science fiction game or a more naturalistic score for a fantasy. He can create individual themes for different characters. Just as in the movies, he creates aural cues when action scenes are imminent, as well as tense music for moments of suspense, romantic music, and basic "moving around" music for exploration.

As with many external contractors, there are two sides to working with a composer/musician—the creative side and the administrative side.

The creative side begins with technical direction. The composer needs to know the game's target hardware platform and what kind of music it will support. PCs and all next-generation consoles allow you to use full RedBook audio (regular CD audio), but handhelds and Internet-delivered games probably still require MIDI music, which doesn't sound as good but uses very small files.

Some games use looping music to provide a continuous soundtrack. One key to pulling this off is to make the loops long enough that the player doesn't notice that the music is repeating. Another trick is to create different themes with identical starts and finishes, and stitch them together to provide variation. Your goal is to avoid driving the gamer crazy. A player may spend more than a hundred hours with your game. If all you give him are short, repetitive musical phrases, he'll eventually turn it off.

A more difficult technical and creative task is to write adaptive music, which changes on-the-fly to match the player's actions. This requires writing music in very small segments and embedding flags in the code to signal the rapidly changing gamestates. For example, when the player is approaching an unseen monster, the music expresses a rising tension. When the player first sees and attacks the monster, the music shifts to high action. When the player defeats the monster, the music automatically goes into a victory theme. Creating this kind of music requires very close coordination between the game designer, programmer, and composer.

When you first start talking with a composer, give him as much of the game materials as you can. Make sure that he knows what the game is about. If he's composing for a cutscene, send him the animation so that he can score it like a movie, with the rise and fall of the music paralleling the scene's action. For general game music, communicate the shifting moods to him so that he can interpret them for the player. Just as visual references are useful to artists, musical references will help the composer, so give him examples of what you're looking for. If you have storyboards, send them along as well.

Early on, the composer will send you some rough pieces to see whether you're on the same wavelength. As you discuss them, it will quickly become clear that you and he have different vocabularies, and you might find it difficult to describe what you want. Don't worry too much about this—experienced composers are used to it. Just do the best you can, say what's on your mind, and make sure that before you turn him loose on the overall game, he has delivered some small portion with which you're both happy.

On the administrative side, the composer will be concerned about payment and rights. These can be tricky to negotiate because although there are established norms in other areas of his business (TV and movies), our industry is groping towards a different set of standards.

In Hollywood, composers are generally paid by the song (or score), and they retain a host of rights that provide an income stream from their music for years after they do the work.

In our business, we want to pay by the finished minute, we want to acquire all the rights, and we want to avoid entangling the project in royalty accounting and down-the-road payments. We also want to avoid restrictions that can prevent us from repackaging the game and managing it through its normal lifecycle, from front line, to marked down, to budget, to compilation, with manufacturer bundles and other OEM deals thrown in along the way.

A common compromise is for you to make a one-time payment to acquire all the rights you need for the life of the game, while the musician retains the rights for "noninteractive" use so that he can sell the music again in other arenas.

A game company executive might want you to use existing songs or music from popular groups to increase the marquee value of your game. Not only is it questionable whether this is effective, but it can also be prohibitively expensive and create nightmare back-end problems with royalties and rights.

However, if there is a band whose music you like, you should investigate a synchronization license, which allows you to hire your own performers to make a new version of the famous band's music but at a fraction of the cost.

You should also consider the independent music scene. The artists and bands who pursue alternative distribution channels, such as MP3.com, might be more open to licensing deals than bands who have signed up with the big labels (see Figure 9.2). Working with these "indies" helps you avoid the nightmare of dealing with the legal departments of the major labels.

This whole area of licensing music is a minefield that is best negotiated with a lawyer by your side. Fortunately, a new kind of agreement is evolving—the *new media license.*

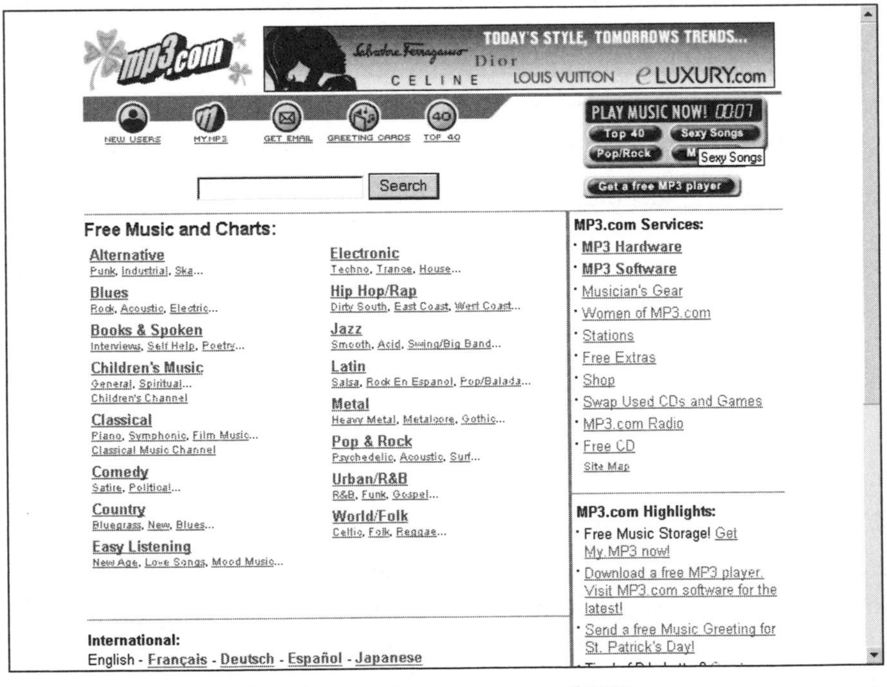

Figure 9.2 MP3.com's main page. Image courtesy of MP3.com.

One day this should make it much easier to license music for Internet and computer game use.

Sound Effects

Not long ago, the only sounds a computer could make were the beeps and boops that came from its tiny speaker. Then came a period of several years when some gamers had sound cards and some didn't. During that time, a PC game designer couldn't make sound an integral part of the game, because he was never sure whether the player would be able to hear it. Now, every computer and console has sophisticated sound capability, and sound design has taken a central role in overall game design. Sounds can be used to immerse the player in the game world, provide feedback for his actions, and give clues that help him along his way.

In the real world, background noises are the soundtrack of our lives. No matter where you go, there is a constant hum of background noise. (One encounters pure silence only in artificial situations, such as anechoic chambers.) In games, background sound effects can be used to establish ambiance and atmosphere. They become part of the stream of concrete details that help make the fictional world seem real.

These ambient sounds give life to a scene. The player doesn't focus on them, but he would notice if they weren't there, just as you would notice if all the background noise around you were to suddenly stop. Some games, of course, won't have ambient sounds—board games, card games, and trivia games are rarely set against an audio background, although they can have event-based sound effects and perhaps some background music as well.

Event-based sounds serve as feedback to the actions the player takes. These can be realistic sounds, such as a golf club swishing through the air and hitting a ball, or artificial sounds, such as the ka-*ching* of an arcade-style game that lets the player know when he's racking up points.

Sounds can also provide gameplay hints to the player. If a gamer playing an action game comes to a door and hears a monster roaring on the other side, he knows to expect danger when he opens that door. If a player in a driving game is out in front and suddenly hears the sound of another car behind him, it is a pretty solid clue that he'll soon be challenged for the lead.

With all these layers of sound available—voice and music as well—the sound designer must be sure to focus the player's attention on the right sound at the right time. Background noises shouldn't drown out dialogue, and the musical soundtrack shouldn't obscure vital sound clues.

In movies, two people add sound effects: the sound FX editor and the foley artist. The sound FX editor creates the big noises—jets taking off, bomb explosions, subway trains screaming through a station. The foley artist creates the small noises—footsteps walking down a gravel path, the click of a key in a lock, the tinkle of ice cubes as they fall into a glass. "Foley" is named after Jack Foley, a Hollywood pioneer who helped studios make the transition from the silent era to talkies. Using a bunch of old props and a lot of ingenuity, he re-created noises in a sound studio that weren't easily captured on a movie set, and then synced them to the action on the screen. Many techniques he invented are still being used in studios around the world today.

In games, both the big and small sound effects are selected or created by the sound designer. His job is easier than Jack Foley's was, because now entire sound libraries are available for purchase. Every sound designer has one, but he generally uses it only as a starting point. It is not uncommon for a sound guy to go out into the world, armed with a microphone and digital recorder, to capture the natural sounds that occur around us. Then he returns to his studio to twist them electronically into the screaming dive of a wounded jet fighter or the pulsing heartbeat of an alien monster.

The bane of the sound designer's life, however, is the storage and playback practices that degrade the quality of the sounds he has so lovingly assembled. The problem with really good sound is that it requires really big data files. If space were not a consideration, all sounds would be sampled to maximize the dynamic range and be stored with no loss of data so that they could be exactly reproduced within the game. The reality, however, is that to conserve space and enable fast streaming, the sounds are generally sampled at a lower rate and compressed using a lossy algorithm that reduces the overall quality.

To deal with this, the sound designer and audio programmer must collaborate to find the compromise that best suits the majority of sounds in the game. For example, human voices (especially female ones) require a higher sampling rate than sound effects such as doors slamming and machines running. The lower the sampling rate for voices, the more hissing is introduced and the harder it becomes to understand what is being said. If your game has a lot of dialogue, try to get a high sampling and bit rate. If it has little dialogue and is heavy with environmental effects, a lower sampling and bit rate can be perfectly adequate.

When you work with an external sound designer, you will probably be paying him based on the number of sounds you ask him to provide. You should require him to work out a naming convention with your tech lead so that the files are easy to identify and track. Tell him as much as possible about the game, so that he can bring his own experience and creativity to the task.

Keep audio in mind from the very start of the development process. The most common complaint of the audio team is that they are brought in too late. If your budget won't allow you to have a sound designer on board from the beginning, use the same strategy you use for the external writer: Call him in early to consult on the fundamentals, and then bring him back sporadically as needed. Also, don't forget that you can buy extensive sound effects libraries on license-free CDs for only a few hundred dollars. This might not replace the need for a sound designer, but it will keep you moving forward until you're ready to bring him in.

Video

Shooting FMV (Full Motion Video) had a wave of popularity that has now receded. Most action games deliver their cutscenes with in-engine graphics. These graphics are less complicated to produce, leave control in the hands of the game creators, cost less, don't interrupt the suspension of disbelief with a jarring visual style, and involve fewer legal hassles.

If you plan to include FMV anyway, your very first step should be to hire a producer. The complicated business of hiring actors, finding or designing costumes, booking a studio, renting equipment, finding props, hiring a crew, doing the shoot, and overseeing post-production is no job for an amateur. You especially need someone to handle the regulations of unions such as the Screen Actors Guild (SAG), the Directors Guild (DGA), and the Teamsters (see Figure 9.3).

There are plenty of independent directors and producers in almost every city, and they can handle all these details for you. They hire the studio and equipment, find the talent and crew, and handle the morass of paperwork. Tell them up front the budget you have to work with, and then make sure that you understand the trade-offs they'll have to make in order to stay within that budget.

Most likely, you will be filming in a studio against a solid-color background and compositing the actors over a prerendered background later. This process is called *chromakeying*. The first part of the word comes from the single-color background. This color (*chroma*) is selected to provide the most contrast with the subject. When you are filming people, this color is usually green or blue because there are no green or blue tints in human flesh. During postproduction, the chroma is deleted, and the actor is composited (or *keyed*) against a prerendered background.

In the studio, time is money, so make sure that you are as prepared as possible. You can easily spend as much on a two-day video shoot as you spend on the rest of the game put together. Be ready to answer questions and make decisions, but mostly, just put yourself in the hands of your producer and try to stay out of the way.

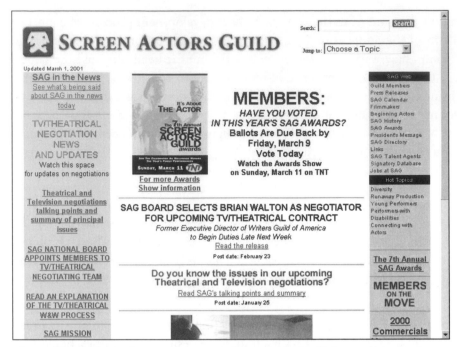

Figure 9.3 Hiring union members more than pays for itself, due to the professionalism they bring to the final product. Image courtesy of the Screen Actors Guild.

Motion Capture

The most realistic human animation is generated through motion capture. This is done in a special studio, where a technician places optical sensors on key spots on an actor's body and then makes a digital recording of his movements (see Figure 9.4). The recording is then imported into a graphics package and manipulated by an animator.

When this technology was young, you were likely to end up with an overwhelming amount of data that would take you longer to sort through than it would have taken to do the animation by hand. Now, however, most houses provide "cleaned up" data that is much easier to use.

You must do as much preparation for a motion capture session as you would for a full video shoot. Make a list of the number of actors you will need, and write out the specific moves you will need to capture from each actor. Rent a rehearsal studio prior to the shoot so that the actors can get the moves right without an entire crew standing by while you coach them. Make sure that they wear the motion capture gear during the rehearsal so they'll get used to it.

Figure 9.4 A motion capture session. (Note the optical sensors on the black costume.) Image courtesy of Vicon Motion Systems

Hire actors who are approximately the same height, weight, and body type as the characters in the game. Practically speaking, this can be tricky because game characters often have exaggerated body dimensions, which leads to difficulties matching the real-world data to the skeletons of the game characters. Fortunately, software is now being developed to help compensate for these problems.

Each studio has its own fee structure, but you can expect to pay a flat day-rate for the facility, labor, and equipment, plus a price per second for hand-tweaking the data afterward. You must arrange separately with the actors for their fees and releases. If your budget is tight, some companies also sell stock data that you can purchase and apply to models you have already created.

For a comprehensive look at motion capture, including tips and tricks for setting up the character and running the session, check out *Understanding Motion Capture for Computer Animation and Video Games* by Alberto Menache.

Language Localization

These days, more than half of a game's revenue is likely to come from outside the United States. Game publishing has become a worldwide business, and making multiple-language versions of games is standard practice. Furthermore, many publishers insist on releasing localized versions on the same day worldwide, which means that the localization process must be included in the original production schedule rather than tacked on afterward.

The worst way to localize is to wait until development is almost over, go back through the code, strip out all the language-related elements, and ship them off to a translator. Pasting in these translations line by line when they come back is time-consuming and prone to error. Dealing with other problems as they pop up can also be devastating to the schedule.

Instead, the best way to localize is to plan for it from the start. While the game is still in design, be on the lookout for translation problems that could arise. If the solution to a puzzle depends on a pun, for example, is there a version of the pun that will work in other languages? If not, throw out the puzzle.

While the interface is being designed, remember that words in foreign languages (especially German) can be up to three times longer than their English counterparts. This is important when allocating space for things like menus. Status bars in particular can be a problem, because their width is limited to the width of the screen. Consult with a translator ahead of time to see whether suitable abbreviations can be used to save space. (If you are using a localization firm, they are certain to have encountered this problem before and might have a solution at hand.)

When it comes to displaying text messages, don't hard-code the size of text boxes. English is a compact language, and different grammatical structures can cause a translated sentence to be considerably longer than the original. Instead, size the text box dynamically so that it can automatically expand to fit whatever it contains. Likewise, if your game requires the player to type in information, make sure that your entry fields are much larger than would be necessary for English.

Another trap created by the compactness of English is that animations linked to dialogue are likely to be too short. This isn't just a problem of inferior lip syncing. If a cutscene contains dialogue between two characters, and the camera cuts back and forth between them as they speak, the timing of the cuts is almost certain to be wrong for the foreign language versions. Make sure that your localization team has the cutscene animations *before* they do the translations, so that they can trim the dialogue to fit.

Avoid sprinkling text strings throughout your source code. Instead, create one file that contains all the text that is to appear on the screen. This saves countless hours when it comes time to extract text for translation and countless days when it is time to integrate the translations back into the game. If what you send to your localizers is one big file, with each line properly numbered, you might be able to complete the localization within days instead of weeks or months.

Find out early on whether your game will be localized into Asian languages. If so, your programmers need to assign two bytes for each text character, instead of one.

Don't generate text or speech algorithmically. In other words, don't construct sentences on-the-fly. In the early days of game development, when space was excruciatingly tight, it wasn't uncommon to cobble together words and sentences based on a set of rules, because it was much more efficient to store the rules than it was to store all the variations of the words themselves. Consider the following:

You search the man but don't find his key.

Depending on the game situation, you might need to change the subject of the sentence (*you*) to *he* or *she* and to change the objects (*man* and *key*) from singular to plural. In code, it wouldn't be too difficult to store all the variations. When these changes are plugged into the sentence, it looks something like this:

You/(s)he search(es) the man/men but do(es)n't find his/their key(s).

The code could very efficiently check the situation for specifics and spit out the right sentence. That's how you would do it algorithmically.

However, if you were to store all these sentences separately, you'd have something like this:

You search the man but don't find his key.

He searches the man but doesn't find his key.

She searches the man but doesn't find his key.

You search the men but don't find their keys.

He searches the men but doesn't find their keys.

She searches the men but doesn't find their keys.

Even though the latter method requires more storage, it is the correct one to pursue if your game is to be localized. Space is cheap, and the last thing you want is for one of your programmers to develop algorithms for generating text using multiple foreign languages and grammar.

Avoid hard-coding drive letters and paths for your filenames. Not all countries use *C* to designate the main hard drive.

Avoid embedding text in graphics, especially text that is critical to playing the game. The cost of generating and storing multiple versions of the art is likely to be prohibitive. Similarly, use icons on buttons wherever possible, instead of words. When translated, the words are likely to take up more space than is available on the button.

Provide context to your localizers. If you send a list of single words to translate, you might get back translations that are technically correct in that they apply to one meaning of the word, but that completely miss the mark for the meaning you have in mind. This isn't surprising, given the multiple meanings that words in our language must carry. For example, if you saw the word "cleave" by itself on a list of words to translate, would you assign it the meaning "cut off," or the meaning "adhere to"?

Finally, remember that localization applies to more than just words. Different countries have different standards about what can appear in games. The most notorious example is that Germany will not permit the image of a swastika to be published, causing problems for games staged in the World War II era. Other countries, such as Brazil, have tough standards concerning violence and bloodshed. Discuss your game with your localization firm (or internal group) early on, and find out what adjustments you must make to accommodate local customs.

The Manual

Writing the manual is another task that many companies turn over to external resources, and it is more difficult than most gamers realize. By the time the final line of code has been written, all the in-box materials are already sitting in a warehouse waiting for the game discs to show up. Game features change right up to the moment the master disc goes into duplication, yet by then the manual is already printed. (This is why so many games come with readme files.)

If you are in charge of getting the manual produced, your first mission is to ensure that the gamer has enough information to install the game and get it running. Your second mission is to tell him how to play it. As game boxes get smaller and smaller, manuals have shrunk as well. Most are now designed to fit inside a jewel case. You might not have room for the elaborate backstory that used to come with most games.

The way many companies handle the job is to have someone (usually the designer or producer) create a rough draft during the pre-alpha phase of production. This draft covers the major features of the game and explains the controls, but has many portions marked TBD (To Be Done). At this point the draft is turned over to the manual writer, who usually works with an assistant producer or lead tester to track the game while it is in progress, filling in all the TBDs as the information becomes available. The writer might request screen shots or other graphics to help explain the features, or just to make the manual look more interesting. The writer also coordinates with the legal department to make sure that the manual has all the notices required by licensors, as well as the trademark and copyright information for the game itself.

Oddly enough, one of the touchiest tasks when writing the manual is making sure everyone on the team is happy with the credits. Because our industry doesn't have Hollywood's clear job delineations, figuring out exactly who did what on a game can be a mess. Usually, the producer draws up an initial credits list and circulates it privately to the department heads for comments and corrections. When it comes back, he posts it to the team and waits for the storm. This can be especially difficult because it happens in the middle of crunch mode, when everyone is operating on too little sleep and too much caffeine. Compromises are made, egos are soothed, and most producers consider themselves lucky to escape the task with everyone still speaking to one another.

The writer continues to playtest the manual against the game right up until his deadline. After the manual is in production, the producer assumes the responsibility of tracking last-minute changes to the game and creating a readme file with anything that didn't make it into the manual.

Legal Issues (Getting the Rights)

An important part of working with external resources is ensuring that you acquire the rights to use the work you are paying them to do. Under current U.S. copyright law, a piece of art, music, writing, or code belongs to its originator from the moment it is created. This is true whether or not the individual takes any formal steps to register his work. The only way you can acquire the rights to his work is if he explicitly assigns them to you, and for this, you need a written document. A verbal agreement will not do.

Acquiring these rights is tedious but necessary. Failure to obtain signed agreements from every contractor can result in the game not being published in the first place or its failing to become an asset should your company be sold. (An acquiring company will want to ensure that they have complete rights to the title so that they can republish it without fear of legal problems.)

The best way to go about this is to be relentlessly methodical. First, you need a rights-transfer agreement that has been blessed by your legal advisors. Usually, this is a work-for-hire agreement that broadly assigns all rights to you. Then, assign an AP to get that agreement signed by every single contractor you work with, at the moment you begin working with them. This includes every voice actor, composer, and artist, no matter how small each one's contribution is. You will also need each contractor's legal name and social security number or Fed ID# for tax purposes, so you might as well lock down the agreement at the same time.

A good rights-transfer agreement allows you to do demos, run ads, and use the material in other games or sequels, all without having to go back to the creator for additional permissions.

If you or a contractor want to incorporate a piece of existing material into the game, remember that you must acquire the rights to it as well (unless it is in the public domain). Whether it is a snippet of a song, a clip from an old TV show, or even an old movie poster—if it has already been created, someone owns it, and you must acquire the proper rights before you can use it.

Small developers have a tendency to overlook these legal issues, figuring that no one will ever pay attention. This is a mistake. Not only is it just plain wrong to use someone's work without permission, but it would also be folly to create what could be a breakout hit, only to see its success blocked by some legal entanglement.

In all these matters, the only way to make certain that you're on safe ground is to work with a lawyer. If your company does not have a legal department, try to find a lawyer who is experienced in intellectual property law in general and entertainment products in particular. A good place to start is by looking at firms who make presentations at the annual Game Developers Conference. Their attorneys are well versed in all these issues. They have sample contracts and agreements that are reasonable starting points for negotiations with contractors, and they can provide advice that will steer you clear of trouble.

PART III

DEVELOPMENT

CHAPTER 10

PROJECT LIFECYCLE AND DOCUMENTS

S ome games are developed in six months. Others take many years. No matter how long projects last, each one goes through certain well-defined phases that have become standard across the industry. This chapter looks at these development phases and describes the documents and other tasks that accompany them. Appendix A also contains guidelines and templates to help you create many of these documents.

Concept Development

Concept development is the fuzzy front end of game design. It lasts from the moment someone first comes up with a game idea until the day the game goes into preproduction. The team is very small during this period. It consists of the designer, the tech lead, a concept artist, and a producer (who may spend only part of his time on the project).

The main goal of concept development is to decide what your game is about and to write this down so clearly that anyone can understand it instantly. During this phase you decide on your major gameplay elements, create concept art to show what the game will look like on the screen, and flesh out the story (if there is one).

If you work for an independent developer, this phase probably won't be funded by another company. Unless your studio has an amazing track record, it is unlikely that you will find a publisher willing to pay you to sit around and think up new ideas.

The documents that come out of concept development are the high concept, the game proposal (or "pitch doc"), and the concept document.

The High Concept

As discussed in Chapter 1, "Getting to 'Yes,'" the high concept is a one- or two-sentence description of what your game is about. It is the "hook" that makes your game exciting and sets it apart from the competition.

A strong high concept is also valuable during the development phase, because it helps you decide which features to include and which to leave out. If game development is like trying to find your way through a jungle of possibilities, the high concept is a path that has already been cleared so that you don't get lost. Any feature that doesn't contribute to the game's main focus is a direction you don't need to explore.

The Game Proposal ("Pitch Doc")

The game proposal is the two-page handout that you speak from during pitch meetings as you seek funding for your game. In just a few pages, you must summarize what your game is about, why it will be successful, and how it will make money. The document covers the same territory as the concept doc, but in abbreviated form.

The Concept Doc

This is the fleshed-out version of the pitch document. It is a 10–20 page "leave-behind" for members of the publishing team. They won't have time to review this during the pitch meeting, but they will peruse it afterward to gain a more detailed understanding of your game.

The concept doc should be presented in a professional binder on good paper stock, with an eye-catching cover and excellent game art throughout. It should contain the following sections: the high concept; genre; gameplay; features; setting; story; target audience; hardware platforms; estimated schedule; budget and P&L; competitive analysis; team; risk analysis; and summary.

The High Concept

The high concept is the quick description you would give an executive if you only had 30 seconds to pitch your game.

Genre

Explain which genre your game belongs to, along with crossover elements to other genres if applicable.

Gameplay

Describe what the player will do while he's playing the game. Emphasize any new twists to the genre that your game provides.

Features

This is the list of the features that will make your game exceptional. It can include anything from an unusual graphical style to advanced engine technology. Write this section as if you're writing copy for the back of the game box.

Setting

Describe the world your game is set in. Include concept art, if you have any. If it is a story game, highlight the most interesting features of the setting and explain how they affect the plot.

Story

If your game has a story, take a page or so to summarize the plot. Introduce the main character, identify his problem, describe the villain, and explain how the hero will ultimately defeat him.

Target Audience

Explain who you're developing the game for and why you think it will appeal to them.

Hardware Platforms

List the devices the game will be played on: PC, console, handheld, mobile phone, etc.

Estimated Schedule, Budget, and P&L

Break out the major phases of development and the level of effort associated with each phase, to show how you arrived at the estimates in the pitch doc.

If you work for a publisher, he's likely to require a P&L (profit and loss) estimate at this stage. This is an estimate of all the costs of bringing the game to market, along with estimates of all its anticipated income. Your business division will have templates for these calculations, usually plug-in spreadsheets that have cells for wholesale costs, sales estimates, license royalties, and so on.

(If you're an independent developer making a proposal to a publisher, you won't know his cost structures, and your royalties have yet to be negotiated. So instead of a P&L, you should simply include your development budget. Make sure to break out the amount you want to charge for the preproduction phase, however, because getting that funded is the whole point of this project proposal.)

You can't come up with all the numbers on the P&L by yourself. You have to work with several divisions of the company to come up with reliable estimates:

- The development group supplies the direct costs of creating the game. This is derived by multiplying the man-month estimate by the group's salaries, and then adding in equipment costs, overhead costs, and any external costs (technology license fees, voice recording, FMV shoots, and so on).

- From the production group comes the COGS (cost of goods) estimate. This includes the costs of the physical materials that go into the game box—the disc, the jewel case, the manual, the box itself, and so on.

- The marketing department provides an estimate of how much it will spend to promote the game in magazine ads, TV ads, point-of-purchase displays, sell sheets, and so on.

- From the sales group come the MDF (market development fund) costs that the publisher pays to stores in the retail channel for prime shelf space, end caps, shelf talkers, and ads in their circulars.

- The sales group is also the source for income estimates. Most companies don't give credence to a P&L statement until the sales department indicates that the unit sales estimates can be achieved.

- From the business group come allowances for returns, corporate overhead, and calculations for royalty payments if your game is based on an external license.

The bottom line of the P&L is the ROI (return on investment) number. This must show that the company can make more money investing in your game than in some less risky venture, such as putting the money in the bank and drawing interest for two years. All companies are in business to make money, and if you can't convince them that your game will be profitable enough to justify the risk, it will never be approved.

Competitive Analysis

Make a list of the games that will be competing with yours for sales, and explain the ways your game will be better. If you believe the game is similar to successful games from the past, explain the similarities to those hits and present their sales numbers.

Team

Summarize the credentials of your team and its key individuals, with an emphasis on their experience. You want to show they have the ability to develop the game. Publishers frequently put as much weight on the team members and their track records as they do on the actual proposal in front of them. The goal of this section is to instill confidence that your group can get the job done.

Risk Analysis

This section lays out all the things that can go wrong and how you plan to deal with problems that might arise. Some common risks that threaten projects are

- Difficulties recruiting personnel
- Late delivery of console dev-kits
- Reliance on external sources for key technology components
- Changes in the installed base of the target platform
- Competitive technology developments

This section should also include your comments on which parts of the project are relatively safe. If you have any of the traditional risks covered, such as having a full team already in place or being able to reuse an existing engine, say so.

Summary

Emphasize again the high points of your game and the ability of your team to deliver a quality product, on time and on budget.

Preproduction (Proof of Concept)

Preproduction is gearing-up time. Your goal is to complete the game design, create the art bible, establish the production path, write up the project plan, and create a prototype. This phase is also where you do some technical prototyping that demonstrates the feasibility of any new technology you hope to deliver. Preproduction basically proves that your team can make the game, and that the game is worth making.

If you're an independent developer, your publisher can also use the preproduction period to test the waters and see what sort of relationship you develop with them. If they learn that you're professional, reasonable, and able to deliver on time, they're likely to go ahead. Otherwise, they might write off their loss and move on.

The work products of this phase are the game design document, the art production plan, the technical design document, and the project plan (which itself is actually a suite of documents). Preproduction culminates in the delivery of the game prototype, a working piece of software that shows off how fun the game is to play.

The Game Design Document

By the end of preproduction, you should have a game design document that exhaustively details everything that will happen in the game. The features in this document then become the requirements from which the art production plan and the technical plan are made.

During the development cycle, the game design document should always be the most current representation of everything there is to know about what the player experiences in the game. This should include complete information about the gameplay, user interface, story, characters, monsters, AI, and everything else, down to the finest detail. (See Appendix A for an example.)

Such a document, if committed to paper, would be the size of a telephone directory, impossible to maintain, read by no one, and almost instantly out of date. Instead, put it on your internal network as a set of Web pages. See www.openwiki.com for a methodology that makes this easy.

Maintaining your documents as Wiki pages keeps the design up-to-date, and also gives everyone on the team easy access to everything at all times. The savings to the group over the course of development are enormous.

The Art Production Plan

Preproduction is when you establish the "look" of your game and decide how the art will be created.

The Art Bible

During preproduction, the designer, art director, and concept artist collaborate on setting the artistic style of the game. The concept artist makes reference sheets for other artists to work from, and together the team arrives at a unified look. Establishing this art bible early on helps orient new artists coming onto the project, and ensures the final product will have a consistent style throughout. Most of this art can take the form of pencil sketches, but it is often useful in selling the game to develop a few glossy pieces that capture the high concept and pack a good visual punch.

In the early stages of the game, it is also a good idea to assemble a visual reference library of images that reflect the direction you want the art to take. These images can come from anywhere—magazines, travel books, movie posters, and so on—as long as they're used only for guidance and don't find their way into the final product.

Production Path

The production path is the process by which you go from concept to reality, from an idea in someone's head to actual figures and gameplay on the screen. For example, to create a functioning character in an action game, you must find the most efficient way to go from a designer's spec, to a concept sketch, to a 3D model, to a skin for the model, to animation for the figure, to applying AI to the character, to dropping him into the game and seeing how he works. All the tools you select along the way must be compatible. They must be able to "talk" with each other so that the work you do on one step can be imported to the next step, manipulated, and passed up the line.

Assets, Budgets, Task, and Schedules

The Production Plan also includes the first draft of the asset list, team tasking, equipment budget and costs, etc. (See Appendix A.) Like the Game Design Document, this plan must be updated and kept current throughout the life of the project.

The Technical Design Document

The technical design document sets out the way your tech lead plans to transform the game design from words on a page to software on a machine. It establishes the technical side of the art production path, lays out the tasks of everyone involved in development, and estimates the time to completion of those tasks. (From these man-month estimates, you learn how many people you need on the project and how long they will be with you. This, in turn, has a direct effect on your budget.)

The tech document describes the core tools that will be used to build the game, and it details which of these are already in-house and which have to be bought or created. The document also lists the hardware and software that must be purchased, as well as any changes you need to make to your organization's infrastructure (storage capacity, backup capabilities, network speed) to support development. See Appendix A for a detailed outline of a complete TDD.

The Project Plan

The project plan is the roadmap that tells you how you're going to build the game. It starts with the raw task lists in the tech plan, establishes dependencies, adds overhead hours, and turns all that into a real-world schedule. The final project plan is broken down into several independently maintained documents. (See Appendix A for samples.)

Manpower Plan

The manpower plan is a spreadsheet that lists all the personnel on the project, when they will start, and how much of their salaries will be applied to the project.

Resource Plan

The resource plan calculates all the external costs of the project. Building from the tech plan, it takes the timing of the hardware purchases to support internal personnel, and it estimates when the external costs (voice, music, video, and so on) will be incurred.

Project Tracking Doc

This is where you keep track of whether you're on schedule. Some producers use project management software for this, but many find the programs too inflexible to manage all aspects of the game's development. The producer usually enters tasklist data into the software to create a Gantt chart that reveals dependencies and the critical path, but he may also use a hodgepodge of other homegrown techniques to keep track of the project.

Budget

After applying the overhead multipliers to the manpower plan, you combine these numbers with the resource plan to derive your month-by-month cash requirements and the overall budget for the game.

P&L

The original profit and loss estimate was made during the concept phase. As development progresses and costs become clearer, the P&L must be kept current.

Development Schedule

Many developers chafe against creating a firm schedule and committing to a specific release date, but you owe it to yourself and your company to do exactly that. After a release date has been set, a whole different machine goes into motion. The marketing team books advertisements that will appear in the months running up to the release date. The PR department negotiates with magazines for cover stories, well-timed previews, and feature articles. The sales group commits to end caps in the software stores. Changing the release date of the software is likely to torpedo all the carefully planned efforts of these groups, and your game may sell far fewer units than it could have.

Milestone Definitions

Milestones are significant points in the development process marked by the completion of a certain amount of work, called a *deliverable*. These deliverables should be concrete and very precisely defined, with language such as "Concept sketches for 15 characters, front, side, and back" or "Weapon #1 modeled, skinned, and operational within the game, with a placeholder sound effect, but without animations or visual effects."

Avoid fuzzy deliverables, such as "Design 25% complete." The best deliverables are binary: They're either complete or they're not, with no ground for argument in-between.

Game Prototype

The tangible result of preproduction is the prototype. This is a working piece of software that captures onscreen the essence of what sets your game apart from the crowd, and what will turn it into a hit.

This "look and feel" demo can be the single greatest influence on whether the project goes forward. Publishers like to be able to look at a screen and "get it" right away. If they can't see the vision within a minute or two, they're unlikely to fund the rest of the project.

This is a tough task to pull off, especially if the project requires a new engine, or if one of your hooks is new technology that won't be built until much later in development. When this is the case, most developers simulate what the final product will look like, most often by prerendering material that will be rendered in real time during the game.

Another approach is to prepare standalone demonstrations to prove that the various pieces of planned technology are feasible. These small technical demos might not be much to look at from an artistic point of view, but they show that your goals are reachable. Typical tech demos might show nothing more than a lighting scheme on a few spheres, the camera moving through a featureless "cube" environment, or a bunch of particles bouncing off one another as they stream from an invisible source. The point is to show that the building blocks of your technology are solid. The features you choose to prototype in this way should be the most difficult ones, the ones that present the greatest risk.

The finished prototype not only shows the vision, but also establishes that your production path is working and that you can go from ideas to reality in a reasonable and effective way.

Development

Development is the long haul.

Your development schedule is likely to last six months to two years. Very little software can be designed, coded, and tested in less than six months (although with the advent of Internet gaming and mobile gaming, "small" games are coming back into style). Likewise, games that spend longer than two years in development run the risk of going stale, suffering personnel turnover, having features trumped or stolen by other games, or seeing the technology lapped by hardware advances. Any of these problems can lead to redesign and reworking, which in turn lead to schedule delays.

The deceptive part of development is how much time you seem to have when you're starting out. You have a good plan, and it is easy to think that anything and everything can be accomplished. This phase of the project can be dangerously similar to summer vacation. At the beginning, all you see are weeks and months stretching out in front of you, with plenty of time to accomplish everything that's on your mind. Then, as the deadline draws near, you wonder where all the time went, and you start scrambling to fit everything in.

The trick to surviving this long stretch is to break large tasks into small, manageable tasks that are rigorously tracked. You can't know whether you're behind on a project if you don't track the tasks. You should do this as often as once a week.

One effective task-management technique is to have each developer track his own tasklist, complete with time estimates. These individual lists roll up into a master list, which shows at a glance the estimated time to completion for the entire project. This method is particularly useful for seeing whether one person's task bar sticks out beyond the others. If this happens, that person is the *de facto* critical path for the project, and you should take a close look at his list to see whether some tasks can be handed to someone else.

This method also has the advantage of leaving the developer or artist in charge of his own estimates, instead of imposing them from above. This increases his buy-in to the schedule and makes him less likely to miss deadlines.

If you are an external developer working for a publisher, your progress is tracked for you in the form of contractual milestones. The incentive to stay on schedule is clear—if you don't meet the milestone, you don't get paid. Well-run internal groups use the same structure. Milestones are established at the start of development, and there is usually a monthly, company-wide project status meeting where all the producers get together and go over the status of their projects in detail. During project reviews, senior managers look at whether the project is on schedule, and also how the producer is working to minimize any risks that could endanger the project in the future.

The technical aspects of managing the development process are dealt with in Chapter 11, "Managing Development." In the meantime, here are some nontechnical tips for surviving the process:

- Bring your test lead on at the beginning of development. Add more testers only as you approach alpha.
- Maintain good communication across the team. Keep the project documents updated and accessible, especially the game design doc, tech design doc, and art production plan. Establish internal mailing lists that allow groups to e-mail their peers without clogging the inboxes of the entire group.
- Track your actual expenditures against your budget.
- Maintain the team's identity and spirit. You don't have to use some management guru's oddball exercise for this. Just find an activity that fits the personality of your group, whether it is going to an amusement park, playing laser tag or paintball, or just going out for a movie and drinks every once in a while.
- Work with marketing and PR to keep them supplied with the materials they need. The resulting previews and features will energize your team when their spirits are low.
- When it is time for a trade show, remember that demo versions of the game are like miniature projects—they cannot be tossed off in a few hours of overtime. Demos need their own tasklist and schedule, and they must be included in the technical plan from the start. The dates of major trade shows are known years in advance, so no one should be caught short when the next one rolls around. (See the "External Events" doc in Appendix A.)
- Be ready for a shock or two. We work in a volatile industry, and any project that lasts more than a year is likely to experience at least one management upheaval, corporate buyout, or other calamitous experience. The trick to surviving is to keep your head down and *do the work*. Things are rarely as bad as they seem, and if you stay focused on the job at hand, the corporate storms that rage above your head are less likely to kill you.

■ Have a few features ready to "throw off the back of the wagon" to help you manage scope. (See Chapter 11 for more on this.)

Alpha

The definition of *alpha* varies from company to company, but generally, it is the point at which the game is mostly playable from start to finish. There might still be a few workarounds or gaps, and not all the assets might be final, but the engine, user interface, and all other major subsystems are complete.

As you enter alpha, the focus starts to shift from building to finishing, from creating to polishing. Now is the time to take a hard look at the features in the game and decide whether any of them must be dropped in order to make the schedule. Now is when more testers come onboard to start ferreting out bugs. Now is the first time the game is seen and evaluated by people outside the development team.

The good news about alpha is that it is the beginning of the end. The bad news is that reaching the end is seldom easy.

Beta

At beta, all assets are integrated, all development stops, and the only thing that happens thereafter is bug fixing. Stray bits of artwork can be upgraded, bits of text can be rewritten, but the goal at this point is to stabilize the project and eliminate as many bugs as possible before shipping.

If you're creating a console game that's subject to the approval of the console manufacturer, the final weeks of beta will include submissions to that company so their testers can verify that the game meets their own quality standards. If it is a PC game, it can be sent to an outside testing firm for compatibility testing. This will uncover, you hope, any pieces of hardware (or combinations of hardware) under which the game won't run.

The last portion of beta testing has come to be called *crunch time*. During these weeks, people have been known to stay in the office for days at a time, sleep under their desks, eat nothing but carryout, ingest massive amounts of caffeine, and become strangers to their families. All in all, it is a weird twilight world where the only important thing is finishing the game.

When this goes well, you end up with a dedicated team who believe that they're working on something special, and who are willing to make sacrifices in other areas of their lives to see this creation come out right. The people work hard because they *want* to, because it is important to them, and because it is fun. Their motivation comes from an internal desire rather than an external mandate. If you've ever worked hard with a group of people to achieve a cherished goal, you know how exhilarating and rewarding it can be.

On the other hand, when it goes poorly, you have people who feel pressured to put in long hours so that they won't lose their jobs, who don't care what's in the game as long as it gets done, and who feel bitter and exploited. If you've ever had to grind away at a pointless task that was doomed to failure anyway, you know how mind-numbing and soul-deadening that can be.

When it goes really poorly, crunch time turns into a *death march*, which is any period of extraordinary effort that lasts more than one month. You should avoid this at all costs. The benefits of overtime are lost in mistakes caused by exhaustion. Apathy sets in. The team breaks down. You're very likely to deliver the game later than if you just kept plugging along in the first place. If you ever find yourself saying, "We can make the deadline if everyone works two months of mandatory overtime," take a deep breath, step back, and reevaluate.

Crunch time is inevitable on any project, and when it arrives, be prepared to walk on eggshells. As time runs out, emotions run high and tempers can flare. One of the hardest parts of making a game is the last-minute agonizing over how important any given bug is, and these decisions are likely to be made in a supercharged atmosphere with too little time and not enough sleep. In these final days, try to keep your sense of proportion, understand that there is rarely a "right" decision. And remember that even if you disagree with what's happening, you still need to work for the good of the game.

Finally, when you're putting together the release-candidate discs, always work from a punchlist and have two people check off each task as it is performed. Trusting a single exhaustion-addled engineer to remember all the ins and outs of creating the final disc is a recipe for disaster.

Code Freeze

In the last few days of beta, you are likely to be in a code freeze, when all the hard work is done and the preparation of candidate master discs begins. Each of these discs is sent to testing, and the only changes allowed to the code base are those that specifically address showstopper bugs that turn up in testing.

RTM (Release to Manufacture)

The game is released to manufacture when one of the candidate releases has been thoroughly tested and found to be acceptable. You can finally celebrate.

Patches

On the PC side of the house, it has become almost inevitable that a game will need to be patched after its release. Contrary to the opinions expressed on Internet message boards, this isn't necessarily because the developer has rushed a poorly tested product out the door. In a world where literally thousands of hardware combinations exist, it is impossible to test all of them. If a consumer finds that his particular combination of BIOS, graphics card, sound card, monitor, CPU, operating system, keyboard, mouse, and joystick causes problems in the game, most developers will work with him to figure out the source of the problem. If the problem is pervasive enough, the developer will issue a patch.

Upgrades

An upgrade is different from a patch. It represents additional content that's been created to enhance the original game. Companies create upgrades for a number of reasons. In some cases, it is simply to extend the life of the original game. (If add-ons appear, retailers are more likely to keep the original on the shelves.) In other cases, it is an effective strategy to keep part of the team gainfully employed while a smaller group goes on to the early stages of their next project.

In any case, an upgrade is a mini-project and needs to be handled like one, with testing, milestones, and all the other elements of good software management.

CHAPTER 11

MANAGING DEVELOPMENT

Before it is anything else, building a game is a software development project. Because the end product is entertainment, many try to compare the game development process to producing a movie or writing a book. You can't. The techniques you use to manage the process should be taken from the realm of software engineering.

Many excellent books have been written on managing software development. Four of the best are *The Mythical Man-Month* by Frederick Brooks, *Peopleware* by DeMarco and Lister, *Rapid Development* by Steve McConnell (see Figure 11.1), and *Debugging the Development Process* by Steve Maguire. None of these books require technical knowledge on your part. Whether you're a designer, a producer, a programmer, or an executive, you should read these books and apply the techniques that work best for you and your team.

Figure 11.1 *Rapid Development* should be required reading for everyone involved in making games. Image courtesy of Steve McConnell.

Agile Development

Since the first edition of this book was published, a quiet revolution has taken place in software development. For years, developers and managers alike have struggled with the chronic problems of software projects that are delivered late, over budget, and with poor quality. In 2001, the advocates of several new development methodologies suddenly realized that their ideas had much in common. They met and codified a new approach they labeled *agile development*. The core of agile development is to deliver "customer satisfaction through early and continuous delivery of useful software components." (In this context, the "customer" is the game publisher.)

Agile development is most useful in projects where the requirements are not well understood at the beginning, where new technologies must be created, and where the customer is willing to be deeply involved in the development process. This perfectly describes most major games in development today.

Note, however, that not all games will benefit from agile development. Expansion packs and some sequels, for example, have well-known requirements and stable engine technologies. These projects are better suited to more traditional methodologies.

The proponents of agile development value the following:

- **Individuals and interactions** over processes and tools
- **Working software** over comprehensive documentation
- **Customer collaboration** over contract negotiation
- **Responding to change** over following a plan

"That is, while there is value in the items on the right, we value the items on the left more." (www.agilemanifesto.org)

The principles behind this manifesto are as follows:

1. Satisfy the customer through early and continuous delivery of valuable software.
2. Welcome changing requirements, even late in development.
3. Deliver working software frequently, as often as every few weeks.
4. Business people and developers must work together daily throughout the project.
5. Build projects around motivated individuals. Give them the environment and support they need, and trust them to get the job done.
6. Face-to-face conversation is the most efficient and effective method of conveying information.

7. Working software is the primary measure of progress.

8. Promote sustainable development. The sponsors, the developers, and the user should be able to maintain a constant pace indefinitely.

9. Continuous attention to technical excellence and good design.

10. Simplicity—the art of maximizing the amount of work *not* done—is essential.

11. The best architectures, requirements, and designs emerge from self-organizing teams.

12. At regular intervals, the team reflects on how to become more effective, and then fine-tunes and adjusts its behavior accordingly.

Let's apply these principles to the task of managing game development.

Managing Development

To manage a software project successfully, you must do the following:

1. Understand your design goals.

2. Develop a reasonable tech plan and schedule.

3. Understand the problems that can occur, and work to avoid them.

4. Know how to recover when your project is in trouble.

Design

The game design document is the equivalent of the requirements analysis used in the world of formal software development. It lists the features the game should have, describes the user interfaces, defines the art requirements, and so on.

Starting to code without a design and tech plan is a mistake that many teams make, especially if they're under schedule pressure from the very start. However, study after study has shown that shortchanging the critical *upstream* activities—such as effective planning, design, and establishing the scope of the project—result in cascading problems later in the process. Take the time at the beginning of the project to understand your design goals.

If your team is using agile development, it's easy for the game designer to protest that he shouldn't waste time writing up a complete document, because everything's going to change anyway. But even if things are going to change, the team has to start somewhere. The designer must make the effort and do the most complete imagining of the game that he can. Only then can the team decide which portion to attack first.

The mechanics of creating and documenting this design are covered thoroughly elsewhere in this book, so let's move on to developing a tech plan and a reasonable schedule.

Planning and Scheduling

At the risk of brutally simplifying one of the most complicated tasks known to man, the best way to create a schedule for a software project is to go through three steps:

1. Estimate the size of the project.
2. Estimate the effort in man-weeks or man-months that it will take to build something of that size.
3. Apply the man-month estimate to the number of people on the team, and spread it out over a calendar schedule, while making sure to allow for overhead activities such as meetings, holidays, vacations, and so on.

If this three-step process is so simple, why doesn't it always work? Why do studies show that two out of every three software projects significantly overrun their schedules?

Let's take a quick look at the way that many projects are built:

A team comes up with an idea for a game. It's on a new hardware platform for them, but in a genre with which they're familiar. They make up a feature list, and their producer presents it to management. A vice president likes the idea, does a quick ROI, and says that he'd be willing to fund it for about x dollars. However, it has to be done within a certain time frame.

The producer goes back to the group with a date that's two months prior to the VP's date so that he'll have a private fudge factor. The team members look at the schedule and adjust their vision of the game. They throw out some features, eyeball the rest, and say, "Maybe it will work." They dive into coding right away while waiting for the dev-kits to arrive.

After a while, the team has a working prototype of the game up and running. It's two months later than expected, because the dev-kits came in late and they couldn't hire the right people, but at last everyone can sit down and see where they are. The producer isn't worried about the delay, because he had the two-month fudge factor built in all along.

The vice president (if he hasn't left the company by now) gets excited and thinks the game can be a hit, but only if they can add a multiplayer mode and still make the date. The team works hard, but as they come up on the deadline, it becomes evident that they won't make it. The producer adds more people to the team, starts holding a daily 5:00 p.m. "project status" meeting, and institutes mandatory ten-hour days, six days per week.

The original release date comes and goes. Marketing screams. The team slips ever further behind, but keeps banging away on a ten-month death march until the product finally ships. The team stumbles across the finish line exhausted and barely alive—and, of course, they're criticized by everyone because the game was late.

What just happened here?

Scope

The first problem is that no one sat down to figure out the size of the project.

In the world of formal software design, there are many approaches to estimating the size of a project, but it remains an extraordinarily difficult task. You can buy estimation software, bring in outside experts, estimate the number of function points or the total lines of code, you can eyeball the different modules and add up the components to get a total, and so on.

All these methods are reasonable, and it might be useful to try a few of them to see whether the results jibe with each other. However, in our industry, the most reliable method of estimating a game's size is to compare the features with those of a similar game you've worked on in the past.

Naturally, this means that the more experience you have, the more accurate your estimates will be. Nevertheless, because our business is driven by innovation, parts of the project are sure to be new to you, whether they're the individual features, genre, hardware platform, point of view, art style, gameplay modes, or whatever. For each of these, your estimates are likely to be off because you either overestimate or underestimate the complexity of the unknown tasks. This means that it is important for everyone to recognize that estimates made early in a project have a high margin of error. As the project progresses, the unknowns become known, and the margin of error decreases.

You can improve the accuracy of your estimates by using historical data rather than relying on personal memory. Use timesheets to track what people are working on. Keep records of how long the various modules actually take to design, code, test, and debug. Look at published postmortems in *Game Developer* magazine and on gamasutra.com to see how long it took other teams to overcome the same sorts of problems you're facing now.

If you're an agile team, you also have the benefit of focusing your estimation efforts on the next discrete portion of development, rather than on the entire project. It's much easier to estimate the scope of a task when it's relatively small and you have a concrete set of requirements (user stories) in front of you.

Whatever estimation method you use, be aware that *scope* is the single biggest factor in determining a project's schedule. Big projects take longer than small projects. The more features you have in a game, the more time you must allow for designing, building, debugging, integrating, and testing them. Because of this, increasing the size of the game results in greater than a one-to-one increase in the effort. If you have a schedule problem, the first places you should always look for relief are features and scope. According to *Rapid Development*, "Cutting the size of a medium-size program by one-half will typically cut the effort required by almost two-thirds."

External Pressures

The second problem in this scenario is that the schedule and budget were set by an executive who wasn't involved in the project, without any reference to the effort necessary to deliver the features.

> "We need the game to fill the hole in our third quarter."

> "If we miss Christmas, we're sunk."

> "It's a football game—we can't bring it out in March!"

There are many good business reasons to target a particular time of the year for the release of a product. However, creating an inflexible schedule and budget without regard for the feature set is a recipe for disaster.

Before you sign up for a schedule, it's absolutely critical for everyone up and down the line to agree that it should be based on a reasonable level of effort for the features you plan to deliver, rather than on an arbitrary date. If the date is fixed (as it sometimes must be), you need to adjust your feature set and task lists to fall within the schedule.

Padding

The third problem in this scenario is that the producer privately padded the schedule.

Producers pad schedules because they figure that something's bound to go wrong that the tech lead won't anticipate. They hide the padding from the team, because they think that an aggressive schedule will motivate the team to work harder, whereas a "relaxed" schedule might fall prey to Parkinson's Law: "Work expands to fill the time available for its completion."

When managers create a short schedule, they believe that they're acting responsibly to prevent the programmers from running wild. They believe that by holding the development team's feet to the fire, they'll get the game faster than they would otherwise.

This is wrong. It creates credibility and trust problems when the deceit is discovered, as it will be. Besides which, when a team is faced with a short schedule, the first thing they do is abandon the practices that enable them to be efficient and fast. They grab whoever is available for the project, rather than finding the people best suited to the tasks. They jump into coding right away, without taking the time to understand the requirements or how the various pieces will fit together. Design is shortchanged. People start working 80-hour weeks right off, and they burn out within a month.

The more rational technique is to create a *bottom-up* schedule. Ask the developers to make their own estimates. Determine the calendar schedule that comes out of those estimates, and *then* decide what to do about it. If the schedule doesn't match management goals, either don't do the project or change your goals. You'll be helping yourself in the end. If you start by imposing an unrealistic schedule, you will cost your company money by canceling the project late in the process, when you realize that it won't hit the schedule, or by extending the schedule (or worse, pouring on more resources in the middle of the schedule), even though time and money have already been spent on inefficient ways to meet the first schedule.

Either way, you lose. The best thing to do is work with the developers from the start to achieve a reasonable, efficient schedule, and modify the project's features, scope, and goals to be achievable within the time available.

Altered Requirements

The fourth problem in this scenario is that features were added without adjusting the schedule.

Another torpedo in the hull of a good schedule is a sudden change in scope. The VP might be exactly right that a multiplayer mode is necessary to put the game over the top. The team may even agree. However, it's unrealistic to think that such a major feature can be added to a game without changing the schedule.

While agile teams specifically welcome altered requirements as the project is in progress, the customer must participate with the team in assessing the impact on the schedule and making the necessary tradeoffs to keep the overall project in line with the company's goals.

Developer Optimism

The fifth problem in this scenario is that the team was overly optimistic.

The problem of creating overly optimistic schedules cannot be put entirely in the hands of management. Sometimes developers shoot themselves in the foot with their own scheduling practices. They create a short schedule because they *think* that this is what the boss wants to hear. More unscrupulously, they sometimes underestimate a project to get funding for it, believing that, by the time the discrepancy becomes apparent, most publishers would rather provide additional time and money than cancel.

The three most common developer problems, however, are that they don't take enough time to plan properly, they forget or overlook important tasks that belong on the schedule, and they're just plain optimistic. Studies show that developers generally underestimate the time it takes to perform their own tasks by 20% to 30%.

The Heart of the Problem

The sixth problem in this scenario is that no one was really *sure what they wanted to build until they saw the prototype.*

No matter how complete the game design is when you start, it still provides an incomplete picture of what the final game will be like. Often, the only way to get a clearer picture is to build what has been specified and then examine it to see whether it's *fun*.

This is the most intractable problem of game development. Fortunately, it can be anticipated and managed.

In practice, building a game is a process of constantly adjusting the design. From concept development through preproduction and development itself, you're constantly making decisions that will affect the schedule. The more you build, the more you know *what* you want to build. If the game isn't fun, the design must change. If the design changes, the requirements change, and therefore the schedule changes too.

In a moment, we'll examine some lifecycle models that help address this conflict, but this dilemma remains as the core reason why so many games are late and go over budget.

When all is said and done, it's important to understand that a game's features, schedule, and cost are *always* imprecise until the day it ships. This doesn't mean that you cannot lock down the schedule and cost. You can—if you're flexible about the features. Neither does it mean that you cannot have all the features you want. You can—if you're flexible about the schedule and cost.

Nor does it mean that you should throw up your hands and declare that all is anarchy and chaos. Make estimates, but express them in ranges. At the beginning, the ranges are wide because so much isn't known. As the project progresses, more becomes known and the ranges narrow. Toward the end, you can have an excellent (if not absolutely precise) idea of how it will all come to completion.

The unfortunate truth is that if everyone involved with the project isn't willing to participate in the horse-trading around the fundamental tradeoffs of schedule, features, and cost, your project is doomed.

Selecting the Right Lifecycle Model

The discipline of software engineering recognizes several formal approaches to design and development. Some of them are best suited to very small projects, with only one programmer and just a few thousand lines of code. Others are suited to very large projects, where there can be 50 or more developers and millions of lines of code. Most game projects fall solidly into a medium category, with teams of four to eight programmers and a few hundred thousand lines of code.

Given the size and nature of our projects, the most appropriate lifecycle models are generally the classic waterfall, the modified waterfall, and iterative prototyping.

The Waterfall

In a perfect world, software development would follow the classic waterfall model. Requirements would be completely defined. Then the system architecture would be designed, followed by detailed design, coding and debugging, and finally testing.

This orderly progression through a defined set of processes works best when everything is well defined up front and will not change. As we've already seen, game development is usually more chaotic than that. The game projects for which the waterfall method is appropriate are usually series sequels in which the basic gameplay mechanics are already known, and other major subsystems, such as the game engine and interface, are already set. If all you're doing is giving the product a facelift, adding a few new features and building some new levels, the pure waterfall is the model for you.

For the record, the waterfall steps are

1. Concept
2. Requirements analysis
3. Architectural design
4. Detailed design
5. Coding and debugging
6. Testing

The Modified Waterfall

The modified waterfall allows for overlapping of steps. For example, you can begin coding some subsections before a detailed design is complete, especially if those subsections are understood and relatively independent modules. If you're working on a trivia game, for example, you can decide early on what the user interface will look like, and the questions themselves can be developed anywhere along the way.

Another genre that lends itself to the modified waterfall approach is the adventure game. Meaningful interaction with the environment is important to the gameplay, but the designer usually won't know exactly what those environments look like until the artists create them. Even though the basic story and puzzles are known when development starts, specific interactions might have to wait until the designer can see the world that the artists have created.

Iterative Prototyping

Rapid iterative prototyping is the best development model for most new games.

Whether you call it extreme programming, crystal, adaptive software development, dynamic systems development, or simply agile programming, the idea is to get a rough prototype up and running quickly, play it, keep what you like, throw out what you don't like, and then go back and build another one. Repeat as needed.

Sid Meier (see Figure 11.2) is famous in designer circles for saying that he always gets the kernel of a new game up and running as quickly as possible, even with just stick-figure graphics, so that he can be playing the actual *game* throughout the development process.

The key to this lifecycle model is to refine the design continually, based on what you've built so far. At the beginning of each cycle, the team sits down to consider what needs to be done next. The customer (in this case, the designer or the publisher's producer) writes out "use cases" or "user stories," succinct statements in plain English of things he needs the game to do. The development team attaches time estimates to these, and then everyone sits down in a horse-trading session. If the customer

Figure 11.2 Sid Meier, designer of the classic games *Civilization, Railroad Tycoon, Pirates!,* and many others. Image courtesy of Firaxis Games, Inc.

learns that a particular request will take two weeks, and that 10 others could be done in one day each, he may decide he'd rather see those 10 features implemented first. Or not. The goal is to intimately involve the customer in the process, so that they take responsibility along with the development team for the decisions as the game is built.

The things you have to watch out for are getting ahead of yourself by building assets that you might later decide you don't need, and the temptation to degenerate to hacking. Each prototype should have its own tight cycle of full development, with requirements laid out, a plan for delivering them, and a schedule for getting it done.

RTS games are perfect candidates for this lifecycle model. As units are created and features are added, unforeseen gameplay dynamics and strategies emerge, some of them good and some bad. Because flexibility is built into the process, the bad dynamics can be weeded out and the good ones allowed to flourish.

Action games might do well to mix the modified waterfall with the iterative prototype for different portions of the development process. The asset-creation portion of the task lends itself to the waterfall model. Creatures, weapons, and environments can all be designed, specified, and built in an orderly process. The gameplay portion of the task lends itself to iterative prototyping, where the AI for the creatures and the operation of the weapons are designed, coded, tested, and refined in a series of prototypes.

Problems

Even if you've planned well, things can still go wrong. Certain problems routinely arise over the course of development. In postmortem after postmortem, you see the same litany: overly optimistic schedules, disruptive team members, feature creep, and more.

Classic Mistakes

In *Rapid Development*, Steve McConnell identifies several classic mistakes that managers make on software projects, and discusses the problems that these mistakes cause. The following is a list of some of those mistakes, along with tips to help you avoid them:

- **Undermined motivation.** Game developers aren't usually motivated by the same things that inspire the general workforce, and not all developers are motivated the same way. Get to know the people on your project, and give them reasons to do a good job that make sense to *them*. Ham-handed attempts at motivating the team are likely to blow up in your face.

- **Weak personnel.** When you choose your team, don't necessarily pick the people you can bring onto the project the fastest. Skill levels can vary among programmers by as much as a 10–1 margin. Waiting to get better people can be the smartest decision you make on the project.

- **Uncontrolled problem personnel.** When a person doesn't work well with the team, bad things happen. The worst is that the rest of the team's morale suffers as they see unacceptable behaviors tolerated or even rewarded. You must work to convince the problem person that the team's goals are his own. If his behavior doesn't change, get him off your project as soon as possible. His absence will be more than compensated for by the rest of the group's continued productivity.

■ **Noisy, crowded offices.** According to *Peopleware*, programmers who have their own offices, with doors they can close and phones they can turn off to avoid interruptions, are up to 2.6 times more productive than those working in "bullpen" or cubicle environments. Get private offices for your programmers, or, failing that, try to sequester them in a quiet area of the building. If your office has a P.A. system, either disable it or discourage its use. One study shows that each employee in an intellectually demanding job should have 100 square feet of dedicated work space, and 30 square feet of work surface. Also, no one should work with a blank wall closer than 8 feet in front of him. Although some teams benefit from having everyone in one big room, which can do wonders to improve both communication and esprit de corps, you need to provide a reliable "quiet time" each day, when team members know they'll be able to focus on difficult tasks without the threat of interruption.

■ **Contractor failure.** Maintaining your schedule can be a nightmare when you're relying on an external group to deliver a vital piece of technology or art. See Chapter 9, "External Resources," for an extensive discussion of managing external resources.

■ **Requirements gold plating.** If a project is too ambitious in too many areas, you're headed for trouble. Choose your battles. Instead of trying to innovate in every facet of the game, thereby adding enormous uncertainty to your schedule, perhaps you should be content to rely on the tried-and-true in a few areas, embracing them for their predictability and low risk.

■ **Developer gold plating.** Managers aren't the only ones who ask for extra features. Very often in the course of development, team members themselves think up cool new features they want to add to the game. Often, they don't realize the effect these unplanned additions have on the schedule. (It's especially hard to say no to one of these features when a team member offers to implement it "on my own time." The problem here is that few game elements stand completely on their own. The extra feature might have to be supported by additional art, AI, programming, or even changes to the design.) Each proposed feature must be scrutinized to determine how much it really costs to implement, what its full effect is on the team, and whether it adds to the fun of the game. Tradeoffs become a way of life here. When you've identified the core set of features that the game can't ship without, everything else becomes a nice-to-have that goes on the trading block as the team decides which features they want to kill so that other features can live.

- **Insufficient management controls.** You must be able to track your progress in meaningful ways to determine whether you're on schedule. Break down the development process into discrete chunks of no more than two months. This not only gives you specific goals against which you can track your progress, but also gives the team a series of goals to accomplish and successes to celebrate, rather than one long slog toward a distant finish line.

- **Omitting necessary tasks from estimates.** Some tasks never seem to make it onto the task list, but nevertheless take up valuable time. New-hire interviews. Project meetings. Code reviews. Creating screen grabs for marketing. Days missed because of trade shows or industry events such as E3, SIGGRAPH, or GDC. You need to include these things in your estimates.

- **Misunderstood tasks.** Sometimes a task makes it onto the schedule, but there is a "disconnect" about what the person who requested the task really wants. What do you do, for example, when marketing asks you to prepare a trade show demo? Showing pieces of the latest version in a back room is vastly different from releasing a playable demo to the public. Make sure that you know what you're being asked to produce before you schedule the time for the task.

- **Distributed development teams.** If your team is geographically dispersed, you must work hard to make sure that communication doesn't break down. Build more travel than usual into your budget, and make sure that people use it. (Even if there doesn't seem to be a point to getting together for a given meeting, the simple act of gathering people together in one room *always* results in ideas emerging that otherwise wouldn't.) Make sure that your design documents are available to everyone on your internal Web site. Upgrade to high-speed Internet access as part of your infrastructure, both for your home office and for your off-site workers, especially if they are artists, level designers, or anyone who will need to transmit large files.

- **The Not-Invented-Here syndrome.** Many developers are mistrustful of software that wasn't developed in their own shop. Yet often it's better to buy technology than to build it. For each of the game subsystems (and the tools used to develop them), make a survey of what's available elsewhere within your organization or off the shelf. Save your own developers for working on the features that will make your game great.

- **Pop-up tasks.** Throughout the course of development, management will ask you to provide people for unplanned tasks that just seem to pop up. It could be anything from sending someone to the European office for a demo to having your artists prepare high-resolution screenshots for a magazine cover. You need to budget in some time for this at the beginning of the project. When that budget is exceeded, you must say no, or at least be able to explain the effect it will have on the schedule so that management can decide for themselves how important their request is.

- **Waiting too long to fix bugs.** Some developers claim that there's no point in fixing bugs until near the end of the development process. This is wrong. Fixing bugs not only uncovers other, hidden bugs, but also creates more bugs! According to *The Mythical Man-Month*, "Fixing a defect has a substantial (20-50 percent) chance of introducing another." Bugs should be fixed as they're found. This significantly reduces the unknowns in a project and makes the schedule more accurate as the end approaches.

Many of these problems can be avoided if you schedule some of your own time each week for risk management. Look ahead to see what problems could be coming your way. Think about how to prevent them, and develop strategies for dealing with them if they happen anyway.

Recovery

The deadliest problem in the earlier scenario is that the team didn't know what to do after they had fallen behind.

Ineffective Strategies

When projects start to slip, managers typically have one of several reactions:

- **Plan to catch up later.** "They're two days behind, but we're only two weeks into the schedule, so there's plenty of time to make it up." Most often this is coupled with some sort of denial that a slip has actually occurred. A slip of two days after two work weeks is actually a twenty-percent slip! The remedy to this is to track your project closely enough to recognize when slips are occurring, and to address them immediately.

- **Require mandatory overtime.** "Everyone will just have to work harder." Although asking for small amounts of voluntary overtime can sometimes be effective for a short time just prior to major milestones, studies show that extended periods of mandatory overtime result in a significant drop in productivity. When you require mandatory overtime, several things happen: As developers tire, they make more mistakes, which results in more testing and reworking. People who are required to spend more time in the office start to attend to personal tasks on company time, reducing their effective work time. Most importantly, their motivation plummets, and motivation is the single greatest predictor of productivity.

Instead of requiring people to work overtime, it is much more effective to ask them to concentrate on making the best use of their 40-hour work week.

- **Add people to the project.** "If it's a question of man-months, let's throw on more men." If you're at the beginning of a long project, you think that you're under-staffed, and the tasks can be sensibly reapportioned across the team, adding people may indeed be the right solution. However, if you're well into a project and you've fallen behind, adding people will almost never help you catch up. New people must come up to speed on the project, which means that other team members have to take time away from their own tasks to train them. The volume of e-mail increases, team meetings take longer, and communication becomes more difficult. As noted in *The Mythical Man-Month*, ". . . when schedule slippage is recognized, the natural (and traditional) response is to add manpower. Like dousing a fire with gasoline, this makes matters worse, much worse."

- **Hold more meetings.** The more extraneous tasks people have, the less work they accomplish. The problem actually goes deeper than that. Intellectual work requires entering a state of *flow*, where the mind becomes fully immersed in the problem. Studies show that this process takes about fifteen minutes. Every time you interrupt someone, all the mental balls he was juggling fall to the ground, and he has to begin the process all over again. Creating a workday full of reports, meetings, and interruptions almost guarantees that creative work will be delayed.

  This isn't to say that important meetings should be abandoned, however. One of the most effective techniques of extreme programming is the daily "stand-up" meeting. This is a very short session at the beginning of each day when the team gathers in a room, and each person (including managers) says in 30 seconds or less what he'll be working on that day. No one sits down, which encourages brevity. Everyone gets a quick understanding of the project's status, and managers can take note of issues that will need follow-up later. The whole thing should never last more than 10-15 minutes.

- **Close their eyes and make a wish.** "It's probably not as bad as it looks, and everything bad that could happen already has. Probably." When managers engage in wishful thinking, they're hoping against hope that things will turn out right without requiring them to act. This never works. Software projects must be constantly monitored and managed. Problems that aren't addressed as soon as they come up become worse as time passes. The captain who keeps his ship on course with a series of gentle nudges reaches port more quickly and safely than the captain who steers by dead reckoning and lashes the wheel in place so that he can go flog the sailors.

The Back of the Wagon

If these strategies for recovery aren't effective, what strategies are? As we've seen, the biggest single factor affecting a project's schedule is its scope.

(You can see what's coming, can't you?)

The single most effective way to cut a project's schedule is to decrease its scope.

Obviously, scoping the project appropriately at the beginning would be a big help. However, if you run into trouble along the way, reducing the number of features you plan to deliver is the single fastest way to get back on track. Every feature you eliminate creates savings in design, asset creation, implementation, integration, testing, and debugging.

This still requires careful planning, however. Pulling features out of a game at the last minute can leave holes, create bugs, and demoralize the team. The solution is to prioritize, identifying the difference between core features and nice-to-have's from the very start of the project. This has enormous benefits:

- If you gear your development toward finishing the high-priority items first, the team will be motivated to work efficiently so that they'll have time to implement the features on their wish list.

- You create the most important fixed assets first, which means that you won't get caught short at the end. This also means that you'll be less likely to waste money creating fixed assets that are never used.

- If everyone knows ahead of time that a feature might be cut, they are less emotional if it has to be killed. This is especially true if it's someone's pet feature that he's been working on feverishly, only to learn at the last minute that it won't be in the game.

- You won't create gaping holes in your design by killing a feature. You knew all along that it might get cut, so you made sure that the game would be complete without it.

In short, if the schedule and cost are the wolves that are chasing you, it helps if you have a few features ready to push off the back of the wagon to lighten the load and keep those wolves at bay.

Other Recovery Strategies

After scope, the second biggest variable in the schedule is the team's level of productivity. The largest influence on productivity is motivation, so try to keep everyone invested in the project. Piling on the pressure only leads to a vicious circle of increased stress, more mistakes, decreased motivation, and more schedule slips.

Instead, If your project is in serious trouble, recovery is likely to come from a combination of strategies. Identify some short, discrete tasks that can be easily tracked so that people get used to feeling successful. Eliminate problem personnel. Make changes to the workplace to create a more developer-friendly atmosphere. Identify core features, and eliminate any activities that aren't geared toward delivering them.

Whether or not you pursue any or all of these strategies, the most important thing is that you regain the confidence of the team by creating a plan everyone believes in, even if it means pushing out the schedule.

Management Style

As you ponder these issues, remember that the corporate management styles of the past simply don't work in the game industry. Executives cannot remain aloof from the process and issue dictums that work their way down through the corporate hierarchy, being interpreted by successive layers of managers until they reach the peons who do the actual work.

If you're a manager, you must become part of the team. Just because you're fulfilling certain functions that are traditionally associated with leadership doesn't mean that you can dictate everything about the job to your "subordinates." As DeMarco and Lister remind us in *Peopleware*, "The manager's function is not to make people work, but to make it possible for people to work."

Here are some approaches to the job that can help:

- Don't issue orders. Ask people for their input.
- Don't hand down the schedule and features as if they were carved in stone. Develop the feature list and schedule with the team. Make sure that everyone knows how important the project is to your company's fortunes.
- Don't discourage people from telling you about problems. Actively seek out problems so that you can kill them before they become bigger.
- Don't panic when problems arise. Gather all the information you can, and work with the people who have the skills to come up with potential solutions.
- Don't personalize problems. When something goes wrong, stay focused on the potential solutions.
- Don't make decisions in a vacuum. Get the facts. See whether the team can reach a consensus decision, but if they can't, be prepared to make the final decision yourself.

- Try to create a work environment where people have several uninterruptible hours of flow time each day. Keep paperwork tasks to a minimum.

- Don't hide information from the team because "they can't handle it." Be honest about the factors that affect your project.

- Don't hide turbulence within the company. Lay out the facts as you know them, both good and bad, and let the team draw their own conclusions. Better that they hear the facts from you than the rumors on some Web site.

- Don't work nine to five and expect everyone else to put in punishing hours. Establish a schedule that allows everyone to work reasonable hours.

- Don't go home at 5:00 during crunch time "because you have nothing to do." Stay with the team through the evening to help in any way you can, even if it's just going out to pick up the food.

- Don't dangle false promises in front of the team to get them to make sacrifices for the project. If extraordinary performance is called for, arrange for meaningful rewards at the end of the project, and make sure that those rewards are delivered.

We work in a volatile industry. Change begets uncertainty and fear. You owe it to your team to create the best possible environment, despite the chaos that surrounds them. If you are habitually honest, realistic, and dedicated to making great games, the people around you will be happier and more productive, and so will you.

PART IV

THE BUSINESS

CHAPTER 12

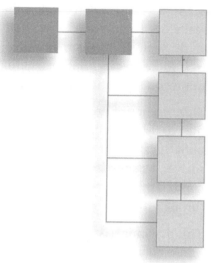

THE BUSINESS

"**B**uild a better mousetrap and the world will beat a path to your door."

If only it were true. The fact is, your mousetrap has to be financed, marketed, and sold before you can open your door to find the world waiting outside.

In this chapter, you'll learn how games are sold, what the other members of the publishing team do, and how development deals are put together.

How Mainstream Games Are Sold

It used to be that a new game had four to six months after its release to find an audience. Advertisements were timed to appear a few weeks after the initial shelf date, because marketers didn't see any sense in promoting something the public couldn't buy yet. Magazines focused on reviews instead of previews, because they wanted to see the final product before passing judgment. TV ads were unheard of.

No more.

Today, a game has as little as two weeks to prove that it belongs on retailers' shelves. Chain stores have specific targets for "turning" their shelves and are strict about enforcing them. If your game isn't meeting those goals soon after it comes out, your sales group will come under immediate pressure for markdowns (sometimes called *price protection*) or returns.

Many developers don't realize that when their game goes onto a store shelf, it hasn't really been sold yet. The retailer has the right to return it to the publisher for a 100% credit against future products. This creates an interesting struggle between the retailer, who wants to carry only games that sell well, and the publisher, who wants *all* his games to stay on store shelves as long as possible.

This balance of power is usually even: The retailer wants a supply of games to sell, and the publisher wants a place to sell his games. Sometimes, however, the equation becomes unbalanced. If the retailer has a large backlog of the publisher's games languishing on his shelves, he can refuse to bring in more until the deadwood is cleared out. On the other hand, if a publisher has a hot new game coming out, he can try to muscle other games through the door on its coattails.

This dynamic has prohibited small, independent publishers from flourishing. When you have only one or two games per year, you're too risky a proposition for the retail channel to deal with. They're afraid (and rightfully so) that if one of your games isn't successful, they'll have no realistic chance of getting back their money and will be stuck holding the bag. With larger publishers, new products are always coming along, and it's in the best interest of both parties to clear up inventory problems as the year goes by.

Before a retail buyer will pick up a game, he has to be convinced that it will sell. He uses various guidelines to help with this decision: the pitch from the sales force, the sell sheet, the box art, the industry buzz, and above all, preorders. This means that the marketing, PR, and sales campaigns all must be geared to create maximum consumer demand for your game *before it even ships*!

Games almost never start slowly and then ramp up. Generally, their largest sales come within four weeks of their release, and their shelf life is determined by how slowly their weekly sell-through numbers degrade thereafter. Exceptions are rare and usually are caused by chance factors, such as a popular movie suddenly sparking interest in a particular subject.

This pressure to create advance demand is why you see advertisements for games that won't be out for six months. It's why publishers push magazines to run previews of their games. It's why Web sites have sprung up devoted to games in development. More than anything else, it's why there's such pressure on the development team to deliver the game *on time*.

Consider the leaps of faith a publisher must make when he accepts your word that you'll "go gold" on a particular date:

- The operations group books a time slot at the disc duplication plant months in advance, especially before the busy Christmas season. For console games, a slot is reserved in the console company's manufacturing queue. If your game is late, another slot might not be available, and the game could miss Christmas altogether.

- The marketing group must commit to magazine ad space months ahead of time. The ads are going to run whether or not your product is ready. If you're late, the game could hit the stores with no current advertising push, because the ads ran months ago and no money is left in the budget for new ones.

- The sales group buys premium space in stores for your game. End caps and other special promotions are slotted out well ahead of time by the retail channel. If your company signs up for one of these and your game doesn't show up on time, the company pays for it anyway, and someone else gets the benefit of that premium placement. Then, when your game does come out, you will sell-in only a few copies per store . . . and they'll probably be displayed spine-out, on the bottom shelf, and in the wrong section!

- The PR department pushes, prods, begs, and pleads for premium magazine editorial coverage timed to hit the streets just before your game is due out. If you miss your ship date, the buzz will fade away, no magazine will give you that coverage again, and your game will come out in obscurity.

- The marketing group can also decide to advertise your game on television, but they don't just want to throw out 30-second spots randomly across the broadcast day. Ad slots on programs with the right demographics for your game could be in heavy demand and should be booked well in advance. Furthermore, the sales bump from a television ad is immediate and short-lived, so it's pure folly to do one for a game that isn't available on the shelves. Put yourself in the shoes of your marketing director. Would you commit in October to a $1,000,000 TV campaign for December, while at the same time your developer is telling you that the game "will be done when it's done"?

The Publishing Team

Let's take a look at the team that creates this carefully orchestrated campaign. Knowing what they do and how to work with them is vital to your success.

Public Relations (PR)

Well before your game comes out, the people in your PR group will start beating the drum for it. Their targets are trade magazines, Web sites, general-interest magazines, newspapers, even radio and television. Their success is measured in previews, reviews, feature coverage, and the biggest prize of all: magazine covers (see Figure 12.1). Their

Figure 12.1 Magazines like *Computer Gaming World* have an enormous influence on gamers' opinions. Used with permission of *Computer Gaming World.*

weapons are anything they can lay their hands on: demos, videos, concept art, interviews with the development team, and above all, screenshots.

PR professionals spend their lives cultivating relationships. If people can't trust them, those relationships are shot. Thus, they have the delicate task of always telling the truth, even when it's embarrassing, yet doing so in a way that puts the company and its products in the best possible light.

They have to stay in touch with people without getting in their faces. They have to be professional at all times, which is especially difficult when so many business occasions take the form of social events. They have to send out materials relentlessly, and then make follow-up calls to people who don't have time to talk to them.

They have to work hard to understand all the products they're promoting. They can't just mindlessly repeat what a developer has told them, because many of the journalists they talk to play more games than anyone else in the business. They know that they're not going to "snow" a magazine editor about your game. Instead, they try to bring out what they believe are its good points, and explain why they think it deserves coverage and a good review.

To do all this, they need materials and information that only the developer can supply.

Marketing

The marketing team has two goals: to help you target the game for a particular market, and to persuade everyone in that market to buy your game.

To do the first, they study demographics. They advise the business group on the appropriateness of particular licenses. They try to determine whether certain features of your game will help or hurt your chances with your target group. They tell you which of these features will affect the game's rating, and how that rating will affect your sales. They help you understand cultural differences that can determine how your game is received in foreign countries.

To reach their second goal, persuading people to buy the game, they create an image for the game and try to let everyone in the target market know about it. Their primary weapon is advertising. (Here, we're making an artificial distinction between marketing and public relations. In reality, PR is usually part of the marketing department, and the two groups work hand in hand to achieve maximum exposure for the game.)

When the marketing group is developing an image for your game, they're likely to fall back on the original high concept. They'll incorporate that message into all the various materials they develop, from magazine ads and sell sheets to Web banners and TV spots.

Marketers think in terms of impressions. How many times has someone been exposed to your message? How many times does he have to see it before he remembers it? When they're selecting which media to use, they think in terms of cost per thousands. They're very selective, however, about *which* thousands they're targeting. It does no good to promote a game to people who have little chance of buying it. Your marketing group will work out a plan that reaches as many people in your target audience as possible, for as little money as possible.

Their decisions will be affected by your positioning strategy. Does your game target the hardcore or casual gamer? Each demographic requires its own marketing strategy. Can you achieve maximum sales by starting with the hardcore gamer and building word of mouth from these key influencers? Are you better off taking a mass-market approach and promoting the game to casual gamers, so that everyone is eager to buy it the day it's released? This decision doesn't affect just the marketing campaign—it affects the game design itself. If you're targeting the hardcore gamer, you need to create competitive features and depth of gameplay. If you're going after the casual gamer, the game must be easily accessible and can't have any of the common barriers to purchase, such as graphic violence, sex, or foul language.

The marketing group can also suggest specific features that will help the game find a broader audience and give it longer legs. For example, creating chat capabilities and lobby areas in online games helps build a stronger community, and enables the game to survive longer and attract more people.

If development and marketing aren't talking with each other throughout the game development process, you're just asking for failure.

Sales

The sales force maintains personal relationships with the channel buyers who order your game in bulk. These buyers work for chain stores, national or regional distributors, "club" stores, video rental chains, and even original equipment manufacturers (OEMs). Each of these customers requires a different approach, and each approach requires different game material to support it.

Chain Stores

Chain stores make money only if they constantly turn over their inventory. Customers rarely think about this, but the continuing need to *move* product is the driving economic force behind every retail business. That's how they pay the rent. At some level, retail executives aren't concerned with selling your game at all—what they care about is getting enough money to pay for the space your game is taking up.

In suburban malls and other prime retail locations, rents are high. Games that don't sell quickly aren't paying for the space they're taking up, so they're sent back and replaced by other games that do. This is why we've become such a "hits" business. Retailers don't care about providing a broad selection if most of that selection doesn't move. If they could get away with stocking only one product that sold enough to cover their costs, that's the only product they'd carry. There is no romance in retail.

As we have seen, this leads buyers in the chain stores to want a continuing relationship with large publishers who have a lot of product to move. They also want the publishers to pay for promoting games at the retail level. This MDF (Market Development Fund) money is used to buy special positioning in the store, and ads in the store's flyers and newspaper circulars. (When you receive an advertisement that's crammed with small pictures of software products, it's not because the store has singled out those products to recommend. Each of those square inches is actually an advertisement bought and paid for by a publisher.)

Generally, the amount of MDF a store asks a publisher to pay is a percentage of the anticipated sales for the year. At the beginning of the year, the chain sends around a booklet containing various combinations of end caps, shelf talkers, circulars, stand-ups, mobiles, storefront pyramids, and so on. The more business a publisher does with the chain, the more programs he's expected to commit to. (If you're a developer being paid royalties, the money that pays for this can even be deducted from your royalty basis.) Among the most effective of these in-store promotions is a rolling demo of your game, or better still, an interactive demo that hooks customers on the spot.

Most chains also have an annual meeting where they gather all their managers for training and inspirational sessions. A portion of this meeting is usually reserved for a miniature trade show where publishers push their latest products from 8 × 10 booths. Less fancy than the big shows such as E3, Comdex, and CES, these events generally feature lightning-fast game demos and giveaways of T-shirts, tchotchkes, and other products. The goal of the sales group is to tell store managers about upcoming products so that they'll recommend your games to their clerks and customers.

Distributors

Not every retailer buys directly from the publishers. Many go through national or regional wholesalers. This enables "mom and pop" stores to carry less inventory but still access a wide range of products. This arrangement benefits the publishers as well, because they have fewer relationships to manage.

The sales group's job is to encourage the wholesaler's representatives to be aware of and promote the game. The distributor usually has a telephone boiler-room filled with salespeople, each of whom keeps in touch with a number of small retail stores. It's not unusual for a publisher to organize a special day at the wholesaler's place of business to promote his products. He comes in with promotional material such as T-shirts and caps, and spends the day with the group. He sets up a continually running video of his products that the reps can look at during their coffee breaks. He can also offer a SPIFF to the group (Sales Performance Incentive Fund; no one seems to know where the extra *F* comes from). He gives them direct cash rewards based on the amount of his product they sell on that particular day, and gives a prize to the person who moves the most units while he's there. Overall, his goal isn't just to get a sales bump for that particular day, but also to educate the sales reps about the game so that they'll promote it to their customers in the future.

OEM (Original Equipment Manufacturers)

An *OEM* is a company that makes hardware, including computers, graphics or sound cards, joysticks, and mice. These companies want to bundle software with their hardware to add extra value to their products, and to distinguish themselves from their competition.

OEM deals are large-volume, low-unit-price deals that get your game out to a general audience that might not otherwise see it. The profit per unit is usually quite small, but it's guaranteed and usually paid up front. An OEM deal can require the development group to prepare a special version of the game that's optimized to work with that particular piece of hardware and show off its features.

Selling the Salesmen

The members of your sales team lead hectic lives. Always traveling, they're in a constant cycle of pushing new product while managing down the old. When they go on a sales call, they might have only one hour of the buyer's time to pitch 30 or more products. At a trade show, they have only minutes. The games they regard as the most important get the most time, and you want your game to be one of them. How do you do this? By making sure that they know what your game is about, and by cooperating with your marketing group to create good support materials.

If you're a designer or producer, part of your job is to sell your own sales team on the project. Explain to them why they'll make money on it. You have to get them enthusiastic about it before they can get anyone else excited. The *real* secret is to get them hooked on your game—no one sells a game like one of its fans!

If you're an independent developer or a small publisher who distributes through a larger organization, it's also smart to participate with the sales force on their calls to buyers. First of all, no one can represent your product as well as you can. Second, it helps the sales force understand your product. Third, it provides a change of pace in the middle of the sales presentation, which both the sales rep and the buyer will appreciate. If you're given this chance, make sure that you can present the game swiftly and efficiently. Finally, it keeps your game from getting lost at the bottom of the sales rep's bag.

Promotional Tools

We've established that the PR, marketing, and sales groups need information and materials about the game so that they can promote it to the outside world. To do their jobs, they need screenshots, concept art, videos, sell sheets, interviews with the development team, demos, and so on. What we *haven't* established is how they can get these things without disrupting the development schedule.

The only answer that makes sense is to build the time it takes to supply these items into the development schedule in the first place. The smart producer works with every department from the start, finding out what they'll need and when they'll need it, so that he can make a plan and deliver it all on schedule.

The developers have to recognize that these materials will help their game in the long run, and they need to schedule in the time to create them. The publishing groups have to recognize that if they ask for more than what has been planned, they must be prepared to step gingerly.

When a chasm develops between the development group and these other departments, it's most often because one group doesn't understand what the other needs in order to be successful. In extreme cases, you'll find people lined up on opposite sides of the chasm throwing rocks at each other. When that happens, the game itself falls into the chasm and dies.

Demos

Why is creating a demo such a big deal? Isn't the game up and running in some form every day? Why can't we just dump everything onto a CD and send it out?

First of all, the everyday version of a game in development is nothing like the finished product. It's loaded up with debug code—perhaps as much as 50% of the code in the build at any given time is mere "scaffolding" to help the developers build the game itself. This code can make the game run slowly and interfere with gameplay. Often, to show the product properly, you have to strip out the debug code, which can involve a lot of work. Imagine if every time the Pope wanted to show off the progress on the Sistine Chapel, Michelangelo had to remove all the scaffolding from the room and then put it back again afterwards. (Not that our games are comparable to that great work of art, but you get the idea.)

In addition, game demos come in several flavors, depending on where in development the game is, the purpose of the demo, and its intended audience. As you saw in the preceding section, a demo can last anywhere from just a few seconds (for example, when it's part of a video) to several hours (when journalists come onsite for an in-depth look at the game while it's in development). Typical demo lengths are

- **Five seconds or less.** Clips or screenshots for a video.
- **Thirty seconds to two minutes.** A highly distilled presentation of the high concept, usually something a buyer can "get" in under two minutes.
- **Five to ten minutes.** A narrated, looping video that shows screenshots and gameplay, useful for trade shows, PR kits, Web site downloads, and in-store kiosks.
- **Ten minutes and up.** An interactive demo used on magazine demo disks, trade show stations, Web site downloads, and in-store kiosks.
- **Hours.** An in-depth presentation of many facets of the game over the course of a day.

Typical audiences for demos include:

- **Journalists.** Gaming fans who are always looking for something new. They're likely to be impressed by technological advances.
- **Buyers.** Harried people without much time. They're looking for a quick presentation of the high points that will make the game a hit.
- **Trade show audiences.** Industry insiders looking for the flashy stuff that signals "the next big thing."
- **The general public.** Gamers who want to play a demo and figure out whether the game is fun.
- **Internal company groups.** Coworkers who need to learn what the game is about and what its features are, so that they can promote it to the outside world.

Demos aren't easy to make. They aren't "free" spinoffs of the regular development process. They have a different purpose than the overall game; a different rhythm, design, and execution. They should be designed with input from PR, marketing, and sales to maximize their effectiveness with the intended audience. They have to be programmed and tested. They are, in effect, mini-projects unto themselves.

Also, it is wise to assume that anything you give to someone outside the company will eventually find its way into the hands of the public. Each demo should represent the game at its very best. No one should ever say to the development team, "Just throw together a quick demo so I can drop it off with a buyer next week." You might all be embarrassed when it shows up on the Web the following week.

The wise producer will sit down at the beginning of the project with the tech lead and people from PR, marketing, and sales to discuss the best times in the development cycle to create various demos. The tech lead will be happy to do this, because it gives him specific targets to shoot for, and he wants everyone to have the best promotional tools possible. (See the TDD template in Appendix A for an example of how these requirements can be worked into the technical schedule.)

Special requests always come up. If a leading magazine wants to put your game on the cover, no one will turn it down because this week's schedule doesn't include time to show off the game. But everyone has to be aware of the level of effort involved in impromptu demos, and they need to know that the extra work can throw the game off its schedule.

Interviews

Developers tend to think that the benefits of their projects are self-evident, so often they're not the best ambassadors for their own games. Nevertheless, journalists like to have access to the people who actually create the games. If you're a PR manager, try to set up interviews for editors with people on the development team. When you do this, try to go beyond the designer (who gets too much credit in the first place), and try to get coverage for the entire team. Perhaps there's a subteam that the journalist could focus on. If the game has great art, for example, see whether you can get coverage for the art director and his group. If the AI is a thing of beauty, try for a story featuring the tech lead and AI programmer. Not only will this help promote the game, but it will improve the team's morale. This, in turn, will make the game better.

If you do arrange an interview with a developer, let him know whom he's talking to and what that person's main interest is likely to be (programming, art, design, and so on).

Screenshots

In the PR wars, the game with the best screenshots wins.

Never turn an early version of your game over to a magazine or Web site and let them do their own screen grabs. They may use the wrong settings or pick a boring location. Your screenshots should be carefully chosen by someone on the team to show off the game to its maximum advantage. A picture is worth a thousand words, but only if the person creating it knows what he wants to say (see Figure 12.2).

The demand for screenshots before a game's release can be insatiable. Web sites are always clamoring for new and exclusive shots. Your PR group will be pressured for literally hundreds of unique shots before your game is released.

Figure 12.2 Skillfully created screenshots show games like *SimCity 3000* at their best. © 2000 Electronic Arts. All rights reserved.

There are two problems with this. First, it takes time and expertise to create a great screenshot. Second, if you're not careful, you'll overexpose your game, and people will feel that they've seen it all by the time it's released. Some producers solve the first problem by assigning one individual (usually an AP) to create all the screenshots. They solve the second problem by sequestering certain portions of the game and never releasing screenshots from those areas before the game comes out.

Sell Sheets

Sell sheets are usually one-page flyers that the sales force gives out to the retail trade. They contain an unusual mix of information. One part resembles the back of a game box, with a feature summary and attractive graphics or screenshots. Another section contains information of interest to the retail buyer, such as the size and nature of the marketing campaign (TV, radio, magazine), the anticipated release date, how many boxes are in a case, and so on.

Consumers never see these sheets. They're printed up only for use within the trade. However, they can be graphically linked to the advertisements or other marketing materials.

The Bottom Line

Even with all this activity, the publishing team can only open the door. Your product has to walk through it. Their jobs are all about access and relationships. If you support them well, they'll have a greater chance to succeed. But in the end, it's your game that must carry the day.

Business Development

Whether you're a publisher's producer working with an outside developer or an independent developer selling your wares to a publisher, at some point you'll find yourself sitting down to negotiate a development deal.

Both sides presume that lawyers will craft the final language of the contract. But before you bring the lawyers in, you should have already agreed on the major points of the deal. The lawyers' job is then to crystallize in unambiguous language what's been agreed on, ensure that the contract has the right form and language to commit each side to its obligations, and make provisions for the failure of either side to deliver on those commitments.

Each side should make all its intentions explicit in the contract. Unspoken agreements and unwritten understandings go up in smoke when the person you made those agreements with leaves the company, and all that's left behind is the written word.

What follows is a discussion of the deal points that need to be negotiated in most development contracts. Lesser issues, such as boilerplate language, aren't addressed.

Advances

An advance is a royalty that's paid before it's earned. Generally, for every unit a publisher sells, he pays the developer a percentage of the money received (see the next section, "Royalties"). The advance is money paid by the publisher to the developer *before* the product has sold those units. Generally, advances aren't recoupable. That is to say, after a publisher makes a payment to the developer, he usually can't get it back.

When a game has sold enough units to cover these advances, it's said to have *earned out*. Money paid to the developer after this point is commonly called *the back end*.

Publishers want the developer to get the lowest advances possible, not just for their own cash flow, but also as an incentive to the developer to make a great game so that he'll get to the back end. If a developer gets huge advances, he knows that the odds of earning out are slim, and there's correspondingly less incentive to extend himself on the game. Ideally, what the publishers want is a partnership in which the developer is participating in the risk. The more the developer shoulders the up-front costs, the higher his royalty will be.

The developer, on the other hand, wants the advances to be high enough to cover the costs of running his business while the game is in development. It's in neither party's best interests for the developer to go belly-up halfway through the project. On top of that, the developer wants to build in a little profit up front, because the publisher always retains the option to kill the game at any time. This can leave a developer who has been counting on reaching the back end high and dry. Sometimes this particular contingency is addressed by establishing a *kill fee*.

The negotiation over advances is always about each side finding the other's "point of pain," and determining whether an accommodation can be reached whereby both sides are only a *little* uncomfortable.

Royalties

Royalties vary greatly, and the percentage changes depending on how much risk the developer is willing to take on. Development houses that fund all their own development and don't take advances from the publisher are entitled to a higher royalty, because they're taking on that extra risk.

The basis of the royalty is also important. Usually, it's the wholesale price paid for the game (*not* the retail price), minus the COGS, marketing, and shipping. Other items that the publisher will request and the developer will resist are MDF, license fees, and the publisher's distributed overhead costs.

The royalty percentage is likely to decrease as the game is managed through its lifecycle. When the wholesale price drops below a certain percentage of its original price, the royalty can disappear altogether. Then the publisher can get rid of old product without being hampered by royalty accounting.

If a publisher and developer are working on more than one game at a time, the publisher can seek to cross-collateralize the games. This links the finances of the two. The practical result is that the publisher can withhold royalty payments on one product if the other product hasn't earned out its advances. This is favorable to the publisher and will be resisted by the developer.

Reserve Against Returns

Because retail stores can return 100% of their stock to the publisher at any point, a game isn't truly sold until it has sold through. In other words, until the customer takes it to the checkout lane. (Even then, things can get dodgy, because some stores give limited return rights to their customers. Even a unit that has sold through can sometimes find its way back to the publisher.)

Because publishers hate to go back to a developer and try to extract money they've already paid, they build in a reserve against returns. Whenever a royalty is due, the publisher holds back a certain percentage of it, just in case the game eventually comes back from the retailer. This reserve ranges from 15% to 30%. The higher number favors the publisher, and the lower number favors the developer. Generally, the reserve is liquidated over a period of twelve to eighteen months. Here again, the higher number favors the publisher; the lower number favors the developer.

Milestones and Deliverables

Advances are generally hooked to *milestones*, which are significant points in development marked by the completion of a certain amount of work, or a *deliverable*. An initial advance is usually paid on the signing of the contract, but the rest of the payments hinge on completion of the deliverables. The milestones should be broken out in an appendix to the contract, and their deliverables should be defined very precisely. This protects both sides. If you're a developer and you've done the work, you want to be paid. If you're a publisher and the developer hasn't done the work, you don't want to pay. The best way to keep this hassle-free is with concrete deliverables (see the "Milestone Definitions" section in Chapter 10). The best deliverables are binary: They're either complete or they're not, with no room for argument.

It's entirely reasonable for the milestone dates and deliverables to change over the course of development. This happens all the time. Just make sure that the new deliverables are as specific as the original ones, and be sure to issue an amendment to the contract. (That's why it's easier to put them in an appendix in the first place, rather than sprinkling references to them throughout the document.)

Make sure that the mechanism for accepting milestones is defined in the contract. Generally, the publisher wants a certain amount of time to review the work and declare whether it satisfies the milestone. It's to the developer's advantage for this period to be as short as possible.

Rights

See Chapter 9, "External Resources," for a discussion of rights and intellectual property. Generally, each side of the table wants to retain as many rights as possible. If you're a developer with an original intellectual property (IP), think long and hard before assigning it to a publisher. If you're a publisher, think equally long and hard about throwing millions into developing and promoting an IP that the developer can walk away with after two years.

Proprietary Technology

The publisher needs to have access to all the code necessary to publish and maintain the game. The developer should have the right to hold onto his own game engine and tools. Some negotiation must take place here, but the issue should be explicitly addressed within the contract so that no disputes arise over who owns what after the companies go their separate ways.

Term

It's important to have a fixed length of time (or *term*) to any agreement. Neither side wants to create obligations that go on forever.

Termination

The effects of terminating the deal should be spelled out in the deal itself. If either side needs to terminate for breach, the method should be spelled out, as well as the consequences.

Confidentiality

This is usually not a big-deal point, and it can be covered in a separate NDA (non-disclosure agreement). At issue is deciding what's considered a trade secret or confidential information, the methods used to safeguard this information, and the conditions under which the information can be revealed. Typically, each side agrees to guard the other party's confidential information in the same way it guards its own. If the information is published or otherwise becomes available through a third party, they agree that the restrictions against discussing it are removed.

Ancillary Revenues

Usually, there's a provision in the agreement for royalty revenues from hint books, action figures, and so on. You won't get rich from these merchandising deals, but you do want to encourage the publisher to pursue them, primarily because they help elevate the game's image (and therefore sales) to core customers.

"Indie" Development

Not all developers are concerned with creating games that follow the mainstream model. There is a flourishing community of independent game makers who develop games "on their own," without the benefit of publisher advances (or the hindrance of publisher input!).

Indie developers are typically one-or-two-man shops who self-fund the development of relatively small games, which they then market through non-traditional means, usually a shareware try-before-you-buy model. The developer has complete control over the development process, the creative content of his game, and the ways in which it will be promoted and sold.

Indie games are generally sold online, either directly to customers through the developer's Web site or through a license arrangement with an Internet portal site. Most indies allow the customer to try out the game before purchasing it. They may give him access to the full game for a short period of time, or let him play a subset of the larger game that will whet his appetite for the full set of levels or features.

The challenges that face indie developers include the following:

- **Getting the game done.** Most indie developers have other jobs, at least when they start out. Finding the time to bring a game to completion is a daunting task.

- **Marketing.** Once you've created a game, you have to let people know it's out there. With little or no marketing budget, indies have to use guerilla marketing and PR techniques to get exposure for their products.

- **Collecting the money.** You want to make it as easy as possible for customers to pay you. For most people, that means credit cards. Some indies establish their own merchant accounts, which allow them to process credit card payments. Others turn to shareware registration companies or order-processing services who will handle payment and fulfillment for a fee.

- **Working alone.** Going your own way can be a difficult road. Indies often fail to benefit from the experience of others, and they sometimes feel isolated from the development community. One way to remedy this is to join the Association of Shareware Professionals (www.asp-shareware.org).

The rewards for "going indie" are many. You have the freedom to set your own hours, develop only the kinds of games you want, and be the captain of your own ship. For more information on the indie life, check out the following links:

http://www.infinisource.com/shareware.html

http://www.upload.it/

http://www.dexterity.com/articles/

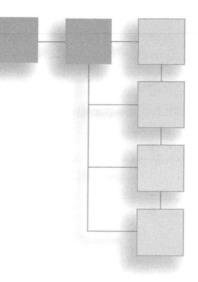

CHAPTER 13

BREAKING IN

I f you are not working in the industry yet, this chapter gives you some pointers on how to break in.

The bad news: Lots of other people have the same goal, so you face stiff competition.

The good news: The industry is large, and it has a high turnover rate. If you're talented, enthusiastic, well prepared, persistent, and willing to relocate, you'll almost certainly catch on somewhere.

General Advice

As you've seen in this book, games emerge from the collaborative effort of specialists with varied areas of expertise. What employers want from an applicant depends on the position he seeks, but we can make some generalizations.

Getting Ready

Before you get in touch with a game company, you must acquire skills that make you useful. No one wants to hear an applicant say, "I've been playing games all my life, and I just *know* I can learn to program if you'll only give me a chance." Companies want to hear from people who already have the necessary skills.

For some, this means formal education in university-level courses. Whether you're a programmer, an artist, a writer, a musician, or a manager, it's important that you master the fundamentals of your trade.

For others, formal education is just a distraction. Many of the most highly regarded people in the business have little or no college education and are largely self-taught.

Going to college is still recommended, however. Having a degree comes in handy if you decide the industry isn't for you and you need to make a career change. A college education also helps you become a more well-rounded person. By learning about the world outside your area of expertise, you bring a broader perspective to the problems you face within your specialty. Also, if two candidates for a job are equally matched professionally, the more interesting person is likely to get the job, simply because the team would rather work with him.

You should have a passion for playing games—but it's not enough merely to *play* them. You must *analyze* them (see Figure 13.1). Try to understand what works and what doesn't. Decide what you would have done differently if you had designed it. If you dislike a popular game, try to figure out what makes it appealing to others.

Figure 13.1 Web sites like Gamasutra.com are devoted to all aspects of making games. Image courtesy of Gamasutra.com.

Figure 13.2 Hotbeds of game development in the United States.

Be willing to relocate. In the United States, the game business is concentrated in California, with strong communities in Washington state and Texas (see Figure 13.2). Other companies are scattered across the country. If none of them are nearby, you must be ready to pack your bags and go where the jobs are.

Remember: Above all, "luck is what happens when preparation meets opportunity."

Your Demo

Showing a great demo is the single fastest way to get hired in this business. Game companies are more interested in capabilities than credentials. No matter what your area of expertise, you're far better off *showing* that you can do the work than merely *saying* you can.

This is true of everyone, from programmers and artists to musicians and level designers. The tools used to build games are widely available, but you must show that you've mastered the ones that are relevant to your specialty.

Creating a demo shows many things to prospective employers:

- **You can do the work.** Your mastery of the tools will be evident to the professionals who use them every day.
- **You are self-motivated.** You took it upon yourself to create a substantial piece of work without a boss looking over your shoulder.
- **You have initiative.** You figured out the best way to communicate your skills.

- **You can finish what you start.** Anyone can *begin* a piece of work. By turning in a professional-quality demo, you show that you can follow through and get the job done.
- **You are enthusiastic.** No one without a strong desire to work in the industry is going to go through the pain of putting together a great demo.

Naturally, your demo should strut your best stuff. Don't include old work simply because you have it lying around. Use only your best material, and update the demo as your skills improve.

Once you've prepared yourself, it's time to make contact.

The Cover Letter and Resumé

The purpose of a cover letter is to get your resumé into the right hands. It should be brief and professional. Right away, you should mention the position you're interested in, and list any special reasons why you're qualified for the job. Everything else should go on the resumé itself.

Your resumé should be targeted at a professional in your field, not someone in human resources. It should contain a detailed summary of your skills, as well as any other information that reflects well on your ability to do the job. This can include university coursework, nonprofessional experience, and even hobbies you think are relevant.

In both of these documents, neatness counts. Check for spelling errors. Have a friend read them to catch any mistakes you might have missed. Communicating well is an important part of every job, and this is your first chance to show that you are up to the task.

Studies show that up to 25% of job hunters lie on their resumés. In this business, that's a foolish and dangerous tactic, and it's almost certain to be uncovered during your interview. Don't do it.

The Interview

Prepare for an interview the way you would a test. Try to learn ahead of time as much about the company as you can. Play its most recent games. Check industry news sites for recent stories about it.

Check with your interview contact ahead of time about what you should wear. At most places, it simply doesn't matter, but crossing it off your list of things to worry about will make you more relaxed on that day.

Be on time.

Some companies give you a test before you arrive. Others hit you with one when you walk in the door. Still others don't do any testing at all. These tests can be anything from a personality/compatibility test to an academic-style exam that checks your specific knowledge in your field of expertise.

Each company has its own way of conducting interviews, so be ready for variations.

One-on-one interviews generally focus on your professional knowledge (see Figure 13.3). You'll be asked how you put your demo together, the problems you faced, the solutions you considered, and why you made the choices you did. You might face very specific technical questions. If you don't know the answer to any question, say so. Don't try to fake it.

Group interviews are likely to take place over lunch with the team you'd be working with. The purpose of the lunch is to see whether your personality seems to fit the existing

Figure 13.3 You can add to your professional knowledge by reading magazines like *Game Developer*. Image courtesy of *Game Developer*.

team. Questions here are likely to be softer. What game genres do you like? What's your favorite game, and why? What music do you listen to? What books do you read? Be prepared to talk about "off-duty" interests; otherwise, you might come across as flat and boring. There's no point in trying to tailor these responses. Be yourself and hope for the best. Also, try to order food that comes in bite-size pieces so that you can concentrate on talking rather than eating.

Lunch is also a good opportunity to learn what it's like to work for the company. Ask your potential coworkers about the corporate culture, the workload, and the management style. If you're from out of town, ask about housing, traffic, and other lifestyle issues. If there has been a recent news story about the company, ask how it has affected the lives of the employees.

At the end of the interview day, you're likely to spend time with someone from human resources. Ask him or her about the company's benefits package and the organization's plans for the future. Know your salary requirements ahead of time, and be prepared to discuss them. Don't accept any job offer on the spot. Always allow yourself 24 hours to think it over and come up with any follow-up questions you might not have thought of during the interview.

Applying for Specific Positions

Each subdiscipline of game making has its own requirements, and what it takes to break in varies from position to position.

Programmers

Programmers are the most likely applicants to be given an actual test. Companies want to check your knowledge of physics and math, your familiarity with C or C++, and your ability to solve programming problems.

Your resumé should list your formal software training, your languages, and the types of programs you've created in the past.

Your demo should be small, working pieces of code that demonstrate skill in your particular specialty, whether it's engine programming, graphics, AI, audio, UI, tools, and so on.

If you're thinking of taking classes to learn programming, consider a basic computer science degree. This will give you a broad background against which you can specialize later.

Artists

Artists live and die by their demo reel. If you can create great art, it doesn't matter what formal training you've had.

What *will* matter, however, is whether you can use art tools such as 3DSMax and Maya. Art and technology are more intertwined than ever before, and you must know these tools the way other artists know charcoal and ink, paper and canvas. Be sure to include your knowledge of these tools on your resumé.

If you're thinking of getting some formal training, go for a degree in either fine arts or industrial design. Try to take classes in drawing, anatomy, geometry, color, and lighting. Be sure to pick a school that has courses in computer graphics, so that you can keep up with the tools being used in software development houses.

Level Designers

The only way to convince a game company that you can design good levels is to show them levels you've already built.

There's no formal training for this, no class you can take. Nevertheless, the training is available informally on the Web. Pick a popular game, learn how to use its editor, and become part of the MOD community. Submit your levels to contests. Invite critiques from users. Over time, your work should improve to the point that you're ready to show it to an established game company.

In the meantime, pursuing a liberal arts education will give you the background to create varied, interesting levels set in any period or culture. Even imaginary ones!

Producers

It's unusual to enter the game business as a producer, unless you've gained project management experience elsewhere in the software community. The most common path to becoming a producer is to start in testing and learn the business from the ground up. From testing, it's a small step to assistant producer (AP). As an AP, you learn the duties of a producer. As time goes by, you take on more and more responsibilities until one day you're given a game of your own.

Testers

Testing is the one area where you don't need any experience before you can apply. It helps if you've participated as a volunteer tester in open betas, but even that is not necessary. What companies are looking for are thoroughness and good communication skills.

No one is expected to stay in testing forever. It's generally regarded as the "mail room" of the industry, a stepping stone you can use to get to the job you *really* want.

Composers and Sound Effects Technicians

Breaking in as a musician or sound effects technician is very, very hard. Game companies receive hundreds of demo tapes and CDs each year, and many of them are never listened to. Persistence seems to be the answer. Attend the Game Developers Conference. Form personal contacts. Build a good Web site. Keep mailing out demos. The only way you're going to get work is if you can persuade someone to listen to what you've done.

Game Designers

Almost no one breaks into the industry as a game designer. Usually, people start in another role in the company, become proficient in that field, and then take on more and more design tasks until one of their original designs gets the green light.

To prepare yourself, learn what everyone else on the team does. You have to know enough about programming, art, and sound to understand the limitations of the medium. You have to keep up with technical advances so that you can design new gameplay around capabilities that didn't exist a few years ago (see Figure 13.4).

Figure 13.4 GameDev.Net has a cross-section of information about all aspects of game development. Image courtesy of GameDev.Net.

Beyond that, there's no formal training for this job. Read a lot of good books. Read a lot of junk. Watch movies, TV, and cartoons. Read magazines about scientific breakthroughs. Play games, and then read the reviews and postmortems. Listen to different kinds of music. Try to learn "what everyone knows." Games are mass-media entertainment and a part of the popular culture. You should be immersed in that culture, and you should also have a broad knowledge of the older culture that lies beneath it.

Finding Job Openings

The obvious first step to discovering who's hiring is to check game companies' Web sites for employment announcements. You should also read the Web sites that cover the industry, because many of them carry ads as well. (See Appendix B, "Resources," for a partial list of these sites.) *Game Developer Magazine* also carries employment ads in the back of each issue, as do several general-interest gaming magazines.

There are ways to dig a little deeper, however. Many of the development companies who do the contract work for larger publishers don't have the resources to advertise. To smoke out their job openings, go to their Web sites or even to the sites dedicated to individual projects. Sometimes a tech lead or producer will drop by and mention that he's looking for someone, well before the posting makes it to the company's official employment site.

An even more proactive strategy is to find out who the producer, tech lead, or art lead is on a given project and e-mail him directly.

Some companies have internship programs. If you're still in school, write to the publisher of your favorite game and see whether they have any openings. After you're on the inside, everything else depends on making good contacts and doing good work.

The common denominator underlying these strategies is to make personal contacts any way you can. Former Speaker of the House Tip O'Neill used to say, "All politics is local." In much the same way, all business is personal. Network as much as you can. Go to GDC. (If you can't afford the conference fee, go as a volunteer.) Join the IGDA and attend the local chapter meetings. If you want to become part of the industry, start by *being* a part of the industry. This is another area where the cliché is true: Persistence pays.

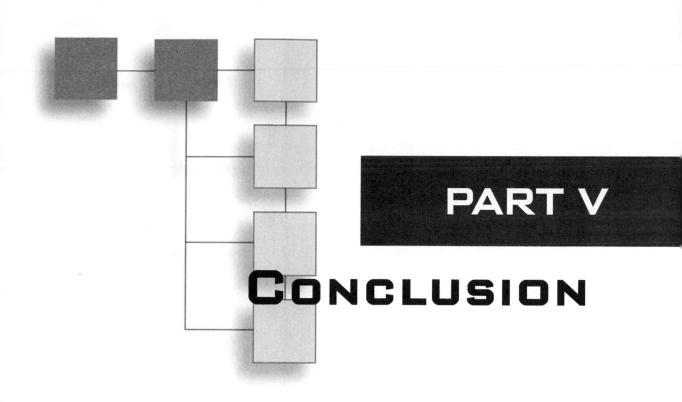

PART V

CONCLUSION

CHAPTER 14

CHAPTER 14

THE HERO'S JOURNEY

The realities of this business are harsh. Hours are long, projects are mismanaged, schedule pressure is relentless, and games never turn out the way you want. Collaborating is difficult, quality is often traded for money, projects are cancelled, and people routinely fear for their jobs.

Is it worth it?

In Joseph Campbell's classic *The Hero with a Thousand Faces,* he writes that a fictional hero must leave his community and go on a dangerous journey to recover something of value. Having survived the ordeal, he must bring back that prize to his community so that all can benefit from it. Those prizes are not easily won. Not only must the hero brave many dangers to acquire the prize, but when he returns home, he might also have to convince the community of its worth upon his return.

For a project team, the prize is the game. The team takes the journey together and, battling against all odds, they create something worthwhile—a game that reflects their collective vision and skills. When it's done, they present it to the community, which passes judgment on its value.

If you want to contribute to this team, you must undertake your own hero's journey. Whether you are a programmer, a tester, a designer, an artist, a musician, or a producer, you must acquire your own special expertise, your own unique vision to add to the creation.

This is not easy. You must study, serve an apprenticeship, and master your trade. Even then, you can never afford to stop learning. You must undertake the hero's journey not once but many times. Again and again, you must *do the work*.

But is it worth it?

A game's value is hard to pin down. It can be a mindless diversion or a mighty epic. It can help the player fill a lonely hour, or immerse him so deeply into another world that he has trouble maintaining contact with this one. It can have a story, theme, plot, and moral, or consist of stacking falling boxes on one another. Presumably, all these games have value to *someone*, because people keep paying money for them. Only you can decide which of these experiences is worth trading a slice of your life to create.

If you can look at a game design and see something of value to you, perhaps it's worth your labor to convert that potential to reality. If you see nothing of value and can think of no way to add any, perhaps you should think twice before signing up for the team.

We all have only one life to live, and we must each decide what we want to accomplish in that lifetime. Only the luckiest of us has the opportunity to combine his innate creativity with his livelihood. If we can harness that creativity to contribute a line to the human play, surely there is some value in that.

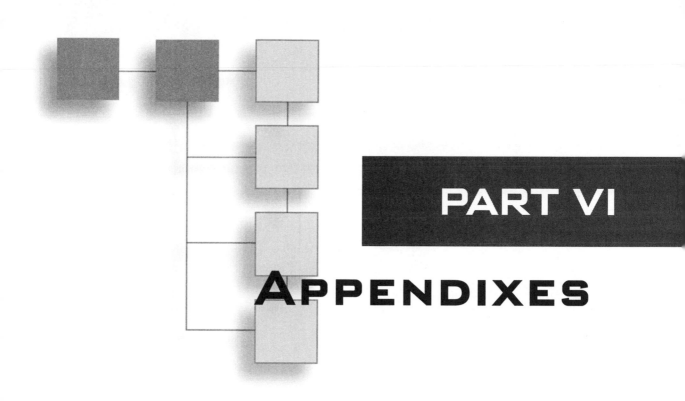

PART VI

APPENDIXES

PROJECT DOCUMENTS

T his appendix contains guidelines, outlines, or templates for creating most of the documents you'll need in the course of a project.

Lack of good communication is the single biggest obstacle to efficient software development, so it's worthwhile to think carefully about how these documents can best be developed and maintained.

The larger a document is, the less likely people are to read it. And in paper form, large documents are almost impossible to maintain. A good solution is to maintain your documents on an internal Web page, and it's best if everyone on the team can modify the information. Go to www.openwiki.com for a very powerful, *no-cost* solution to this problem.

The rest of this appendix will assume that you're maintaining your documents online.

Index to Documents

The "home page" of your internal Web page should contain a list of the major project-related documents. In turn, these documents may contain links to other sub-documents that are maintained by the teams working on particular areas of the game.

1. Index to Documents
2. High Concept
3. Pitch Doc
4. Concept Doc
5. Game Design Doc (GDD)
6. Art Production Plan
7. Technical Design Doc (TDD)
8. Test Plan
9. Project Plan
   a. Manpower Plan
   b. Resource Plan
   c. Project Tracking Doc
   d. Budget
   e. P&L
   f. Development Schedule
   g. Milestone Definitions
10. External Events
11. Current Risks
12. Credits List
13. Change List & Project Archives

High Concept Doc

This is a very short document, no more than a few sentences, that answers the question, "What is your game about?" See Chapter 1 for more details and examples. It may seem strange to devote an entire document to this brief document, but it's important to do so.

Like a company's mission statement, it's useful to print this up and post it around the office so everyone has a visible reminder of what they're trying to create. It should also be maintained in a prominent place on the organization's internal web.

If the high concept changes while the game is in development, that's a major event that should receive a lot of attention. If this happens, make sure to update this document and post new copies where everyone can be reminded how the basic course of the project has changed.

Game Proposal ("Pitch Doc")

This is the one- or two-page executive summary of the game that you give to prospective publishers during your pitch meeting. Ideally, it would be accompanied by a playable prototype of the game, as well as a more complete concept doc (see next section).

The game proposal document should have the following sections. See Chapter 1, "Getting to 'Yes'," for additional details.

1. High Concept. The one- or two-sentence statement of the experience you're trying to create.

2. Genre. A single sentence that places the game within a genre or a hybrid of genres.

3. Gameplay. A paragraph that describes what kinds of actions the player can perform during the game.

4. Features. A list of the major features that set this game apart, including anything from technical advancements to artistic style.

5. Setting. A paragraph about what makes the game world and its occupants unique and interesting.

6. Story. If the game has a story, summarize it here in a paragraph.

7. Target Audience. A single sentence that describes the demographic you're trying to reach.

8. Hardware Platforms. A list of devices your game can be played on.

9. Estimated Schedule and Budget. Your estimate of how long the game will take to develop and how much it will cost.

10. Competitive Analysis. A list of existing and planned games that will compete with yours.

11. Team. Names and credentials of the design, tech, and art leads. Also, list the games the organization has shipped.

12 Summary. A restatement of why this will be a great game, and why your team is the one to develop it.

Concept Doc

As discussed in Chapter 10, this is a more detailed version of the pitch document. It's too large to use in a presentation meeting, but you should leave it for the publishing team to give them a more in-depth understanding of your game.

1. High Concept. The one- or two-sentence statement of the experience you're trying to create. This shouldn't change from the pitch doc.

2. Genre. A discussion of the genre your game falls under. This section should include comparisons to other titles in the genre.

3. Gameplay. A description of the kinds of actions the player can perform during the game, along with some examples.

4. Features. The pitch doc listed the features that set this game apart. Here, you should go into more detail about why each of these features is important, and how you'll implement them.

5. Setting. Describe the game world in detail, and explain what makes it and its occupants unique and interesting.

6. Story. If the game has a story, describe it here in greater detail than in the pitch doc. Include the major characters, their motivations, and how they achieve (or fail to achieve) their goals.

7. Target Audience. Explain why the game will appeal to the target demographic you've identified.

8. Hardware Platforms. A list of devices your game can be played on. If you plan to develop different features for the various platforms, use this section to explain how the game will be different on each one.

9. Estimated Schedule and Budget. Break out the major phases of development, and the level of effort associated with each, to show how you arrived at the estimates in the pitch doc. Also include a P&L estimate if you have one. (See Chapter 10 for details.)

10. Competitive Analysis. List the games you'll be competing with for sales, and explain how your game will stack up against them.

11. Team. List the names and credentials of the design, tech, and art leads, as well as other key team members. Also, list the games the organization has shipped. Publishers place as much importance on the team as on the concept, so make sure this section convinces them that your organization is capable of delivering the product you're proposing.

12. Risk Analysis. Explain the risks the project faces, and how you plan to minimize them.

13. Summary. End on a high note. Emphasize again why this will be a great game, and why the publisher should have confidence in your team's ability to deliver it.

Game Design Doc (GDD)

This is the document that everyone involved with the game comes to for an understanding of the game's details.

Different parts of the document will take shape over time. You won't be ready to write final dialogue on the first day of product development, for example, but you should know how many characters you'll be asking the art team to create. Similarly, you won't have a detailed level walkthrough on day one, but you should know what will happen in each level, what equipment the player will start with, and what new toys he'll acquire.

What's important for you to realize is that at some point, you'll need to document all the information below, and you must keep it current. Failure to maintain an up-to-date game design document (or, more accurately, *set* of documents) will cause team members to waste their time creating features whose specifications have been altered, or that may no longer be needed at all.

You'll notice that a change list is not included as part of this document. While it's important to keep a change list for many documents (especially formal agreements between companies), it's hard enough to get people to read the *current* design document, much less slog through information that's out-of-date. Instead, see the final document in this appendix, which contains a separate change list and project archives.

The following game design doc template can be used for an action game, and it can be modified for games in other genres as needed. Please note that many of the "lists" should actually be maintained as linked spreadsheets or tables. Also note that the order of the sections is somewhat arbitrary; you should order the sections in your own GDD in the way that makes most sense to you.

See Chapter 10 for additional notes about developing and maintaining the game design document.

1. **Game Name**
   a. Copyright Information
2. **Table of Contents**
3. **SECTION I: PROJECT OVERVIEW**
   a. Team Personnel (with contact information for each individual)
      i.   Production Team
         1. Producer
            a. Office phone
            b. Home phone
            c. Cell phone
            d. E-mail

      2. Assistant Producer
         a. Same contact info as above
      3. Etc.
   ii. Design Team
      1. Design Lead
      2. Level Designer #1
      3. Writer #1
      4. Etc.
  iii. Programming Team
      1. Tech Lead
      2. Additional Programmers
   iv. Art Team
      1. Art Lead
      2. Additional Artists
    v. QA Team
      1. QA Lead
      2. Additional Testers
   vi. External Contractors
      1. Mocap Company
         a. Contact Name
         b. Contact Phone Number
         c. Company Address
      2. Composer
      3. Sound Effects House
      4. CGI house
      5. Voice Director
      6. Etc.
b. Executive Summary
    i. High Concept
   ii. The Hook
  iii. Story Synopsis and Setting
   iv. Genre & Scope (such as number of missions or levels)
    v. Visual Style (2D? 3D? Isometric? etc.)
   vi. Engine (and editor?)

    c. Core Gameplay (What does the player *do*?)
   - i. Single-player
   - ii. Co-op?
   - iii. Multiplayer?

    d. Game Features
   - i. Gameplay innovations
   - ii. Advances in AI
   - iii. Artistic techniques and achievements
   - iv. License tie-ins (if applicable)
   - v. Other features that will make this game better than others like it on the market

    e. Project Scope
   - i. Number of distinct locations
   - ii. Number of levels/missions
   - iii. Number of NPCs
   - iv. Number of weapons
   - v. Number of vehicles
   - vi. Etc.

    f. Target Audience

    g. Delivery Platform(s)

4. **SECTION II: STORY, SETTING, AND CHARACTER**

    a. Story
   - i. Back story
   - ii. In-game story (What happens during the game)

    b. Environments
   - i. Area #1
     1. General description
     2. Physical characteristics
     3. List of levels that take place in this area
   - ii. Area #2
   - iii. Etc.

    c. Characters
   - i. Player Character(s)
     1. Personality
     2. Back story

3. "Look"
4. Special abilities
   a. Ability #1
      i. When it's acquired
      ii. How the player invokes it
      iii. Effect it has on the world
      iv. Graphic effect that accompanies it
   b. Ability #2
   c. Etc.
5. Weapon set
6. Regular animations
   a. Walk, run, climb, roll, swim, crouch, crawl, idle, etc.
7. Situation-specific animations
8. Statistics (if applicable)

ii. Allies
1. Ally #1
   a. Personality
   b. Relationship to player character
   c. Back story
   d. "Look"
   e. Special abilities
   f. Weapon set
   g. Regular animations
   h. Situation-specific animations
   i. Statistics
2. Ally #2
3. Etc.

iii. Bad Guys
1. Ultimate bad guy
   a. Personality
   b. Relationship to player character
   c. Back story
   d. "Look"
   e. Special abilities
   f. Weapon set

        g. Regular animations

        h. Situation-specific animations

        i. Statistics

      2. Sub bosses

      3. Grunts

    iv. Neutrals

      1. World NPCs

        a. NPC#1

          i. Attitude towards player character

          ii. Function in the game

          iii. Animation set

        b. NPC#2

        c. Etc.

        d. Level Flow (A flowchart that summarizes the action of each level, and the cutscenes or mission briefings (if any) that take place between them)

5. **SECTION III: COMBAT**

  a. Weapons

    i. Weapon #1

      1. General description and most effective use

      2. When it is first acquired

      3. Art (if available)

      4. Statistics (for both primary and secondary fire)

        a. Type of ammunition

        b. Shots per clip

        c. Fire rate

        d. Reload rate

        e. Damage inflicted

        f. Range

    ii. Weapon #2

    iii. Etc.

  b. Spells

    i. Spell #1

      1. Description

2. When it is first acquired

3. How the player invokes it

4. Statistics

    a. Range

    b. "Refire rate"

    c. Damage

    d. Area of effect

  ii. Spell #2

  iii. Etc.

c. Inventory Items/Gadgets

  i. Item #1

    1. Brief physical description of the object

    2. When it is first acquired

    3. What it does

    4. Art (if available)

    5. How the player equips it

    6. Statistics

  ii. Item #2

  iii. Etc.

d. Powerups

  i. Powerup #1

    1. Brief physical description of how the object is represented in the world

    2. When it is first acquired

    3. Art (if available)

    4. What it does

    5. Statistics

      a. Effect

      b. Duration

  ii. Powerup #2

  iii. Etc.

e. Melee (hand-to-hand) combat (if applicable)

  i. Attacks

  ii. Defensive moves

  iii. Combos

f. Vehicles (if applicable)

  i. Capacity

  ii. Speed

  iii. Armor

  iv. Weaponry

  v. Combat statistics

  vi. Etc.

6. **SECTION IV: CONTROLS**

a. PC Keyboard/Mouse Commands

  i. Default keys for movement controls

    1. Move forward

    2. Move backward

    3. Strafe left

    4. Strafe right

    5. Jump

    6. Etc.

  ii. Default keys for using weapons

    1. Primary fire

    2. Alt-fire

    3. Reload

    4. Previous weapon

    5. Next weapon

    6. Etc.

  iii. Inventory access and manipulation

  iv. Menu access

b. Console Platform #1

  i. A picture of the controller explaining what each button does

  ii. Movement controls

  iii. Weapon controls

  iv. Action controls

  v. Combos

  vi. Force-feedback options

c. Console Platform #2

d. Etc.

7. **SECTION V: INTERFACE**
   a. The Camera
      i. Standard view
      ii. Alternate views
      iii. Player-controllable options
   b. HUD
      i. Worldview (what the player sees)
      ii. Status information
         1. Health
         2. Energy
         3. Armor
         4. Weapon equipped
         5. Ammo remaining
         6. Mission objectives?
      iii. Crosshairs (targeting reticule)
      iv. Radar or proximity map?
   c. Menus
      i. Game screen flow diagrams (schematic of how all the game's various screens are accessed)
      ii. Start Menu
         1. Install
         2. Play game
         3. Explore CD (bonus features)
         4. Uninstall
         5. Quit
      iii. Main Menu
         1. Single-Player
            a. Load game
            b. Save game
            c. Play training level
            d. Set difficulty level
         2. Co-op

         3. Multiplayer
            a. Connection instructions
            b. Character/team selection
      iv. Game Menus
         1. Remap player controls
         2. Display (video)
         3. Audio
         4. Music
         5. Map
         6. Advanced
         7. Help screen
         8. Quit
      v. Inventory Menu
      vi. Credits

8. **SECTION VI: ARTIFICIAL INTELLIGENCE (AI)**
    a. NPC #1
      i. Statistics
         1. Field of view
         2. Range of view
         3. Etc.
      ii. Internal states & the triggers that change them
         1. Idle
         2. Guarding an area
         3. Patrol
         4. Follow
         5. Search
         6. Etc.
      iii. Movement
         1. Pathing
      iv. Combat decisions
         1. Friend/foe recognition
         2. Targeting decisions
         3. Attack with ranged weapon

       4. Attack with melee weapon

       5. Take cover

       6. Team-based decisions

       7. Etc.

  b. NPC #2

  c. Etc.

9. **SECTION VII: DETAILED LEVEL/MISSION DESCRIPTIONS**

  a. Level #1

    i.   Synopsis

    ii. Introductory material (Cutscene? Mission briefing?)

    iii. Mission objectives (player goals)

    iv. Physical description

    v.   Map

    vi. Enemy types encountered in-level

    vii. Weapons/powerups available

    viii. Level walkthrough, including scripted sequences and non-interactive scenes. This should also include any puzzles the player must solve, as well as the solutions to those puzzles.

    ix. Closing material (Cutscene? Debriefing? Statistics menu?)

  b. Level #2

  c. Etc.

10. **SECTION VIII: CUTSCENES**

  a. Cutscene #1

    i.   List of actors

    ii. Description of setting

    iii. Storyboard thumbnails

    iv. Script. This should be done in screenplay format, as if you were writing a movie. Include the action, suggested camera angles, location descriptions, etc. You must also include all lines of dialogue that are to be recorded or displayed on the screen. Refer to any of the screenplay books in Appendix B for samples of this format.

  b. Cutscene #2

  c. Etc.

11. **SECTION IX: SCORING, CHEATS, EASTER EGGS, & BONUSES**
   a. Score
      i. How score is tracked
      ii. How score is communicated to the player
   b. Cheats (God mode, all weapons, etc.)
      i. Cheat #1
         1. What it does
         2. How it's activated by the developer
         3. How it's unlocked by the player
      ii. Cheat #2
      iii. Etc.
   c. Easter Eggs/Bonus Material
      i. Easter Egg #1
         1. What it is
         2. How it's activated/unlocked
      ii. Easter Egg #2
      iii. Etc.

12. **SECTION X: GAME MODES**
   a. Single-player
   b Split-screen/co-op (if applicable)
   c. Multiplayer game types (if applicable)
      i. Gametype #1 (such as "Capture the Flag")
         1. Description of gameplay
         2. Min/max # of Players
         3. Rules
         4. Respawning
            a. Delay
            b. Respawn locations
            c. Default weapons
         5. Victory conditions
         6. Scoring
         7. Maps
      ii. Gametype #2
      iii. Etc.

13. **SECTION XI: ASSET LIST**
  a. Art
    i. Model & Texture List
      1. Characters
        a. Player character
          i.   Undamaged
          ii. Damaged
        b. Allies
        c. Bad guys
        d. Neutrals
      2. Weapons
        a. Weapon #1
        b. Weapon #2
        c. Etc.
      3. Equipment/Gadgets
        a. Item #1
        b. Item #2
        c. Etc.
      4. Environmental Objects
        a. Object #1
        b. Object #2
        c. Etc.
    ii. Animation list
      1. Characters
        a. Character #1
          i.   Move #1
          ii. Move #2
          iii. Etc.
        b. Character #2
        c. Etc.
      2. Weapons
        a. Weapon #1
          i.   Firing animation
          ii. Reload animation
          iii. Projectile in flight animation (if appropriate)

    3. Destructible or animated objects in the world

      a. Object #1

      b. Object #2

      c. Etc.

  iii. Effects list

    1. Weapon effects list

      a. Firing effects

      b. Hit effects

      c. Etc.

    2. Environmental effects

      a. Decals

      b. Smoke

      c. Sparks

      d. Fire

      e. Explosions

      f. Etc.

  iv. Interface Art List

    1. Icons

    2. Buttons

    3. Menus

    4. Windows

    5. Etc.

b. Sound

  i. Environmental Sounds

    1. Walking/running sounds on different surfaces

    2. Foley sounds of character actions within the game

    3. Explosions

    4. Doors opening and closing

    5. Etc.

  ii. Weapon Sounds

    1. Weapon #1

      a. Firing sound

      b. Hit sound

      c. Reload sound

        2. Weapon #2

        3. Etc.

    iii. Interface Sounds

        1. Various clicks, beeps, etc., as the player maneuvers through the menus

        2. Alert/acknowledgment sounds as the player picks up objects or his game state changes

c. Music

    i. Ambient

        1. Loop #1 + duration

        2. Loop #2

        3. Etc.

    ii. "Action"

        1. Loop #1 + duration

        2. Loop #2

        3. Etc.

    iii. "Victory" loops

    iv. "Defeat" loops

    v. Cutscene music

        1. Piece #1

            a. General description of mood and accompanying action

            b. Duration

        2. Piece #2

        3. Etc.

d. Voice

    i. Actor #1 lines

        1. Line #1. Each line in the game must have a unique identifying file name. This will help both the recording process and localization. Don't forget to include various screams, yells, grunts, laughs, and other "non-word" lines.

        2. Line #2

        3. Etc.

    ii. Actor #2 lines

    iii. Etc.

14. **SECTION XII: LOCALIZATION PLAN**
    a. Languages with full text and voice localization
    b. Languages with text localization only
    c. Text to be localized
       i.   In-game text
       ii. Game interface text
    d. Voice to be localized
       i.   (See "Voice" section of asset list above)

15. **SECTION XIII: MAJOR EVENT PLANNING**
    a. Trade Shows
       i.   Trade Show #1
            1. Date
            2. Materials needed for event
            3. Demo description and specifications
       ii. Trade Show #2
       iii. Etc.
    b. Special Publicity Events
       i.   Event #1 (such as "Editors Day" to show off game)
            1. Date
            2. Description of event
            3. Materials needed for event
            4. Demo description and specifications
       ii. Event #2
       iii. Etc.
    c. PR/Marketing Support
       i.   Date when concept art will be available
       ii. Date when first screenshots will be available
       iii. Plan for creating additional screenshots throughout project
       iv. Plan for making team available for interviews
       v.   Etc.
    d. Sales Team Support
       i.   Projected date of first "sell-sheet"
       ii. Demo loop for retail outlets
       iii. Other materials
       iv. Etc.

      e. Prerelease Demo

          i.   Date

          ii.   Scope

          iii. Content

16. **SECTION XIV: TECHNICAL SUMMARY**

      a. Single-Player

          i.   PC

              1. Minimum system requirements

              2. Recommended system requirements

              3. Number of characters viewable at once

              4. Max # polys per character

              5. Max # polys per level

          ii.   Console Platform #1

          iii. Etc.

      b. Multiplayer

          i.   Type of connectivity (Splitscreen? LAN? Online?)

          ii.   Max # simultaneous players

          iii. Client-server? Peer-to-peer?

          iv. Etc.

17. **SECTION XV: MISCELLANEOUS**

      a. Acronyms used in this document

      b. Definition of terms

18. **SECTION XVI: REFERENCES**

      a. Games

      b. Movies

      c. Books

      d. Art

Art Production Plan

This document and the GDD and TDD are the trio of content-creation documents that must be maintained throughout the project. This is where people will look not only for concept pieces, but also for detailed visuals on all aspects of the game.

1. **Game Name**
   a. Copyright Information
2. **Table of Contents**
3. **SECTION I: ART TEAM (including areas of responsibility and contact info for each individual)**
   a. Art Director
      i. Office phone
      ii. Home phone
      iii. Cell phone
      iv. E-mail
   b. Animators
   c. Modellers
   d. Texture Artists
   e. Effects Artists
   f. CGI Artists
   g. GUI Artists
   h. External Resources
   i. Etc.
4. **SECTION II: EXECUTIVE SUMMARY**
   a. Project Overview from the Art-Creation Perspective
   b. Delivery Platforms
      i. PC
         1. Content creation/conversion plan
      ii. Console Platform #1
      iii. Etc.
5. **SECTION III: BUDGETS (Poly/memory limits for each delivery platform)**
   a. Characters
      i. Main character
         1. PC
         2. Console Platform #1
         3. Console Platform #2

    4. Etc.

   ii. Allies

   iii. Bad Guys

    1. Ultimate Bad Guy

    2. Bosses

    3. Grunts

   iv. Other World NPCs

  b. Levels

  c. Weapons

  d. Other Equipment

  e. GUI

6. **SECTION IV: PRODUCTION PATH (A description of how art will be integrated in the game through the following steps)**

  a. Requirements

  b. Concept

  c. Model

  d. Skin/Texture

  e. Animation

  f. Integration into the Game

  g. Porting Across Different Delivery Platforms

7. **SECTION V: ART BIBLE (CONCEPT ART/STYLE GUIDE)**

  a. Overview

   i. Reference Material

  b. Characters

  c. Environments

  d. Weapons

  e. Equipment

  f. GUI

8. **SECTION VI: FINAL ART (as it becomes available)**

  a. Characters

  b. Environments

  c. Weapons

  d. Equipment

  e. GUI

    f. Screenshots, along with a tracking doc that records when each shot was made available, and to whom. This will be especially useful when magazines are requesting exclusive shots that haven't been used before.

9. **SECTION VII: CUTSCENES**

    a. Cutscene #1

       i. Storyboard thumbnails

       ii. Selected shots from final game

    b. Cutscene #2

    c. Etc.

10. **SECTION VIII: ASSET LIST (This should be maintained in parallel with the list in the game design document)**

    a. Model & Texture List

       i. Characters

          1. Player character

             a. Undamaged

             b. Damaged

          2. Allies

          3. Bad Guys

          4. Neutrals

       ii. Weapons

          1. Weapon #1

          2. Weapon #2

          3. Etc.

       iii. Equipment/Gadgets

          1. Item #1

          2. Item #2

          3. Etc.

       iv. Environmental Objects

          1. Object #1

          2. Object #2

          3. Etc.

    b. Animation list

       i. Characters

          1. Character #1

             a. Move #1

             b. Move #2

        c. Etc.
      2. Character #2
      3. Etc.
   ii. Mocap List (if applicable)
      1. Actor #1
         a. Move #1
         b. Move #2
         c. Etc.
      2. Actor #2
      3. Etc.
   iii. Weapons
      1. Weapon #1
         a. Firing animation
         b. Reload animation
         c. Projectile in flight animation (if appropriate)
      2. Destructible or animated objects in the world
         a. Object #1
         b. Object #2
         c. Etc.
 c. Effects list
   i. Weapon effects list
      1. Firing effects
      2. Hit effects
      3. Etc.
   ii. Environmental effects
      1. Decals
      2. Smoke
      3. Sparks
      4. Fire
      5. Explosions
      6. Etc.
 d. Interface Art list
   i. Icons
   ii. Buttons
   iii. Menus

iv.   Windows

v.   Etc.

11. **SECTION IX: SCHEDULING**

a. Task Lists

b. Man-Month Scheduling

c. Calendar Month Scheduling

d. Milestone Schedule & Deliverables

e. Major Event Planning

  i.   Trade Shows

    1. Trade Show #1

      a. Date

      b. Materials needed for event

      c. Demo description and specifications

    2. Trade Show #2

    3. Etc.

  ii.   Special Publicity Events

    1. Event #1 (such as "Editors Day" to show off game)

      a. Date

      b. Description of event

      c. Demo description and specifications

    2. Event #2

    3. Etc.

  iii.   PR/Marketing Support

    1. Date when first screenshots will be available

    2. Plan for creating additional screenshots throughout project

    3. Plan for making team available for interviews

    4. Etc.

  iv.   Sales Support/Team Support

    1. Demo loop for retail outlets

    2. Other materials

    3. Etc.

  v.   Prerelease Demo

    1. Date

    2. Scope

    3. Content

12. SECTION X: RECRUITMENT
    a. Current Personnel
    b. Additional Team Members Needed
    c. Schedule for Hiring Additional Personnel
    d. Risk Plan for Handling Delays in Acquiring Additional Resources
13. SECTION XI: EQUIPMENT BUDGET AND COSTS
    a. Team Personnel with Hardware and Software Toolset
        i. Team Member #1
            1. Hardware
                a. Development PC
                    i. Specs
                b. Console Dev Kit
                    i. Add-ons (TV, controllers, memory cards, hubs, etc.)
                c. Debug Kit
            2. Software Tools Needed
                a. 2D Art Package
                b. 3D Art Package (+ support?)
                c. Plug-Ins and Add-Ons
                d. Tools and Utilities
                e. Mocap Editing Suite
                f. Other Specialized Software
                g. Etc.
        ii. Team Member #2
        iii. Etc.
    b. Equipment Acquisition Schedule and Costs (Summary of who needs what, when they will need it, and how much it will cost.)
14. SECTION XII: LOCALIZATION PLAN (Every effort should be made to keep text that must be localized from creeping into graphics. Even so, some territories may require the development of different art packages.)
    a. Territory #1
        i. Customized models, textures, etc.
    b. Territory #2
    c. Etc.

Technical Design Doc

The technical design document is a companion piece to the game design document and the art bible. Like the other docs, the TDD should be maintained on an internal Web site and kept up to date throughout the project.

1. **Game Name**
   a. Copyright Information
2. **Table of Contents**
3. **SECTION I: TECHNICAL TEAM (including areas of responsibility and contact info for each individual)**
   a. Tech Lead
      i.   Office phone
      ii. Home phone
      iii. Cell phone
      iv. E-mail
   b. AI Programmers
   c. Gameplay Programmers
   d. Graphics Programmers
   e. Tools Programmers
   f. Scripters
   g. Etc.
4. **SECTION II: EXECUTIVE SUMMARY**
   a. Project Overview from a Technical Perspective
   b. Delivery Platforms
      i.   PC
         1. Minimum specifications
         2. Recommended specifications
         3. Disk budget
      ii. Console Platform #1
         1. Disk budget
      iii. Etc.

5. **SECTION III: ENGINE EVALUATION**
   a. Internal solutions
   b. External solutions from affiliated organizations
   c. Middleware
6. **SECTION IV: PLATFORM-SPECIFIC ISSUES**
   a. Delivery Platform #1
      i.   Strategy and comments
      ii. Platform-specific processes
      iii. Memory management scheme & budgets
      iv. Risks
   b. Delivery Platform #2
   c. Etc.
7. **SECTION V: DEVELOPMENT PLAN**
   a. Use Cases
   b. Game Mechanics
   c. Main Loop
   d. Data Structures
   e. Data Flow
   f. Physics
   g. Artificial Intelligence
      i. Pathing
      ii. Scripting
   h. Graphics
      i.   Rendering
           1. Geometry
           2. Textures
      ii. Animation
      iii. Particle System
      iv. Effects
      v.   Lighting
      vi. Camera

        i. Collision

        j. GUI

            i.   HUD

            ii. Menu Flow Diagram

        k. Fonts

        l. Audio/Video

        m. Special Requirements for Multiplayer Support

8. **SECTION VI: CODING STANDARDS**

    a. Programming Standards

    b. Style Guide

    c. Code Review Procedures

    d. Profiling Plan

9. **SECTION VII: SCHEDULING**

    a. Preliminary Task Lists

        i. Programming Tasks

            1. Core Libraries

            2. Object System

            3. Object System, AI

            4. Engine

            5. Tool Creation

            6. Mapping System

            7. Special Effects

            8. GUI

            9. Game Mechanics

                a. Movement

                b. Inventory

                c. Camera

                d. Weapons

           10. Conversion Support

        ii. Art Task Summaries (Taken from art plan)

        iii. Design Task Summaries (Taken from game design doc)

    b. Man-Month Scheduling

    c. Calendar Month Scheduling

    d. Milestone Schedule & Deliverables

- e. Major Event Planning
  - i. Trade Shows
    1. Trade Show #1
       a. Date
       b. Materials needed for event
       c. Demo description and specifications
    2. Trade Show #2
    3. Etc.
  - ii. Special Publicity Events
    1. Event #1 (such as "Editors Day" to show off game)
       a. Date
       b. Description of event
       c. Demo description and specifications
    2. Event #2
    3. Etc.
  - iii. PR/Marketing Support
    1. Date when first screenshots will be available
    2. Plan for creating additional screenshots throughout project
    3. Plan for making team available for interviews
    4. Etc.
  - iv. Sales Support/Team Support
    1. Demo loop for retail outlets
    2. Other materials
    3. Etc.
  - v. Prerelease Demo
    1. Date
    2. Scope
    3. Content

10. **SECTION VIII: RECRUITMENT**
    a. Current Personnel
    b. Additional Team Members Needed
    c. Schedule for Hiring Additional Personnel
    d. Risk Plan for Handling Delays in Acquiring Additional Resources

11. **SECTION IX: EQUIPMENT BUDGET AND COSTS**
    a. Team Personnel with Hardware and Software Toolset
        i.   Team Member #1
             1. Hardware
                 a. Development PC
                     i. Specs
                 b. Console Dev Kit
                     i. Add-ons (TV, controllers, memory cards, hubs, etc.)
                 c. Debug Kit
             2. Software Tools Needed
                 a. Development environment (compiler/editor/debugger)
                 b. 2D art package
                 c. 3D art package (+ support?)
                 d. Etc.
        ii. Team Member #2
        iii. Etc.
    b. Teamwide Tools
        i.   Network/infrastructure requirements
        ii. Version control system
        iii. Asset management package
        iv. QA tracking package
    c. Summary Table of Equipment and Software
        i.   PCs
        ii.   DVD burners
        iii. DevKits
        iv.   Debug kits
        v.   Network/infrastructure
        vi.   Seats for 3D software
        vii. Seats for 2D software
        viii. Plug-ins and add-ons
        ix.   Other specialized software
        x.   Level editors
        xi.   Mocap editing suite

        xii. Sound processing software

        xiii. Tools and utilities

        xiv. Version control system

        xv. Asset management package

        xvi. QA tracking system

        xvii.Etc.

    d. Equipment Acquisition Schedule and Costs

12. **SECTION X: LOCALIZATION PLAN**

    a. Languages with Full Text and Voice Localization

    b. Languages with Text Localization Only

    c. Text to Be Localized

        i.   In-game text

        ii.   Game interface text

    d. Voice to Be Localized

        i.   (See "Voice" section of asset list above)

    e. Art to Be Localized

        i.   See art production plan

13. **SECTION XI: DATA SECURITY PLAN**

    a. Network Security

    b. Onsite Backup Plan

    c. Offsite Backup Plan

14. **SECTION XII: MISCELLANEOUS**

    a. Acronyms Used in This Document

    b. Definition of Terms

Test Plan

1. **Game Name**
   a. Copyright Information
2. **Table of Contents**
3. **SECTION I: QA TEAM (and areas of responsibility)**
   a. QA Lead
      i. Office phone
      ii. Home phone
      iii. Cell phone
      iv. E-mail
   b. Internal Testers
   c. External Testers
4. **SECTION II: TESTING PROCEDURES**
   a. General Approach
      i. Basic Responsibilities of Test Team
         1. Bugs
            a. Detect them as soon as possible after they enter the build
            b. Research them
            c. Communicate them to the dev team
            d. Help get them resolved
            e. Track them
         2. Maintain the Daily Build
         3. Levels of Communication. There's no point in testing unless the results of the tests are communicated in some fashion. There are a range of possible outputs from QA. In increasing levels of formality, they are:
         a. Conversation
         b. ICQ
         c. E-Mail to Individual
         d. E-Mail to Group
         e. Daily Top Bugs List
         f. Stats/Info Dump Area on DevSite
         g. Formal Entry into Bug Tracking System

b. Daily Activities
   i. The Build
      1. Generate a daily build.
      2. Run the daily regression tests, as described in "Daily Tests" below.
      3. If everything is okay, post the build so everyone can get it.
      4. If there's a problem, send an e-mail message to the entire dev team that the new build cannot be copied, and contact whichever developers can fix the problem.
      5. Decide whether a new build needs to be run that day.
   ii. Daily Tests
      1. Run through a predetermined set of single-player levels, performing a specified set of activities.
         a. Level #1
            i. Activity #1
            ii. Activity #2
            iii. Etc.
            iv. The final activity is usually to run an automated script that reports the results of the various tests and posts them in the QA portion of the internal Web site.
         b. Level #2
         c. Etc.
      2. Run through a predetermined set of multiplayer levels, performing a specified set of activities.
         a. Level #1
            i. Activity #1
            ii. Activity #2
            iii. Etc.
            iv. The final activity is usually for each tester involved in the multiplayer game to run an automated script that reports the results of the various tests and posts them in the QA portion of the internal Web site.
         b. Level #2
         c. Etc.
      3. E-mail showstopper crashes or critical errors to the entire team.
      4. Post showstopper crashes or critical errors to the daily top bugs list (if one is being maintained).

    c. Daily Reports

        i. Automated reports from the preceding daily tests are posted in the QA portion of the internal Web site.

    d. Weekly Activities

        i. Weekly tests

            1. Run through every level in the game (not just the preset ones used in the daily test), performing a specified set of activities and generating a predetermined set of tracking statistics. The same machine should be used each week.

                a. Level #1

                    i. Activity #1

                    ii. Activity #2

                    iii. Etc.

                b. Level #2

                c. Etc.

            2. Weekly Review of Bugs in the Bug Tracking System

                a. Verify that bugs marked "fixed" by the development team really are fixed.

                b. Check the appropriateness of bug rankings relative to where the project is in the development.

                c. Acquire a "feel" for the current state of the game, which can be communicated in discussions to the producer and department heads.

                d. Generate a weekly report of closed-out bugs.

        ii. Weekly Reports

            1. Tracking statistics, as generated in the weekly tests above.

    e. Ad Hoc Testing

        i. Perform specialized tests as requested by the producer, tech lead, or other development team members.

        ii. Determine the appropriate level of communication to report the results of those tests.

    f. Integration of Reports from External Test Groups

        i. If at all possible, ensure that all test groups are using the same bug tracking system.

        ii. Determine which group is responsible for maintaining the master list.

        iii. Determine how frequently to reconcile bug lists against each other.

        iv. Ensure that only one consolidated set of bugs is reported to the development team.

   g. Focus Testing (if applicable)

        i. Recruitment methods

        ii. Testing location

        iii. Who observes them?

        iv. Who communicates with them?

        v. How is their feedback recorded?

   h. Compatibility Testing

        i. Selection of external vendor

        ii. Evaluation of results

        iii. Method of integrating filtered results into bug tracking system

5. SECTION III: HOW TESTING REQUIREMENTS ARE GENERATED

   a. Some requirements are generated by this plan.

   b. Requirements can also be generated during project meetings, or other formal meetings held to review current priorities (such as the set of predetermined levels used in the daily tests).

   c. Requirements can also result from changes in a bug's status within the bug tracking system. For example, when a bug is marked "fixed" by a developer, a requirement is generated for someone to verify that it has been truly killed and can be closed out. Other status changes include "Need More Info" and "Can't Duplicate," each of which creates a requirement for QA to investigate the bug further.

   d. Some requirements are generated when a developer wants QA to check a certain portion of the game (see "Ad Hoc Testing" above).

6. SECTION IV: BUG TRACKING SOFTWARE

   a. Package name

   b. How many seats will be needed for the project

   c. Access instructions (Everyone on the team should have access to the buglist)

   d.. "How to report a bug" instructions for using the system

7. SECTION V: BUG CLASSIFICATIONS

   a. "A" bugs and their definition

   b. "B" bugs and their definition

   c. "C" bugs and their definition

8. SECTION VI: BUG TRACKING

    a. Who classifies the bug?

    b. Who assigns the bug?

    c. What happens when the bug is fixed?

    d. What happens when the fix is verified?

9. SECTION VII: SCHEDULING AND LOADING

    a. Rotation Plan. How testers will be brought on and off the project, so that some testers stay on it throughout its lifecycle while "fresh faces" are periodically brought in.

    b. Loading Plan. Resource plan that shows how many testers will be needed at various points in the life of the project.

10. SECTION VIII: EQUIPMENT BUDGET AND COSTS

    a. QA Team Personnel with Hardware and Software Toolset

        i. Team Member #1

            1. Hardware

                a. Testing PC

                    i. Specs

                b. Console Debug Kit

                    i. Add-ons (TV, controllers, memory cards, hubs, etc.)

            2. Software Tools Needed

                a. Bug tracking software

                b. Other

        ii. Team Member #2

        iii. Etc.

    b. Equipment Acquisition Schedule and Costs (summary of who needs what, when they will need it, and how much it will cost)

Project Plan

The project plan is a suite of documents that the producer uses to estimate costs, track progress, maintain the schedule, and estimate profitability.

1. Manpower plan. This is a spreadsheet that lists when all the internal people connected to the project come on board, and when they finish up. Here is a drastically simplified version:

	January	February	March	April	May	June	TOTAL
Designer	0.5	1	1	1	1	1	5.5
Tech Lead		0.5	1	1	1	1	4.5
Programmer #2			1	1	1		3
Art Lead		0.5	1	1	1	1	4.5
Artists #2			1	1	1		3
QA Lead			1	1	1	1	4
Tester #2				1	1	1	3
Total Man months	0.5	2	6	7	7	5	27.5

2. Resource plan. This spreadsheet lists all the external costs of the project and when they will be incurred. The external costs appropriate to the preceding manpower plan might look something like this:

	January	February	March	April	May	June	TOTAL
3 DenKits	10000	10000	10000				30000
2 Debug Kits			1000	1000			2000
Art Tool #1 (2)		5000	5000				10000
Art Tools #2 (4)		1000	1000				2000
Bug Tracking Tool			5000	150			5150
Composer					5000		5000
Voice				5000	5000		10000
Total Ext Costs	10000	16000	22000	6150	10000	0	54150

3. Project tracking doc. This is usually a Gantt chart generated by the producer using project management software. Each department head supplies a list of tasks, along with the people assigned to them and how long they think the tasks will take. With this information, the producer can see if the project is on schedule, what the critical path to completion is, which resources are overloaded, etc.

4. Budget. This is a spreadsheet of all the costs associated with the project. Line items will include the following:

    a. Internal personnel costs (salaries of people applied to the project)

    b. Hardware costs

    c. Software licenses

    d. External contractor fees

    e. Engine royalties

    f. IP acquisition costs (license fee)

    g. Marketing & PR costs

    h. An overhead multiplier that applies fixed costs (building rent, utilities, travel, personnel benefits, etc.) to the project

5. Profit-and-Loss (P&L) statement. This is another spreadsheet that the publisher uses to estimate the profitability of each project. The projected lifecycle sales estimates from the sales team are compared to the costs from the preceding budget to determine if the game will make enough money to justify the investment.

6. Development schedule. This table breaks out the stages of development, with significant events along the way:

Event	Date
Concept phase	00/00/00 – 00/00/00
Start preproduction	00/00/00
Start development	00/00/00
Milestone #1	00/00/00
Milestone #2	00/00/00
… (Additional milestones)…	00/00/00
Alpha	00/00/00
Beta	00/00/00
Localization deliverable #1	00/00/00
Presubmission (console only)	00/00/00
First submission (console only)	00/00/00
Second submission (console only)	00/00/00
Code freeze	00/00/00
Release to manufacture (RTM)	00/00/00
Shelf date	00/00/00

7. Milestone definitions. Here, the deliverable for each milestone is specified in detail, along with the date it's due. See Chapter 10 for advice about creating concrete, binary deliverables:

Milestone	Date
Milestone #1. General description	00/00/00
Deliverable #1	
Deliverable #2	
Deliverable #3	
Milestone #2. General description	00/00/00
Deliverable #1	
Deliverable #2	
Deliverable #3	
Milestone #3. General description	00/00/00
Deliverable #1	
Deliverable #2	
Deliverable #3	
Etc.	Etc.

External Events

In the course of development, predictable interruptions will occur. These must be included in the project plan from the start. Here is a sample list of events and the team involvement that may be needed to support them:

Description	Date	Team Involvement & Materials needed
Trade show #1	00/00/00	Producer. Designer. Show off non-interactive demo in backroom.
Trade show #2	00/00/00	Producer. Designer. LDs. Interactive demo on show floor.
Trade show #3 (overseas)	00/00/00	No one from the team. Supply "leave-behind" demo to PR crew. Also screenshots for press kit.
PR event #1 (Onsite Editor's Day)	00/00/00	Entire team. Interviews. Working game on several machines. New screenshots.
PR event #2 (License launch by content partner)	00/00/00	Corp. Executives. Screenshots for press kit.
Internal sales team presentation	00/00/00	Producer. Designer. "Highlights" demo. One-page features summary.
Other corporate events	Etc.	Etc.

Current Risks

The current risks document is an assessment by the project manager of the top risks to the project, and how they're being mitigated. Usually this takes the form of a "Top Ten" list, but the number is arbitrary and will change over time.

1. Risk #1
    a. Description
    b. Potential impact
    c. Possible ways to mitigate the risk
    d. Current course of action
2. Risk #2
3. Etc.

Risk	Impact	Mitigation & Current Course
Staffing: Our AI programmer's visa is due to expire in two months.	1) The AI programmer is distracted from his work. 2) If he leaves, the project schedule will slip by at least one month.	1) We are working with the INS to request an expedited visa. 2) We have paired another programmer with the AI lead to minimize the impact of his departure, if that happens.
Infrastructure: Our build server has crashed three times in the past week.	The entire team's progress is slowed when they don't have access to the daily build.	1) Our MIS manager is reviewing the server's security to check for attacks from the outside. 2) We have ordered a new hard drive for the server and will install it next week. 3) In the meantime, we have dedicated another machine to "mirror" the server.
External Resources: The contractor creating the CGI cutscenes missed their last deliverable.	1) No current impact to the schedule. (These cutscenes are not on the critical path.) 2) The movies must be received eventually, however, because most of them are integral to advancing the story.	1) The contractor claims this is a one-time failure due to the illness of a key employee. 2) We have reprioritized the cutscene list to have the contractor complete the essential ones first. 3) We are evaluating other contractors as a fallback in the event that this failure continues.
Etc.	Etc.	Etc.

Credits

This is a document that should be maintained from the very start of the project. On long projects, people come and go, and it's hard to remember everyone who has contributed.

There's no industry standard for assigning project credits. The following format is used quite frequently, but each team may develop its own approach.

1. Production
   a. Executive Producer
   b. Associate Producer
   c. Assistant Producer
2. Design
   a. Lead Designer
   b. Level Designers (alphabetical)
3. Technical
   a. Tech Lead
   b. Programmers (alphabetical)
4. Art
   a. Art Lead
   b. Artists (alphabetical)
5. QA
   a. QA Lead
   b. Testers (alphabetical)
6. Localization Team
   a. Localization Lead
   b. Language #1
      i. Personnel
   c. Language #2
   d. Etc.
7. Executive Team
   a. VP Production
      i. Team

    b. Sales Director

    c. Marketing Director

        i. Brand Manager

    d. PR Director

        i. Project Manager

8. Voice Talent

    a. Character #1—Actor Name

    b. Character #2—Actor Name

9. Mocap Actors

    a. Actor #1

    b. Actor #2

    c. Etc.

10. External Companies & Contractors

    a. Company #1 Name

        i. Person #1

        ii. Person #2

        iii. Etc.

    b. Company #2 Name

    c. Etc.

Change List and Project Archives

The advantage of maintaining "live" documentation is that any time a team member looks something up, he'll see the current specification.

You can't rely on team members to constantly check the documents, however, so it's wise to set up a change notification alert system. Whenever someone changes a document, it should trigger an e-mail to the appropriate team members with a summary of the change.

A list of these e-mails should be maintained so that everyone can see the change history. This list takes the place of a "revision history" or "change list" section that used to be at the top of the project documents. (Note, however, that changes that affect milestones or deliverables are important enough to be tracked separately, most often as formal amendments to the development contract.)

From time to time, the project manager (or his designee) should go through the Web site to ensure that everything is current. If too much old information is cluttering things up, it's best to archive it in a separate area.

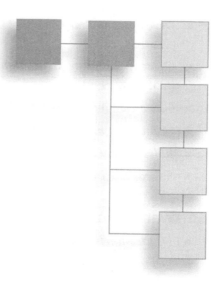

APPENDIX B

RESOURCES

T he realities of this business are harsh. Hours are long, projects are mismanaged, schedule pressure is relentless, and games never turn out the way you want. Collaborating is difficult.

Because the game industry changes so rapidly, the most up-to-date resource will always be the Web itself. Type "game development" into your search engine, and look through the hits. You will quickly find everything you need to know, from development-related Web sites to magazines to schools to headhunters. It should take you no more than a day to figure out which of these are worth further investigation and which are not.

As of the writing of this edition (summer 2004), here are some of the best resources for game developers.

Bibliography

Game Design

- *Andrew Rollings and Ernest Adams on Game Design* by Andrew Rollings and Ernest Adams (New Riders, 2003)
- *The Art of Innovation* by Thomas Kelley (Doubleday, 2001)
- *Chris Crawford on Game Design* by Chris Crawford (New Riders, 2003)
- *Community Building on the Web* by Amy Jo Kim (Addison-Wesley, 2000)
- *Creating Emotion in Games* by David Freeman (New Riders, 2003)
- *Design of Everyday Things* by Donald A. Norman (Basic Books, 2002)

- *Developing Online Games* by Jessica Mulligan and Bridgette Patrovsky (Pearson, 2003)
- *Game Architecture and Design* by Andrew Rollings and Dave Morris (Coriolis, 1999)
- *Game Design: Secrets of the Sages* by Marc Saltzman (Macmillan, 1999)
- *Game Design: Theory and Practice* by Richard Rouse (Wordware, 2000)
- *Rules of Play* by Katie Salen and Eric Zimmerman (MIT Press, 2003)
- *Swords & Circuitry* by Neal and Jana Halford (Premier Press, 2001)

Software Management

- *Death March* by Edward Yourdon (Prentice Hall PTR, 1997)
- *Debugging the Development Process* by Steve Maguire (Microsoft Press, 1994)
- *Game Development and Production* by Eric Bethke (Wordware, 2003)
- *The Mythical Man-Month, 20th Anniversary Edition* by Frederick Brooks (Addison-Wesley, 1995)
- *Peopleware* by Tom DeMarco and Timothy Lister (Dorset House Publishing, 1987)
- *Rapid Development* by Steve McConnell (Microsoft Press, 1996)
- *Software Project Management: A Unified Framework* by Walker Royce (Addison-Wesley, 1998)

Storytelling

- *Aristotle's Poetics*, edited by S.H. Butcher (Hill & Wang, 1989)
- *The Art of Creative Writing* by Lajos Egri (Simon & Schuster, 1972)
- *The Art of Fiction* by John Gardner (Vintage Books, 1991)
- *Character Development and Storytelling for Games* by Lee Sheldon (Course Technology, 2004)
- *The Elements of Style* by Strunk & White (Prentice Hall, 1999)
- *Hero with a Thousand Faces* by Joseph Campbell (Princeton University Press, 1972)
- *Story: Substance, Structure, Style, and the Principles of Screenwriting* by Robert McKee (Harper Collins, 1997)
- *The Writer's Journey : Mythic Structure for Writers* by Christopher Vogler (Michael Wiese Productions, 1998)

Magazines

- *Computer Graphics World* (www.cgw.com)
- *Game Developer Magazine* (www.gdmag.com)
- *Game Studies* (www.gamestudies.org)
- *Develop Magazine* (www.developmag.com)

Web Sites

- www.avault.com/developer
- www.digitalgamedeveloper.com
- www.dperry.com/industry/index.htm
- www.flipcode.com
- www.gamasutra.com
- www.gamedev.net
- www.gameslice.com
- www.gametutorials.com
- www.gdse.com
- www.legendmud.org/raph/gaming/

Conferences and Trade Shows

- **Anime Expo.** Japanese convention for fans of animation, comics, and pop culture.
- **Austin Game Conference.** Focuses on multiplayer and mobile games.
- **Australian Game Developers Conference.** Held annually in Melbourne, this conference is a mixture of keynotes, technical panels, and tutorials.
- **CES (Consumer Electronics Show).** U.S. trade show focusing on consumer electronics devices.
- **ChinaJoy.** Hong Kong digital entertainment expo & conference.
- **COMDEX.** U.S. trade show and conference for IT professionals.
- **Computational Semiotics for Games and New Media (COSIGN).** This European conference focuses on issues of meaning in new media, particularly the application of semiotic-based theories to creating and analyzing computer-based media.
- **DICE Summit.** U.S. single-track conference focused on "the creative endeavor inherent in game development."

- **Digifest.** Canadian festival of digital culture, creativity and innovation.
- **Digital Games Research Conference.** European conference that bridges the academic research community and the professional gaming community.
- **E3.** The annual Electronic Entertainment Expo is the place to see all the games that are in development. If you don't currently work in the industry, you might have to do some work to get a pass. If you have a friend in the business, it's not difficult to arrange.
- **ECTS.** The European Computer Trade Show, held each fall in London, is similar in nature to E3.
- **Eurographics Convention.** European conference for graphic artists.
- **GDC.** The Game Developers Conference is *the* place to meet other game developers, attend lectures on every possible subdiscipline of game development, and see all the latest development tools. (See Figure B.1.) If you can't afford to pay the registration fee, look into the conference associate position, which allows you to attend sessions free in exchange for about 20 hours of volunteer work. Contact them at gdconf.com.

Figure B.1 Legendary game designer Shigeru Miyamoto (*Mario, Donkey Kong, Zelda*) addresses the 2000 Game Developers Conference. Image courtesy of the Game Developers Conference.

- **GDCE.** European version of the GDC, held each fall in London.
- **GCDC.** International Game Developer Conference, held each year in Leipzig, Germany.
- **Graphite.** International Conference on Computer Graphics and Interactive Techniques in Australasia and South East Asia.
- **MacWorld Conference & Expo.** Annual U.S. conference focused on the Macintosh OS.
- **MILIA.** Multimedia content event held each year in Cannes, France. Generally attended by executives, not the rank and file.
- **Project Bar-B-Q.** Unconventional annual Texas conference for industry musicians.
- **Shareware Industry Conference.** Three-day U.S. conference, culminating in the annual Shareware Industry Awards ceremony.
- **SIGGRAPH.** This is the premier U.S. annual gathering of artists interested in computer graphics.
- **3D Festival.** European event for 3D computer graphic artists.
- **Tokyo Game Show.** Japanese trade show & expo.
- **XGDX (EXtreme Game Developer's Xpo)** Annual 2-day game development conference, held in Silicon Valley.

Industry News

- www.avault.com
- www.bluesnews.com
- www.escmag.com
- www.fgnonline.com
- www.gamedaily.com
- www.gamesindustry.biz
- www.next-generation.com
- http://pc.ign.com/
- www.zdnet.com/gamespot/

Organizations

- *Association of Shareware Professionals* (www.asp-shareware.org)
- *Entertainment and Leisure Software Publishers Association (ELSPA)* (www.elspa.com)
- *Entertainment Software Association (ESA)* (www.theesa.com)
- *International Game Developers Association (IGDA)* (www.igda.org)

Schools

With the explosion of interest in game studies, it's impossible to keep track of all the universities, colleges, and other institutions that are offering courses and degrees in game development. The list below was generated from a list of schools and programs who have registered with Premier's Game Developer's Market Guide. If you wish to register a school or program, please go to www.gamedevguide.com.

Argentina

- *Image Campus* (www.imagecampus.com.ar)

Australia

- *Academy of Interactive Entertainment* (www.aie.act.edu.au)

Brazil

- *Tulipa Learning Center* (tulipa.rec.br)

Canada

- *Algonquin College* (www.algonquincollege.com)
- *Center for Arts and Technology – Okanagan* (www.digitalartschool.com)
- *New Media Campus* (www.newmediacampus.com)
- *Replica 3D Animation School* (www.replica3d.ca)
- *Success College of Applied Arts & Technology* (www.thinksuccess.ca)
- *University of Calgary* (www.cs.ucalgary.ca)
- *Vancouver Institute of Media Arts* (www.vanarts.com)

Denmark

- *IT University of Copenhagen* (www.itu.dk)

Germany

- *Games Academy* (www.games-academy.com)

Hong Kong

- *Hong Kong Polytechnic University* (www.mic.polyu.edu.hk)

India

- *GameEdu (Division of University of Northwest)* (www.gameedu.org)

New Zealand

- *Media Design School* (www.mediadesign.school.nz)

Spain

- *La Salle School of Engineering* (www.salleurl.edu)

Sweden

- *Lulea University of Technology* (www.gscept.com)

United Kingdom

- *University of Hull* (www.mscgames.com)
- *University of Paisley* (www.paisley.ac.uk)

United States

- *Academy of Game Entertainment Technology* (www.academyofget.com)
- *Art Institute of California – Orange County* (www.aicaoc.aii.edu)
- *Art Institute of California – San Diego* (www.aicasd.artinstitutes.edu)
- *Art Institute of California – San Francisco* (www.aicasf.aii.edu)
- *Art Institute of Pittsburgh* (www.aip.aii.edu)
- *California Institute of the Arts* (www.calarts.edu)
- *DH Institute of Media Arts* (www.dhima.com)
- *DigiPen Institute of Technology* (www.digipen.edu)
- *Florida Atlantic University* (www.animasters.com)
- *Full Sail Real World Education* (www.fullsail.com)
- *Game Institute* (www.gameinstitute.com)

- *Gemini School of Visual Arts and Communication* (www.geminischool.com)
- *Gnomon School of Visual Effects* (www.gnomon3d.com)
- *Guildhall at SMU* (www.guildhall.smu.edu/)
- *Illinois Institute of Art – Chicago* (www.ilic.artinstitutes.edu)
- *Mercy College, Center for Digital Arts* (www.mercy.edu/cda/)
- *Moraine Valley Community College* (www.morainevalley.edu/cad)
- *Palomar College* (www.palomar.edu)
- *Pratt Institute* (www.pratt.edu)
- *Seattle Central Community College* (www.learnatcentral.org)
- *University of Advancing Technology* (www.uat.edu)
- *University of North Carolina at Chapel Hill* (www.cs.unc.edu)
- *University of North Texas* (www.cs.unt.edu)
- *University of Texas at Dallas* (www.utdallas.edu/)

GLOSSARY

Walk down the halls of any game publisher and you'll hear a flood of confusing jargon, acronyms, and specialized terms. Here's a guide to help you navigate the waters.

2D — Two-dimensional.

3D — Three-dimensional.

AFTRA — American Federation of Television and Radio Artists.

AI — Artificial Intelligence.

alpha, alpha testing — Alpha is an early stage of product development. Alpha testing is generally geared towards resolving gameplay issues.

beta, beta testing — Beta is a late stage of product development, when the game is nearly complete. Beta testing generally focuses on finding and fixing bugs.

boss — The hardest monster to kill in any given environment. He's usually encountered near the end of the level, after the player has dealt with all the "grunts."

build — [Noun] The current version of the game. [Verb] To assemble all subcomponents of the game into a working version.

COGS — Cost Of Goods. The cost to create all the physical objects that go into the game box, including the box itself, the CD or DVD, the manual, the jewel case, and so on.

CPU — Central Processing Unit.

CRPG — Computer Role-Playing Game. *See* RPG.

crunch time — The last few weeks at the end of the project when you're "almost done." During this time, superhuman efforts are often made by the entire team. Laundry goes unwashed, spouses are ignored, and takeout food becomes a way of life. Many games are born in this white-hot crucible of focused talent and energy. Any crunch time longer than one month becomes a *death march*.

CTF — Capture The Flag. Multiplayer gaming mode.

cutscene — A prerendered scene, usually shown between rounds of gameplay, that is designed to move the plot forward.

death march — A crunch time of longer than one month. A highly unproductive way to push software out the door. If you find yourself requiring several months of overtime by everyone on the team to meet the deadline, you need to sit down and reevaluate. Cut the scope or extend the schedule, but don't be fooled into thinking that a death march is the answer.

deathmatch — Multiplayer gaming mode in which players battle each other head to head.

developer—1. A company with whom a publisher contracts to create the software for a game 2. An individual programmer, also known as a *coder*.

DevKit—Developer's Kit. A working prototype of a new console machine that's given to developers, so that they can make games for it before the actual hardware hits the market.

DGA—Directors Guild of America.

DirectMusic—A music delivery system developed by Microsoft for the PC.

Easter egg—A surprise feature or graphic, usually unrelated to gameplay, that's hidden in a game where most players won't find it. An unexpected bonus.

end cap—The display space at the end of the aisle in a retail store.

Flag Day—1. Traditionally, any day when a major change is made that will require everyone to stop what they're doing and incorporate the change into their code. 2. Sasha Meretzky's birthday.

FMV—Full Motion Video. Filmed segments that are inserted into a game.

foo—"Thing." What a game designer calls any unspecified object before he decides what it really is. Interchangeable with frob.

frob—*See* foo.

Gantt chart—A time-based scheduling tool, named for Henry Gantt, a pioneer of scientific management techniques.

GB—Gigabyte.

GDC—The Game Developer's Conference (formerly CGDC). The premier annual event for game programmers, artists, composers, and designers.

going gold—Finishing development. (Sending the gold master off to be duplicated.)

gold master—The master disc from which all other discs will be duplicated.

GUI—Graphical User Interface.

high concept—The one- or two-sentence response to the question, "What is your game about?"

hit points—The amount of damage a weapon inflicts on its targets. Alternatively, the amount of damage a character or monster can absorb before it's disabled or killed.

HUD—Heads-Up Display. A portion of the screen that supplies crucial game-related information to the player.

IP—Intellectual Property. 1. All the ideas, code, art, and other material your company develops. 2. Shorthand for a franchise or brand you license to or from another company.

isometric view—A "top-down" view that has a 3D appearance.

lag—The amount of time it takes for information to travel over the Net. Also called *latency*.

LAN—Local Area Network.

localization—The process of creating foreign-language versions of a game. The term covers a broad range of activities, including translating text, writing subtitles, dubbing voices, altering content that is deemed unsuitable for some markets, and creating new content altogether.

LOD—Level Of Detail. An algorithm that determines how many polygons to display as the player's distance from a model changes.

LOI—Letter Of Intent. A short agreement put in place while a more complete contract is being negotiated.

maguffin—The object around which a story revolves. This word was coined by Alfred Hitchcock to describe an arbitrary device to keep a plot moving. In a game design, it refers to the most important item the gamer must acquire. In other words, it's the object of his quest.

markdown—*See* price protection.

MB—Megabyte.

MIDI—Musical Instrument Digital Interface. A standard that allows a composer to store and play music from data files rather than from recordings.

MMO, MMOG, MMP, MMORPG—Any acronym beginning with MM will be Massively Multiplayer. The O will stand for Online. The G will stand for Game. The P will be some variant of the word Play or Player.

mocap—Motion capture.

MOD—Modification. A version of a popular game that has been changed or added to by the amateur gaming community.

Motion capture—An in-studio process whereby an actor's movements are digitally captured and transferred to a model in an animation program.

MP3—MPEG-3 (Moving Picture Experts Group Layer-3 Audio). A scheme to compress audio for quick transmission and easy playback.

MPEG—Moving Picture Experts Group. A video compression scheme that comes in two flavors, MPEG-1 and the higher-resolution MPEG-2.

NDA—Non-Disclosure Agreement. A document whereby the signee agrees not to reveal a company's trade secrets or other confidential information.

Net—1. The Internet, also known as the Web. 2. A LAN within an office that connects the workers. A central depository for team and company information.

noncompete—An agreement prohibiting an employee from working for another game company while working at his current company, and sometimes for a specific period of time thereafter.

NPC—Nonplayer Character. Any character appearing in a game that's not controlled by the gamer.

OEM—Original Equipment Manufacturer. Usually, a computer maker or a peripheral manufacturer who is interested in bundling your game with his hardware.

P&L (profit and loss) statement—A spreadsheet that estimates how much money a game will make, by calculating the costs of developing and distributing the game and subtracting those costs from anticipated revenues.

PERT chart—Program Evaluation and Review Technique. A project management tool that shows tasks and the dependencies between them.

port—[Noun] A game version created for a different hardware platform than the original. Also called a *conversion*. [Verb] To create such a conversion: "They ported the game from the PlayStation to the PC."

powerup—An item that confers enhanced powers, usually found in action games.

preproduction—The phase just prior to full development. The goal of preproduction is to create a full set of design documents and a proof-of-concept piece of technology.

price protection—The lowering of a game's wholesale price. Usually, this comes in the form of a credit to the retailer for units he has on the shelves but hasn't sold through. The markdown is taken as the game's rate of sales slows down, to encourage the retailer to keep the game in stock rather than return it to the publisher.

Redbook audio—A fancy name for the digital standard developed by Phillips and Sony to record the regular CDs that go in your stereo. So called because the original specification was in a book with a red binder.

ROI—Return On Investment. An estimate of how much money the game will make, usually expressed as a percentage of income to expense. This number is derived from the numbers on the P&L statement.

RPG—Role-Playing Game. A genre in which the player directs a group of heroes on a series of quests, usually in a story-based environment.

RTM—Release To Manufacture. The point at which development stops and the gold master is shipped off for duplication. Also known as *going gold.*

RTS—Real-Time Strategy. A genre of games played in real time (as opposed to turn-based games), in which the player must manage a limited set of resources to achieve a goal.

SAG—Screen Actors Guild.

SDK—Software Development Kit. A set of technologies that that allows a programmer to create applications for a particular platform.

sell-in—The number of units a publisher places in the retail channel.

sell-through—The number of units that are actually sold at retail.

showstopper—A bug that's important enough to hold up the release of a game.

SIGGRAPH—The Association for Computing Machinery's Special Interest Group on Computer Graphics. The premier annual convention for computer artists.

SKU—Stock-Keeping Unit. 1. Technically, each version of a game that requires a different number for retailers to track. 2. More liberally, the name that publishers apply to different platform versions of a game.

SPIFF—Sales Performance Incentive Fund (with an extra F thrown in for good measure). A special one-time incentive for sales representatives to move large quantities of a product in a particular time frame.

storyboard—[Noun] A sequence of pencil sketches that rough out what a scene will look like. [Verb] To create this sequence.

studio—1. An independent development house (or *developer*) that develops game software. 2. A division of a large company that acts as a semi-autonomous unit to develop games. 3. A soundproof room for recording actors' voices, also known as a *voice studio.* 4. An interior location for filming.

SWAG—*See* WAG.

tchotchke—A small, inexpensive promotional item given away at trade shows or sent to buyers and reviewers to create awareness of a game. This could be almost anything with the game's logo on it, with extra points given for tying the item to the theme of the game. Common tchotchkes are T-shirts, caps, paperweights, small figurines, and so on. (The word comes from *tshatshke,* the Yiddish word for *trinket.*)

UBG—Ultimate Bad Guy. What a game designer calls the villain in the early stages of design, before his identity has been developed.

UI—User Interface.

WAG—Wild-Ass Guess. Off-the-cuff estimate. Sometimes SWAG, or Scientific (or Silly) Wild-Ass Guess.

WAN—Wide Area Network.

WIP—Work In Progress. Often attached to an asset's name to indicate that it's not yet final.

WYSIWYG—What You See Is What You Get. Any interface that allows you to see what the material will look like on the computer screen while you're creating it.

INDEX

Gamedev.net

The most comprehensive game development resource

- ☼ The latest news in game development
- ☼ The most active forums and chatrooms anywhere, with insights and tips from experienced game developers
- ☼ Links to thousands of additional game development resources
- ☼ Thorough book and product reviews
- ☼ Over 1,000 game development articles!
  Game design
  Graphics
  DirectX
  OpenGL
  AI
  Art
  Music
  Physics
  Source Code
  Sound
  Assembly
  And More!

Gamedev.net